LUMEN

SUTAPA BISWAS

Ridinghouse

Published in 2021 by Ridinghouse, BALTIC Centre for Contemporary Art and Kettle's Yard on the occasion of the exhibition:

Sutapa Biswas: Lumen
BALTIC Centre for Contemporary Art, Gateshead: 26 June 2021–20 March 2022
Kettle's Yard, Cambridge: 16 October 2021–30 January 2022

Ridinghouse
46 Lexington Street
London W1F 0LP
United Kingdom
ridinghouse.co.uk

BALTIC Centre for Contemporary Art
Gateshead Quays
South Shore Road
Gateshead NE8 3BA
United Kingdom
baltic.art

Kettle's Yard
University of Cambridge
Castle Street
Cambridge CB3 0AQ
United Kingdom
kettlesyard.co.uk

Distributed in the UK and Europe by
Cornerhouse Publications
c/o Home
2 Tony Wilson Place
Manchester M15 4FN
United Kingdom
cornerhousepublications.org

Distributed in the United States and Canada by
ARTBOOK | D.A.P.
75 Broad Street, Suite 630
New York, New York 10004
USA
artbook.com

British Library Cataloguing-in-Publication Data. A full catalogue record of this book is available from the British Library.

ISBN 978-1-909932-64-7

BALTIC & Kettle's Yard
Edited by Amy Tobin
With Emma Dean and Jennifer Powell
Assisted by Guy Haywood, Alina Khakoo, Daniela Riva Rossi and Eliza Spindel

Ridinghouse Publisher:
Sophie Kullmann

Design: Åbäke
Printed in Belgium by die Keure

Publication realised with the kind support of:

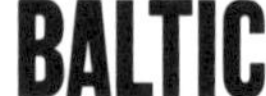

KETTLE'S YARD

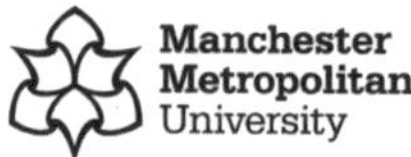

MANCHESTER SCHOOL OF ART

Ridinghouse

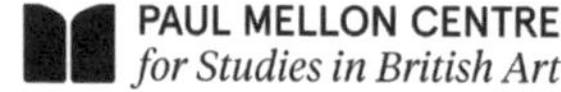

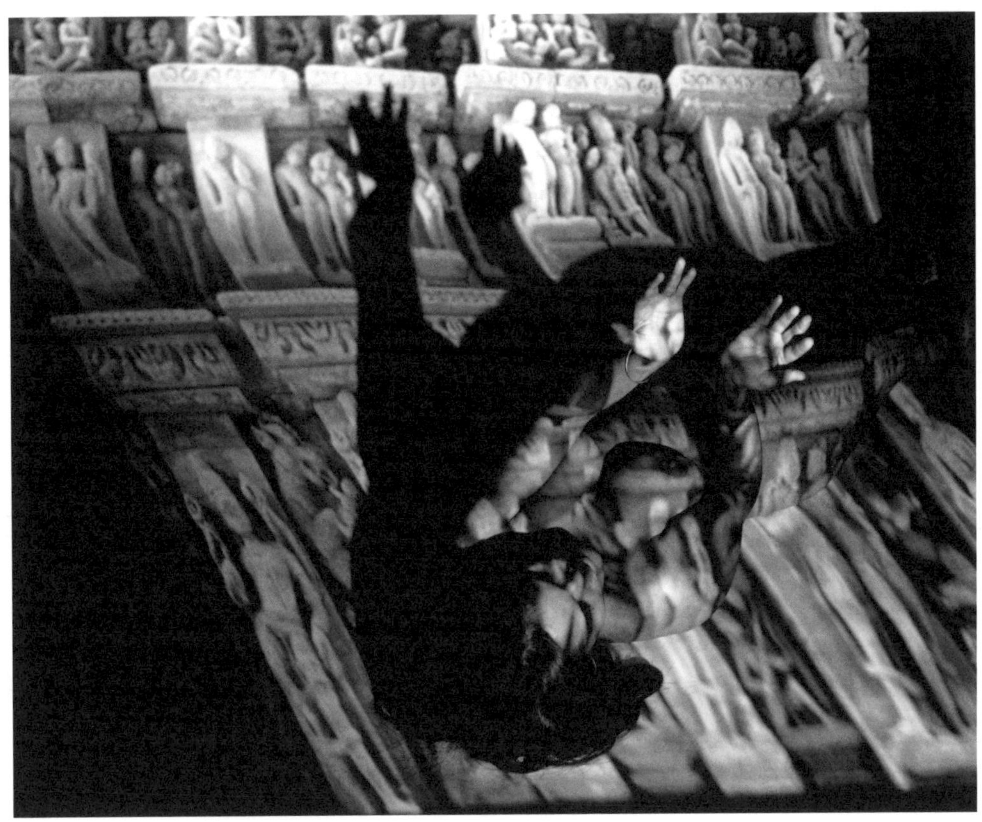

Figure 1
***Synapse IV*, 1987–92**

Preface

Sarah Munro, Andrew Nairne and Jennifer Powell

This book accompanies two exhibitions of the work of British-Indian artist Sutapa Biswas that are companions of one another. A shared passion for Biswas's work and recognition of its ongoing relevance brought BALTIC Centre for Contemporary Art, Gateshead and Kettle's Yard, University of Cambridge together with the artist to embark on this first major showing of her work since 2004. A joint exhibition and book project of this scale was long overdue for an artist whose work has played, and still plays, such a vital role in challenging and rewriting dominant Western narratives of art and its histories. At the heart of both exhibitions is a major new film work, *Lumen*, which is also the title of the exhibitions and this book.

Like many of Biswas's works, *Lumen* feels as though it is deliberately positioned at a junction between dichotomies: trauma and hope, darkness and light, poeticism and violence, memory and loss. Biswas is perhaps still best known for her monumental work *Housewives with Steak-knives* (1983–5), a painting composed of multiple sheets of paper mounted on canvas that was made as a student at the University of Leeds. The painting is hinged and provocatively leans out from the wall, the goddess Kali, who is the subject of the work, confronting the viewer. Kali is a warrior, fighting for our past and future. She is fearsome yet also a protector. Many of Biswas's works in these two exhibitions engage with common themes: her family's own history and the wider role of the matriarch, 'otherness' in its many forms, race and/or gender, and women's bodies and her own, presented not as passive objects but as battlegrounds. Her works are multimedia, ranging from painting, drawing and photography, to film, performance and installation, also incorporating collaged elements.

Biswas played a vital role in the Black Arts Movement in Britain in the 1980s–1990s. Her voice and her art were central in challenging the marginalisation of non-Western histories and the persistent violence of colonialism — a struggle that continues. There is a moment mid-way through *Lumen* when Biswas cuts from the interior of Red Lodge in Bristol to a short piece of contemporary footage shot on the west coast of India. Here, a young boy walks on a tightrope (pl. XXXIII). He is confident in his performance, which is viewed as an enjoyable spectacle by onlookers. But the scene is fragile. The boy's position on the line is precarious, he wobbles furiously from side to side. In some ways this vignette speaks to Biswas's wider practice: her art asks us to push, pull, wobble, bend and break dividing lines — to walk to the edge of them — and to push against the categories of gender, class, race and national identity.

Our heartfelt thanks to the many people in both our institutions and beyond them who have made the exhibitions and this book possible. The exhibition at BALTIC has been curated by Alessandro Vincentelli and Emma Dean, with Adrianne Murray-Neil, Registrar and Production Manager and Thomas Newell, Technical Manager overseeing the build and installation. The exhibition at Kettle's Yard has been curated by Amy Tobin, with Guy Haywood, Alina Khakoo and Eliza Spindel assisting and Tom Noblett managing technical aspects of the installation.

Biswas's new film *Lumen* has been commissioned by Film and Video Umbrella, Kettle's Yard, BALTIC and Bristol Museum & Art Gallery. We are very grateful to the Art Fund, through the Moving Image Fund for Museums, for its additional support. We owe special thanks to Steven Bode, Director of Film and Video Umbrella, for his unstinting commitment to producing *Lumen*, which has benefitted enormously from his skills and experience, along with cinematographer Martin Testar and Mike Jones who provided necessary technical support. Our thanks also to Mark Sealy, Director of Autograph, and Julia Carver, Curator, Bristol Museum & Art Gallery, for their warm collaboration in making *Lumen* and enabling it to reach audiences in both London and Bristol.

Both exhibitions have relied on the generosity and assistance of lenders. Thank you to Cartwright Hall, Bradford; Gallery Oldham; University of Leeds; Tate and Touchstones, Rochdale. Kettle's Yard has benefitted once again from the Government Indemnity Scheme. Accompanying the exhibitions and film presentations, this book offers new perspectives on Biswas's work, exploring subjects and themes that are highly pertinent in an age of contested narratives. Over four decades, Biswas has powerfully addressed these issues through many lenses, speaking out through her art about the potential for positive change in the world.

Praise must go to the writers — Anna Arabindan-Kesson, Alina Khakoo, Courtney J. Martin, Griselda Pollock, Alessandro Vincentelli and Sutapa Biswas — for their insightful contributions, and to Amy Tobin for both her text and role as editor. The beautiful and sensitive design of the book is the work of Kajsa Ståhl.

We also sincerely appreciate the support of Manchester School of Art, Manchester Metropolitan University and the Paul Mellon Centre for Studies in British Art for their financial support.

It has been a pleasure to work with Ridinghouse on this project and we thank Ridinghouse Publisher Sophie Kullmann and her team.

Finally, this ambitious project, encompassing exhibitions, a major new commission, a book and events, could not have been realised without the continuing support of Arts Council England, Gateshead Council, Northumbria University, the University of Cambridge, and regular donors and corporate partners at both BALTIC and Kettle's Yard.

Of course, our greatest thanks are to Sutapa Biswas, a truly remarkable artist, for her active engagement, generosity and constant inspiration to us all over the past three years.

Lumen: An Introduction

Amy Tobin

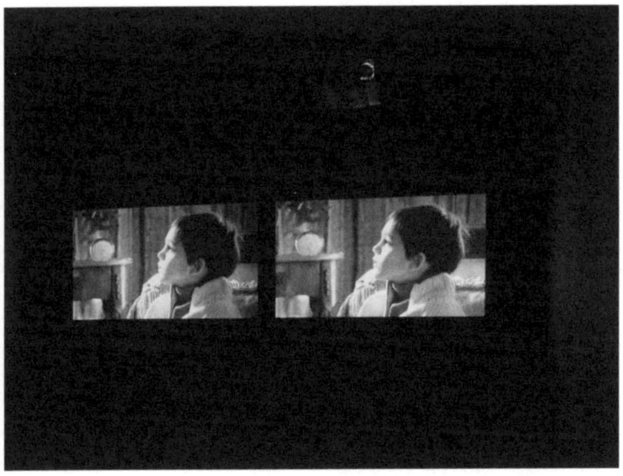

Figure 2
Birdsong, 2004

A lumen is a measure of light, but in Sutapa Biswas's work it is more than a metric. In Biswas's new film *Lumen* (2021) (pls. XXX–XXXXV) — which also gives its title to this book and two exhibitions at BALTIC Centre for Contemporary Art and Kettle's Yard — the word takes on a metaphoric power binding darkness and light. The film is about memory, migration, familial belonging and displacement. It positions intimate histories and archival fragments against the records of Empire, trade, enslavement and colonialism: a moral measure that does not equate. When lumens are used to describe light, they tell us about the intensity or brightness of a light source, natural or artificial, or a compound of the two. This makes a lumen distinct from a volt or a watt, which are units of electrical power. To count lumens is to take account of environmental conditions: to gauge something only otherwise sensed, or indistinctly perceived. Sutapa Biswas's *Lumen* has this effect too, making felt the qualities of life in the wake of colonialism.

Biswas's invocation of lumens asks us to recalibrate. It displaces the language of 'clarity' or 'making visible' that so often attends artworks that disturb or recover occluded histories. Likewise, it pushes past the metaphor of discovery that continues to inform the reception of artists like Biswas who have been excluded from the art world spotlight. *Lumen*, and indeed all of Biswas's work, is more than an instance of exposure or representation anticipating an unknowing audience. Her work does not show what cannot be seen, it makes sensible what hides in plain sight. In this respect, Biswas's work finds a parallel in that of her contemporaries who, as young artists, participated in the exhibitions, debates and activism of the Black Arts Movement in Britain. At a time when 'Black' was a political identity to be claimed as an act of solidarity between artists of colour, the Movement developed a do-it-yourself infrastructure for many artists to stage their first exhibitions. These networks of solidarity provided the mutual support necessary to contend with British racism and its roots in the colonial past.[1]

In the two interviews with the artist in this book, Biswas speaks of her parents' experiences of dehumanising racism after their arrival in the UK, with an infant Biswas and her siblings in the mid-1960s, as well as the small acts of resistance they performed. For instance, Biswas recounts her father's insistence during their visits to South Kensington that the collections of the Victoria and Albert Museum were public and belonged to them, as they did to any other tax-paying citizen. In contrast to recent attempts to portray the ethical responsibility of states to migrants through the roles of host and guest, this claim to a public collection speaks to civic participation as a mode of belonging in and through culture.[2] At the same time, it recognises the colonial provenance of many objects in British museum collections — and the entwined cultures produced by Empire — pre-empting and complicating contemporary calls for reparation and the return of artefacts and artworks.[3]

Biswas's works have long sustained the interweaving of multiple cultural referents and traditions. Take her most famous work *Housewives with Steak-knives* (1983–5) (pl. I) — the subject of a conversation between Biswas and Courtney J. Martin in this volume — in which Biswas has reimagined the Hindu goddess of love and retribution, Kali through Artemisia Gentileschi's *Judith Beheading Holofernes* (c. 1620) (fig. 10). Here, the deity wields a machete and flag with a Xerox image of the original painting, while wearing a necklace of the severed heads of dictators and archetypes. As both Biswas and Alina Khakoo, in her essay on the video-performance *Kali* (1983–5) (pls. V–X), explain, some of these art historical references originated in Biswas's childhood museum visits, and some from her art history courses at the University of Leeds where she also intervened in the course content, as her tutor Griselda Pollock's contributions to this

1. See Eddie Chambers, *Black Artists in British Art: A History from 1950 to the Present*, London: IB Tauris, 2014; Nick Aikens and Elizabeth Robles eds., *Place is Here: The Work of Black Artists in 1980s Britain*, Berlin and Eindhoven: Sternberg Press and Van Abbemuseum, 2019.

2. For instance, see Homi K. Bhabha in conversation with Devika Singh, 'Archives of Home and Homelessness', *Homelands: Art from Bangladesh, India and Pakistan*, Devika Singh and Amy Tobin eds., Cambridge: Kettle's Yard, 2019, pp.101–111.

3. For recent interventions in repatriation debates see Alice Procter, *The Whole Picture: The Colonial Story of the Art in Our Museums & Why We Need to Talk About It*, London: Cassell, 2020 and Dan Hicks, *The Brutish Museums: The Benin Bronzes, Colonial Violence and Cultural Restitution*, London: Pluto Press, 2020.

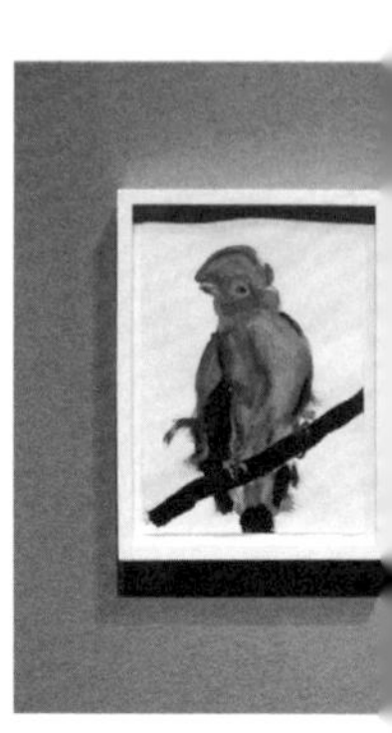

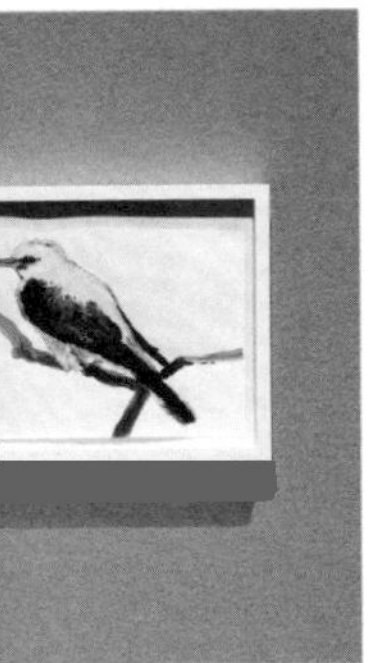

Figure 3
Time Flies, 2004–ongoing (detail)

book attest. Biswas's critique of the elisions in the Leeds syllabus foreshadowed recent calls to decolonise university curricula, and as both Khakoo and Pollock argue, her work and Pollock's receptiveness to it led to change, even if the more profound structural transformation is yet to come.[4]

Biswas's citations work in various ways. Sometimes they are antagonistic; sometimes formative, as in *Housewives*, where Gentileschi stands in for both Western art history and gendered, enraged disenfranchisement. In the later work *Birdsong* (2004) (pls. XXIII–XXV), George Stubbs's painting *Lord Hollande and Lord Albemarle Shooting at Goodwood* (1759) provides the palette for the interior in which the central sequence of the film is shot, while the context of aristocratic wealth and leisure it afforded some, as well as the service it demanded from others — in this case a liveried Black figure in the lower left corner of the painting — provides a subtext. In the film, Stubbs's horse is displaced to a well-appointed living room, where he stands too big for the space. Around him are piles of books some gifted by Biswas's father, and toys belonging to her son, who sits on a settee facing the horse, gazing towards it, inquisitive and accepting. Here the fixed social relations of Stubbs's painting are upset and redistributed in a scene marked by play, fantasy and generational exchange.

Birdsong was prompted not by Stubbs, but by Biswas's son Enzo. As he was beginning to speak, he asked his mother if a horse could live in the family home. Struck by this fantasy and Enzo's articulation of it, Biswas made the film, both realising the wish — in one form — and recording a stage in her child's early life: the movement from 'innocence and wonder' to 'knowing', as the artist Mary Kelly described it to Biswas. While the film features a horse, the title is avian. It is named for and is a birdsong. This comes from an exchange between Biswas and her father in the last days of his life, when they agreed that birdsong could be an earthly substitute for his voice. While the film is a homage to both Biswas's father and her son, the title also shapes the viewer's poetic encounter with the film. Like a song or a poem, it invites the viewer into a rhythm, a disjunctive metric in which the two images that comprise the double channel of the film play slightly out of sync (fig. 2). The tenderness of this lulling cadence belies, to paraphrase the poet Amiri Baraka, the teeth of a political poem's bite and, in this case, Biswas's sustained attention to the legacies of power and oppression in the postcolonial condition.[5]

4. In 2017 Lola Olufemi co-authored a letter calling for the English Department at the University of Cambridge to 'Decolonise the Curriculum'. This prompted a media outcry that treated Olufemi with vitriol. Since 2017 many departments and faculties at Cambridge have recognised Decolonise Groups, while many more have active student groups. This mirrors the activism of student bodies at other UK universities, and in education more broadly. Decolonising Our Minds was set up in 2018 to support the decolonisation of curricula across the higher education sector.

5. Amiri Baraka, 'Black Art', (1965), *SOS: Poems 1961–2013*, New York: Grove Press, 2014, pp.149–151.

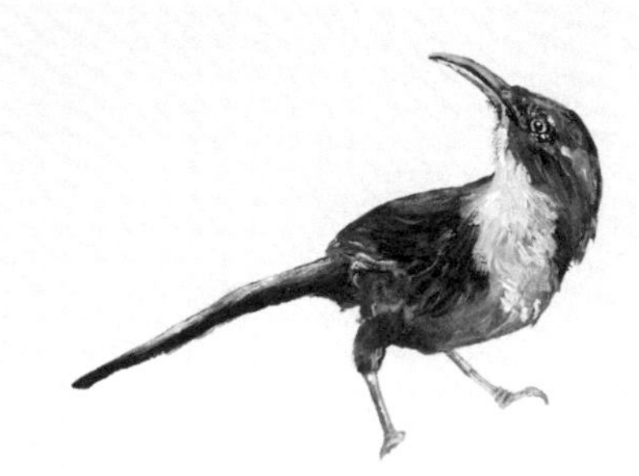

Figure 4
Time Flies, 2004–ongoing (detail)

Birds and horses appear again and again in Biswas's work, from the early painting *Through Rose Tinted Windows* (1996), to her series of watercolours *Time Flies* (2004–ongoing) (figs. 3–4), to *Birdsong, Magnesium Bird* (2004) (pl. XXII) and now *Lumen*. These horses and birds are protagonists, the former pressed into service by human owners and subject to an economy of breeding, the latter itinerant, elusive and vocal. In a recent conversation, Biswas told me that the art critic Guy Brett had made a similar observation about the animals in her work. She said that Brett thought birds were Biswas's spirit animal. The bird is not a stand-in for Biswas, but rather acts like a talisman, providing lines of flight from constraint. Biswas's birds are not always signs for freedom. In *Time Flies*, for instance, a series of acrylic sketches of imagined birds, Biswas makes reference to the work of James Forbes, an artist contracted to the East India Company and deployed to colonial India where he pictured the flora and fauna of the subcontinent. While Forbes took stock, Biswas opened the cage. Her birds are rendered as if in mid-motion, in an open style that deliberately troubles Forbes's static, finely rendered and pseudo-scientific watercolours.

Brett insightfully described Biswas's work as a 'device for awakening memory, gaining a foothold in time and conveying an insight into human lives'.[6] These exhibitions and the essays collected in this book speak to this quality of Biswas's work. At BALTIC visitors will encounter more of Biswas's recent moving-image works, including *Birdsong, Magnesium Bird* (both 2004) and *Light rain* (2014–21) (pl.XXVI) as well as *Time Flies*, all of which weave together the present and the past, the evanescent and the long-lasting. At Kettle's Yard, by contrast, the assembled works speak to the connections and relationships with other women that Biswas has traced across her work. Taking on the matrilineal narrative that structures *Lumen* — which will premiere in both exhibitions — at Kettle's Yard *Housewives* parries with the large-scale drawing *To Touch Stone* (1989–90) (pl. IV) of Biswas's sister, as well as the photographic installation *Infestations of the Aorta — Shrine to a Distant Relative* (1987–9) (figs. 6–7), that Anna Arabindan-Kesson discusses in her essay, among a number of early works, including the photo series *Synapse I* (1987–92) (pls. XI–XIV), which also features in both exhibitions. Kettle's Yard will also exhibit a suite of works Biswas made as the Kashima Artist in Residence in Beppu,

6. Guy Brett, 'Spaces inside Time', *Sutapa Biswas*, exh. cat. London and Portland: inIVA and Reed College, 2004, p.43.

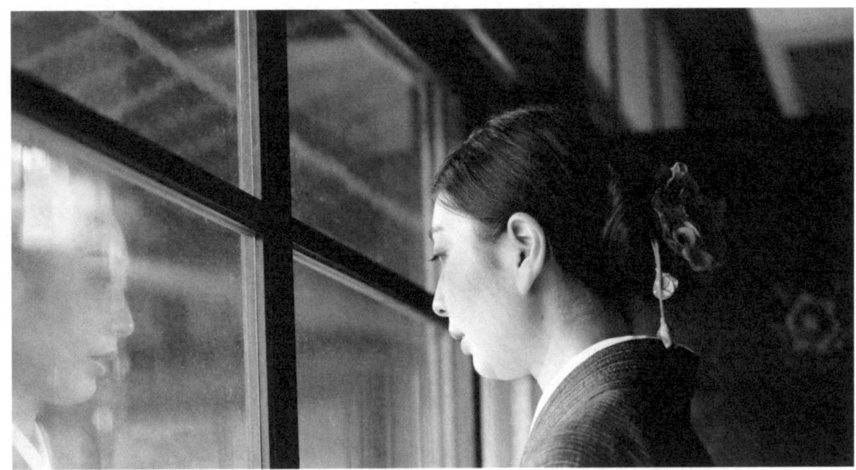

Figure 5
mata ne, 2015–21

Japan in 2015 for which she collated fragments of stories and materials from women of different ages, recomposing and representing them in the film, *mata ne* (2015–21) (fig. 5, pls. XXVIII–XXIX) and the textile work *Stitch by Stitch* (2015) (pl. XVIII). These exhibitions present the first opportunity to see many of Biswas's works in the UK, and her first solo exhibition and publication since 2004.

I began this introduction by discussing *Lumen*, a new film work commissioned by BALTIC and Kettle's Yard with Film and Video Umbrella and Bristol Museums. It is, in an appropriately circular fashion, also where this book will close, as the focus of the conversation between Sutapa Biswas and former BALTIC Curator Alessandro Vincentelli who originated this project in Gateshead. His thoughtful curation has been continued by Emma Dean, who has been a wonderful interlocutor for both Biswas and myself in the production of this book and in the staging of BALTIC's exhibition. Jennifer Powell was also instrumental in the realisation of *Sutapa Biswas: Lumen* in both publication and exhibition form, along with many other colleagues at Kettle's Yard. The many collaborators and contributors to this project are named in the final pages of the book. Lastly, I want to thank Sutapa Biswas for her generosity and implacable hard work, but mostly for the poetic artworks she has created and those still to come.

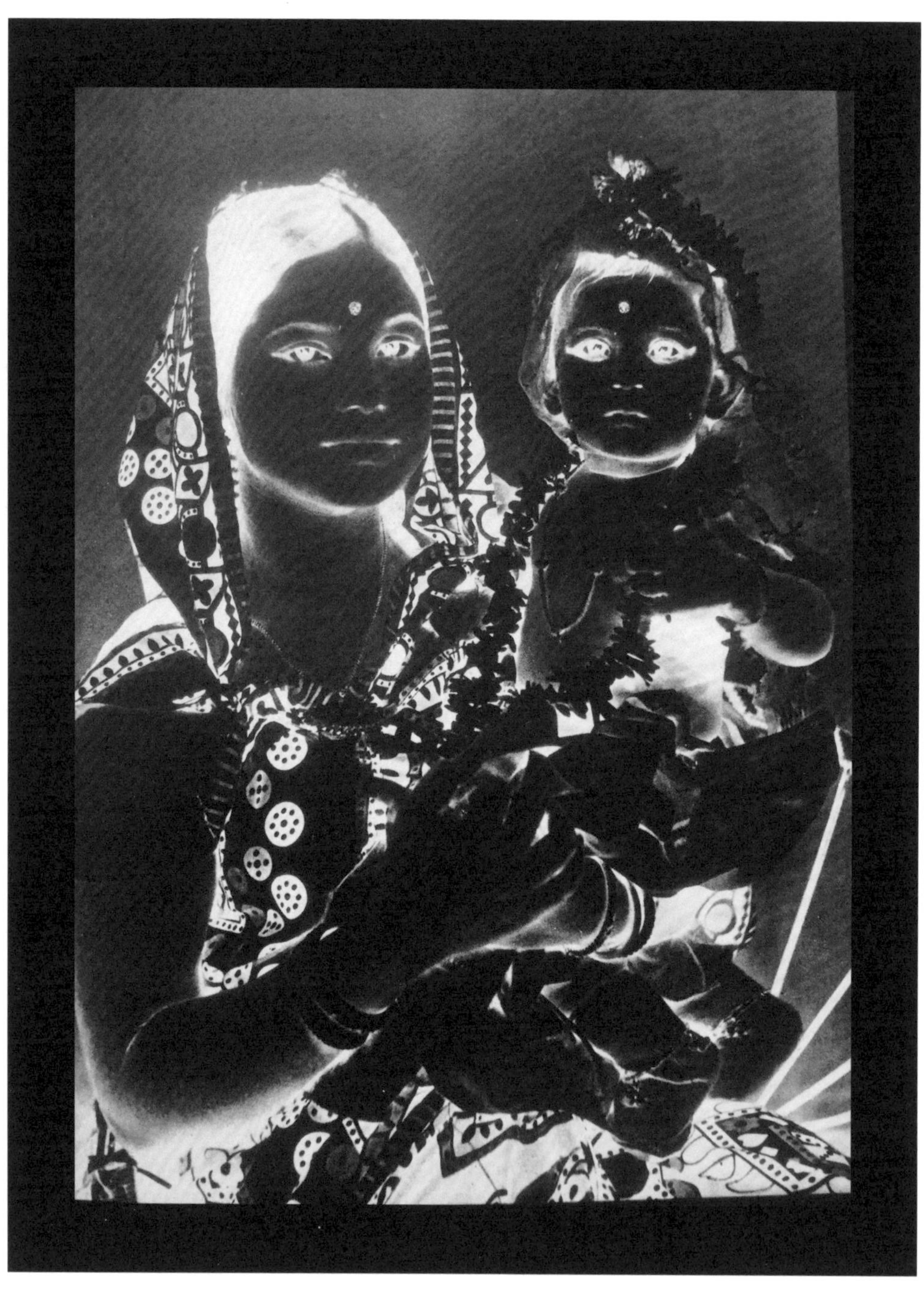

Figure 6
***Infestations of the Aorta – Shrine to a Distant Relative*, 1987–9 (detail)**

Sutapa Biswas & The Space of Diaspora

Anna Arabindan-Kesson

I first met Sutapa Biswas when she was a Fellow at the Yale Center for British Art, in New Haven, and I was a PhD student in the Art History and African American Studies Departments. She was perhaps the first South Asian artist I ever knew, and we were introduced just as my own South Asian-ness — in a predominantly White art history programme — was becoming increasingly difficult to negotiate. I had no mother tongue to call on, and very little to hold onto in the way of cultural practices passed down from my family. But around me South Asia, particularly India, was in vogue. I felt like an imposter and an exotic object, as my colleagues taught me about an art history, a language and a culture that was somehow connected to my place of birth, but of which I knew nothing. In my staunchly Christian middle-class Sri Lankan Tamil family, culture, it seemed, had arrived with the British. So, while a work like *Housewives with Steak-knives* (1983–5, pl. I), powerful and provocative, reminded me of a cosmology that was not mine, I well understood its force. The vehemence, the ferocity, the darkness — and I am also talking about skin colour here — and the wit. It held a familiar sense of mocking vengeance that I also wanted to wield against all those myths of identity and essentialism taught on both sides of the colonial/ colonised divide. Yes, this painting is a savage critique of the colonial underpinnings of modern Britain. Yes, its art historical allusions to Artemisia Gentileschi works through and invites allusions to the marginalisation of Black and South Asian women (artists). Yes, it certainly remains a precursor to the psychic underpinnings and semiotic referents and signs that continue to characterise her work. Yet this is also a painting about the immigrant condition, of being required, but never able to be authentic or essential, of always being called on to stand for something that was never quite there in the beginning.

In taking this personal, even familiar, tone I am not downplaying the intellectual force of Biswas's work. In a field like art history, finding artists whose work visualises ideas as yet unarticulated is akin to finding a home in a place that has been decidedly *unheimlich* to so many artists and scholars. While migration is a key concept in art history, its effects — the frameworks it creates and disrupts — are not always so centrally placed. While Biswas mines migration as a subject, her work is also diasporic in its outlook: it allows, it compels, a viewer to inhabit this orientation to the world, its cultural formations, its referentiality, its liminality and its displacements.[1]

A companion piece to *Housewives*, *The Only Good Indian...* (1985) (fig. 9) was exhibited in *The Thin Black Line* at the Institute of Contemporary Arts, an exhibition curated by Lubaina Himid CBE in 1985. This exhibition was one of three curated by Himid that heralded the arrival on the British art scene of a radical group of Black and Asian women artists. Here the same housewife, as in the earlier work, with a red dress patterned with black-and-white diamonds, sits in front of a television. She has swapped the steak-knives for a potato peeler and she slowly peels the skin from a Tory politician whose head is held firmly in her strong hands. The light from the small television, with another Tory politician on the screen, flickers across her face. As Griselda Pollock wrote in her essay 'Tracing Figures', this piece collapses the public and private. In bringing the domains of the domestic and the political together, it foregrounds the sites of struggle and resistance in which Asian women worked within and against the patriarchal and racist environment

1. I am also thinking here of Ranajit Guha, 'The Migrant's Time', in *The Migrant's Time: Rethinking Art History and Diaspora*, ed. Saloni Mathur, Williamstown, Mass. and New Haven Conn.: Sterling and Francine Clark Art Institute and Yale University Press, 2011, pp.3–9.

of 1980s Britain.[2] This woman, Kali perhaps, dominates this gendered space, transforming it into one of power and satire. Bringing together these icons and mythologies of India and the West, Biswas fuses — as Gilane Tawadros has written — the past and the present in a way that allows for multiple temporalities to appear and to be sustained.[3] I will return to this, but for now we might think of the fusion as another element of this diasporic outlook. It is, of course, partly the space from which we glimpse the complexities of what it means to be a British South Asian woman in the 1980s, but it is also something more: a glimpse of other worlds, of other possibilities, of other referents for meaning-making that exist beyond the frames that hold up our knowledge systems. A diasporic outlook is not about seeking out belonging or even, necessarily, connection: it is a viewing space full of discontinuities, of multiplicity, where ambiguity is itself a political act.

The Thin Black Line also included *Housewives* and a series called *Tracing a History — Whatever Happened to Cricket* in which photographs of shrines and dances devoted to the goddess Kali were interspersed with a narrative letter addressing Leon Trotsky. The text begins with a quote from Alice Walker's essay, 'In Search of Our Mother's Gardens'.[4] Biswas and her contemporaries were inspired by many African American women writers and Black Studies scholars.[5] Their work gave them a language from which to articulate experiences that were often narrowly understood, and acknowledged, in Britain. But perhaps more importantly, the work of these Black women in the United States also confirmed to these British Black artists (and I am using Black here to also mean Asian artists as it was used then) that they were part of a broader, international, set of conversations and experiences: it located them beyond the confines of the UK. The quote from Walker describes the richness of Black women's writing and Black women's experiences as one that challenges the assumptions of what an artist should and could be. Biswas's text — a herstory — weaves descriptions of her mother, reflections on the stories her mother told her and musings on the goddess Kali. Myth and memory interchange, as they often do in the immigrant's story, creating an alternative vision of the encounters and intersections that formed the colonial project, and its relationship to 1980s Britain. Refracted through the subjective experience of Biswas and her mother,

2. Griselda Pollock, 'Tracing Figures of Presence: Naming Ciphers of Absence, Feminism, Imperialism and Postmodernity: The Work of Sutapa Biswas', in *Sutapa Biswas*, ed. Sarah Campbell, London: iniVA, 2004, pp.49–74.

3. Gilane Tawadros, 'Sutapa Biswas: Remembrance of Things Past and Present', *Third Text* 7, no. 22 (1993), pp.47–52.

4. Alice Walker, 'In Search of Our Mother's Gardens', in *In Search of Our Mother's Gardens: Womanist Prose*, New York: Harcourt, 1983 (1st ed.).

5. Including some based in the UK, such as Hazel V. Carby. See Carby, *Reconstructing Womanhood: The Emergence of the Afro-American Woman Novelist*, Oxford: Oxford University Press, 1987 and Carby et al. eds., *The Empire Strikes Back: Race and Racism in 70s Britain*, Birmingham: Centre for Contemporary Cultural Studies, 1982.

this piece expanded terms of debate, around colonialism and Britishness but also around the possibilities of the medium. The images and text are often dissonant, opening up multiple spaces for approaching them. As with other artists like Ingrid Pollard, whose work also drew on the juxtaposition of image and text at this time, the dissonance here manifests a set of meanings that exceed the viewer's grasp. If neither of these forms, as a viewer might understand them, can adequately contain the experiences and the stories that intertwine around them, then these are stories that require altogether different conceptions of what art can look like, and who can make it. They are a reminder, perhaps, of a certain narrowness of vision, of vocabulary and of scope.

In the early 1980s when these works were made, Biswas was an art student completing a degree in the Department of Fine Art at the University of Leeds. It was a programme divided evenly between the history, the theory and the practice of art, meaning students were trained across all three. With faculty like Griselda Pollock and T.J. Clark, it was also a place where politics and aesthetics were seamlessly entwined. The radical aesthetics of Biswas's degree exhibition, which included *Housewives* and the performance piece *Kali* (1983–5) (pls. V–X), emerged from this deep grounding and her deft facility with the theoretical trajectories of Western art history alongside that of the art and cosmology of South Asia. It was also shaped by her family, her academic, Marxist father and their experiences of leaving India. Her work was an articulation of the transnational poetics among which she lived, a position that challenged the systems under which she had studied. In *Kali*, explored in detail in Alina Khakoo's essay in this volume, Biswas made her tutor Griselda Pollock a protagonist in the performance, in order to draw attention to the lack of engagement with issues of race and colonialism in the department's teaching. The course changed after her show. This is an important point, demonstrating how it is often artists who demand the disruption and reassembling of scholarly fields, and so often it is they who provide academics with the frameworks, the words even, to reimagine what scholarship can be.

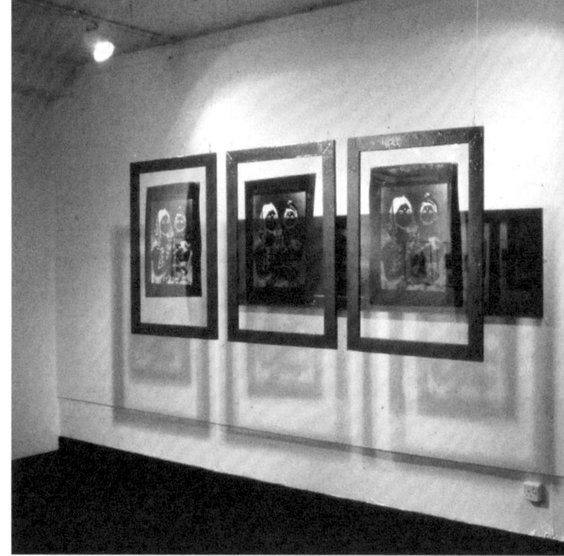

Figure 7
Infestations of the Aorta – Shrine to a Distant Relative, 1987–9

Even now, thirty years or so later, this still rings true and we are still working through the complex ways that artists like Biswas challenged British society and its historical formations, the demands they made for themselves and their communities and their deconstruction of the art world. Biswas's practice was central to, and aligned with, the development of the Black Arts Movement in Britain. While an older generation of Black and Asian artists engaged with the political modernisms of anti-colonialism, this 'second wave' in the 1970s and 1980s signalled a new generation of artists who had grown up in Britain, were art school graduates and were able to find more professional opportunities to exhibit their work.[6] During the late 1980s and well into the 90s, Biswas was exhibiting work in the UK and internationally. This was a moment, then, when Black artists were also increasingly public figures: using aesthetic expression to stake a collective claim on their place in the public sphere, and in the nation itself. While identity acquired a more political meaning, it is also true that 'political struggle acquired a cultural dimension'.[7] Identity politics — and aesthetic experimentation — provided new horizons to explore constructions of subjecthood, questions of belonging and relationships to Britishness in particular.

For artists like Biswas, expanding the limits of media and hegemonic political discourse were one and the same. Stuart Hall described the creative explosivity of the 1980s as a focus of unfulfilled desire.[8] He used the term to refer to the shifts and contestations that emerged from that period, and into the decades following. However, it is also an evocative way to describe the very nature of the work that emerged: desire as a response to the erasure and marginalisation that these artists faced in Britain and as Britons. For Black and Asian women artists, this marginalisation existed on multiple levels and was felt within and beyond the art world, and indeed their role in the formation of the Black British Art Movement is still often under-written.[9] Living in and with these forms of unfulfilled desire characterises this particular moment and the ways that the political became subjective for artists like Biswas. Desire, and its continual refusal, is a provocative, powerful impetus: it is by its very nature full of contradictions and contradictory experiences, and holds those possibilities in tension.[10]

Describing her work in *The Thin Black Line* exhibition, Biswas wrote, 'All art forms are political and must be read within a socio-historical context. Much of my work is satirical and insists upon the multiplicity of meaning. One of its intentions

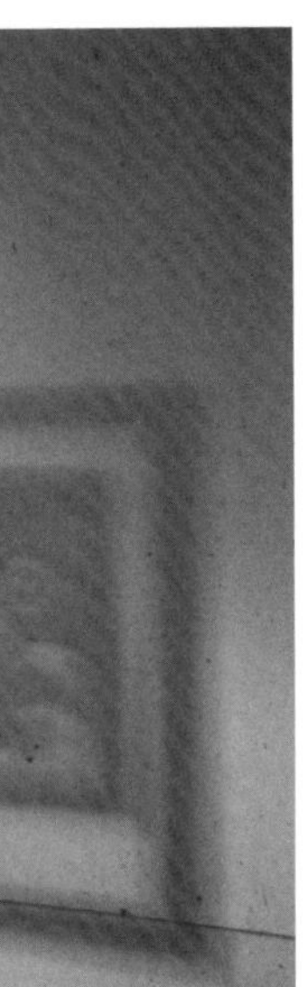

6. For more on this see Eddie Chambers, *Black Artists in British Art: A History since the 1950s*, London: I.B.Tauris, 2014.

7. Stuart Hall, 'Black Diaspora Artists in Britain: Three "Moments" in Post-War History', *History Workshop Journal*, no. 61 (2006), p.19, http://www.jstor.org/stable/25472834.

8. *Ibid.*

9. Lubaina Himid, *Thin Black Line(s)*, Preston: Making Histories Visible Project, Centre for Contemporary Art, University of Central Lancashire, 2011.

10. For more on desire see Eve Tuck, 'Suspending Damage: A Letter to Communities', *Harvard Educational Review* 79, no. 3 (September 1, 2009), pp.409–28, https://doi.org/10.17763.

is to reassess, question and rewrite that history which belongs to imperialism.'[11] This impetus to review, recalibrate and ultimately reconstruct memory is a crucial element of desire, which works not so much from lack, but an absence. The emphasis may not be to fill that void, but rather the void itself — absence — becomes the position from which experience and possibility emerge. This desiring space is also a diasporic one.[12]

At the end of the 1980s Biswas travelled to India, a place she had left two decades earlier. She visited the Ajanta and Ellora temples, as well as those in Orissa and Khajuraha: these are key sites in any survey of South Asian art, as well as any study of the Orientalising gaze that the West turned on India. Her journey there was refracted through her experience of being a British South Asian artist. It was a physical journey, that retraced the psychic affect that attends the migrant experience: the constant movement between here and there, and the feeling of carrying within you multiple places, times, orientations. This was not a return home; it was instead a return to a time recollected, perhaps a return to memory itself.

Memory is an act of willed creation wrote Toni Morrison, a phrase I return to almost daily.[13] What is it that we piece together to create both the memories we rely on and the futures we desire to build? For Biswas this has always been tied to the body of women, or perhaps the spaces that the bodies of women are assumed to occupy. In her work women are not ciphers (remember the *Housewife*); they both propel and ground — they give it its power. In her early paintings, for instance, the exploration of the distinction between myth and reality is often sifted through constructed projections of femininity that are attached, in specific ways, to the bodies of South Asian women. But moving between myth and reality is also another way to address the complicated operations of memory as it frames relationships to movement, to place and to family. After returning from India, Biswas began experimenting with photography. In *Infestations of the Aorta — Shrine to a Distant Relative* (1987–9) (fig. 6–7) Biswas transformed a photograph showing her aunt holding her cousin on their naming day, printing the negatives large-scale and translucent on lithographic film. In the photograph the woman wearing a sari holds the iconic pose of a Madonna and Child, cradling the child in her arms. When the work

11. Himid, *Thin Black Line(s)*, p.22.

12. I am influenced in my thinking on this by the work of Saidiya Hartman and her descriptions of working with incomplete archives, and working from a position of loss, or the inability to ever fully articulate and describe a history that has been erased. Saidiya Hartman, 'Venus in Two Acts', *Small Axe* 12, no. 2 (17 July 2008), pp.1–14, http://muse.jhu.edu/article/241115.

13. Toni Morrison, 'Memory, Creation and Writing', *Thought* 59, no. 235 (December 1984), pp.385–91.

14. Deborah Cherry, 'Suitcase Aesthetics: The Making of Memory in Diaspora Art in Britain in the Later 1980s', *Art History* 40, no. 4 (n.d.), p.800.

was first shown each negative was suspended a few feet from the wall, creating a shadow, but also allowing viewers to walk behind the work so that their shadows mingled with the images cast on the wall and floor. This installation formed part of an exhibition titled *Intimate Distance* held at The Photographers' Gallery, London in 1989 (fig. 7), which examined themes of migration and displacement, through photography. Along with Biswas's work, the exhibition included pieces by Ingrid Pollard, Mona Hatoum, Maxine Walker and Zarina Bhimji.

In her artist's statement Biswas talked about the personal aspects of this work, and particularly the relationships created and transformed through distance between mother and child, aunt and niece.[14] The work's title *Infestations of the Aorta — Shrine to a Distant Relative* also recalls the pain — pathologised and anatomised — of loss. Yet a shrine is also a place where memory accumulates, where loss gives shape to remembrance. A shrine is a conduit, like an aorta. It connects the living and the dead, offering a way to navigate the haunting absence that distance brings. Incorporating viewers into this work as she does, compelling them to move between image and shadow, invites an interrogation of constructions of myth and reality. By forestalling access to either an 'original' or 'stable' photographic image, Biswas destabilised Western notions of representation that pivot on identification and differentiation. Staging this defamiliarisation through the intimacy of familial relations, she also decentred the cultural history attached to Britishness, by privileging her experience of displacement.[15]

In 1990 Biswas held her MA show at the Slade School of Art in London. Entitled *Sacred Space* (fig. 14), it expanded the installation aesthetic of *Aorta* by carefully organising the viewer's relationship to the exhibition space through colour and light. Here, too, the emphasis was on mythologising the everyday, or at least 'linking everyday events to things that are perhaps not [everyday] like the idea of myth, story, heroes and heroines.'[16] The show was staged in a room that looked out over the School of Oriental and African Studies, a forceful reminder of the imperial project and its Orientalist fetishisation of the South Asian subject.[17] She painted the room white, a whiteness recalibrated daily by the play of natural and artificial light and informed by Robert Rauschenberg's *White Paintings* (1951), as well as

15. See also Gilane Tawadros, 'Sutapa Biswas: Remembrance of Things Past and Present', *Third Text* 7, no. 22 (1993), pp.47–52.

16. Sutapa Biswas, 'Artist's Statement', in *Sutapa Biswas*, ed. Sarah Campbell, London: inIVA, 2004, p.20.

17. The School of Oriental and African Studies (SOAS) was established in 1916 as the School for Oriental Studies, taking its present title from 1936. According to Eleanor Newbigin it was formed for the 'specific purpose of training colonial officials for their postings across the British Empire', although quickly 'imperial civil servants were joined by students whose interest in Asia and Africa was not shaped, primarily, by imperialist designs'. Newbigin, 'What Does It Mean to Decolonise History Teaching and Research at SOAS?', *History Workshop Journal* (11 February 2019), https://www.historyworkshop.org.uk/what-does-it-mean-to-decolonise-history-teaching-and-research-at-soas.

the paintings of Edward Hopper. On these walls she hung several framed images made with pastel, acrylic and pencil drawing. These works, with their white backgrounds, made the distinction between artwork and gallery space difficult to perceive. Viewers were compelled to make sense of the installation while also coming to understand their own position, their own location, in space. The final addition was a series of photographic transparencies, showing barefoot footprints, with text she had written:

> Of memory, we change
> From one conversation to the next
> Always in search of
> The edge of the surface
> And of textures
> There is pleasure
> And sometimes none
> So thinking back to our space
> Marked only by fallen clay
>
> There is both absence and presence
> Of violated territories —
>
> You, whose spirit is dull
> Brought me here
> To the Great Mountain
> Whereupon, I died in the thinness of its air
> From violated territories
> Its boundaries with fierce eyes
> I watch
> This sacred space.[18]

Here, understanding one's position in space was also to experience a sense of dispersal — the footprint across the sand, the human presence disappearing — that was reinforced by the play of light on the transparent surfaces. Readers had to struggle to see what was on them, working against and with their reflections, never quite knowing what was absent from the scene, what was lost or what was there in the first place.[19] In a later exhibition, *Synapse*, held at The Photographers' Gallery in 1992, Biswas brought together a variety of visual sources, working through the repetition and rhythms of certain images and forms. There are five large black-and-white photographs that make up *Synapse I* (1987–92) (pls. XI–XIV), and they resemble a family photo album, showing three figures in the water. But each image also includes a

18. Sutapa Biswas, 'Sutapa Biswas', in *Passion: Discourses on Black Women's Creativity*, ed. Maud Sulter, Urban Fox: Hebden Bridge, West Yorkshire, 1990, p.203.

19. I have relied on earlier descriptions of this exhibition as included in Pollock, 'Tracing Figures of Presence', pp.33–35; Ian Baucom, 'Two Places at Once or The Same Place Twice: The Art of Sutapa Biswas', in *Sutapa Biswas*, ed. Sarah Campbell, London: iniVA, 2004, pp.60–62.

20. Tawadros, 'Sutapa Biswas: Remembrance of Things Past and Present', p.52.

faint impression of the artist herself, her semi-naked body and her hands. She is positioned as if to nestle against or cradle the images, her appearance coming in and out of focus depending on the light. In another work from that exhibition, titled *Frieze* (1992), the image of the figures in the water is frozen and expanded into a panorama that on closer view is revealed to be a series of repeated static moments.

Across these works the medium of photography — its ability to suspend time and space, as well as its ability to animate what is absent — offers Biswas the means to stage the fragmented, transposed nature of memory itself, as a continual mediation of what is and what might have been. In *Frieze*, the splicing and dispersal of these images evokes the uncanniness of physically being in a space, imprinted by a recollection of a past moment. While its panoramic appearance suggests a mastery, a survey, of what can be seen, its fragmentation ultimately refuses this: it provides only impressions, and fleeting ones at that. This is also echoed in *Synapse I* where memories fragmented and reconstituted are evoked simultaneously. This is what returns us to the body too, the body of the woman, the body of the artist who works to reconstruct and protect both what is there and what has disappeared.

What also emerges in these pieces is her shift to an engagement with the subjective experience of this memory work, along with the subject of memory itself. Later photographic works also centre on this relationship. *Scarred Surface* (1992) includes five photographs of hands in indeterminate, closed positions — above an installation of various objects. The dislocated hands, their refusal to reveal themselves, refuse a fixed interpretation, forcing viewers to work out their multiple possibilities. In *Synapse II* (1987–92) (pls. XV–XVI) she uses her own body, moving as if in a dreamscape, to articulate the gendered relationship of bodies and landscape. Unlike the private, domestic realm of *The Only Good Indian...* (fig. 9), here she centres her sexuality and interiority, while 'laying bare the body of the female Other to public scrutiny.'[20] As Tawadros has described, this piece also draws on the Orientalising fetish of photography in which Black and Brown women's bodies were sexualised, consumed and read as signifiers of colonial conquest. The artist's body, however, occupies a terrain that exists somewhere beyond reality, yet not quite in the realm of fantasy: it is a space held in silhouetted darkness, a space in which time — the past and the present — converges, a space willed into creation, shaped by desire, yet formed from an absence. As Tawadros writes, this might be the space of diaspora itself, here brought into being through the terrain Biswas maps with her own body.[21]

During that meeting in New Haven, which was sometime in 2009, Biswas introduced us to *Birdsong* (pls. XXIII–XXV), a film she had made in 2004. For many who have seen this stunning work, I am sure the scene in which the horse stands in the living room, looking directly at her young son Enzo, is quite hard to forget. Surreal yet also haunting, this film evokes those nonsensical yet endearing stories of Peter Pan and Edward Lear (so familiar to any good Sri Lankan schoolgirl). But set as if in an English country estate, with its decorative and ornamental furnishings, the film also animates eighteenth-century conversation pieces, shows them up, stages them as the masquerades they are. My point is that, whether in her early paintings or her later films, Biswas's work dissembles the frameworks of our imagination. Perhaps I should put it this way: she plays on the structures that have both constituted and limited our imagination, and hence the possibilities we might work towards. *Birdsong*, for example, with its jarring yet syncopated juxtaposition of the past and the present, its palette — Stephanie Snyder observed that it is full of the colours of Empire — and its staged lyricism, presents a viewing position onto the colonial project by working through its various political, psychological and art historical referents. Simultaneously, its surreal animation of space also immediately dismantles that project, showing us how its forms of meaning, its logics of vision, even its beauty are the very terms that we continue to see, dream, imagine through. In this moment of decolonising, Biswas's work is biting, leaving no room to hide from our collective nostalgia, our unnamed desires. But as with *Housewives*, its wittiness avoids totalising, there is space to laugh at ourselves, there is a humour that neither aggrandises nor elides the pain of these imperial referents.[22]

These, then, are some of the dreamworlds that Sutapa Biswas has created for us, spaces of diaspora formed from the remnants and legacies of Empire and the fragments and stories of immigration and movement. The worlds she creates are acts of memory: forged from that desiring, diasporic space, where absence catalyses and generates, the worlds she builds, centring South Asian women, illuminate and recalibrate the everyday through the histories we refuse to remember.

21. Tawadros, 'Sutapa Biswas: Remembrance of Things Past and Present', p.52.

22. Stephanie Snyder, 'An Exchange: In Conversation with Sutapa Biswas', in *Sutapa Biswas*, ed. Sarah Campbell, London: inIVA, 2004, p.9.

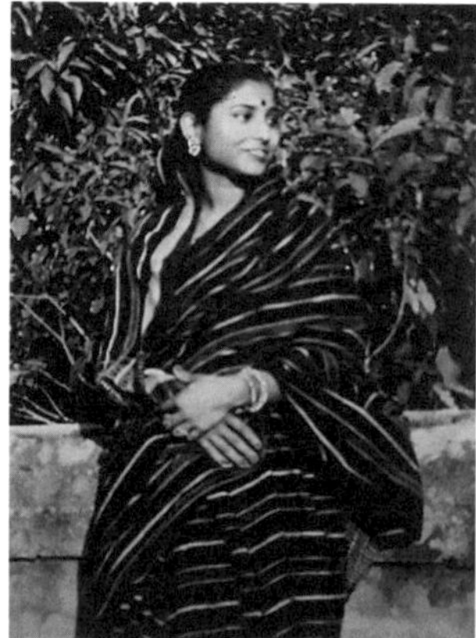

Figure 8
Geeta Rani Biswas, Santiniketan, India, c. 1955. Photographer unknown

Courtney J. Martin in conversation with Sutapa Biswas

On Housewives with Steak-knives

The following interview took place while Sutapa Biswas was a visiting scholar at the Yale Center for British Art in Autumn 2019, where Courtney J. Martin is the Director. Their conversation focuses on Biswas's *Housewives with Steak-knives* (1983–5, pl. I), perhaps her most well-known work, made while she was a student at the University of Leeds between 1981 and 1985. The painting was subsequently included in *The Thin Black Line*, a landmark exhibition of work by Black women artists curated by Lubaina Himid for the Institute of Contemporary Arts in 1985. In 1994 the painting was acquired by Cartwright Hall, Bradford.

I

Courtney J. Martin: *Housewives with Steak-knives* is a contemporary depiction of the goddess Kali, wielding a machete while holding a severed head. How did you arrive at the title and did it relate to women you knew?

Sutapa Biswas: My mother's name is Geeta Rani Biswas. She, her sisters and the women in our close family community were housewives but also worked. I was drawn to the matriarchal role that these women collectively held in the context of the extended family circle, and how in terms of 'surviving England' this felt critical.

CJM: What year did your mother come to England?

SB: My mother travelled to England from India with myself and my four siblings in 1966. My father, having left India under difficult circumstances, arrived in England about six months earlier, in 1965. So, my mother having never been outside of India, after travelling nearly two thousand miles across the country away from her home in West Bengal accompanied by family, boarded a ship in Bombay. For my mum who was born and educated in a society profoundly impacted by the British colonisation of India, travelling by herself with five children must have been daunting. Our route took us on one of the last passenger ships to travel through the Suez Canal in the year preceding the Six-Day War of 1967, to Genoa from where we took a train to Calais, crossed the Channel to Dover and there took another train to London.

CJM: I assume that your mother was born before partition.

SB: Yes, and as a consequence of which both my parents were displaced — in effect twice over. Her family were forced to leave what became East Pakistan after partition. They witnessed the most horrific violence and genocide.

CJM: What's the difference between occupation and colonisation?

SB: People often use the terms interchangeably in reference to India. The term occupation suggests a temporariness. Used to describe the context of the British Raj in India this undermines the degree of systematic rule and violence at a government and military level. The regime was brutal including slavery that extended across the Indian Ocean, and the practice of stripping assets through taxation. When taxation could not be met, land was seized as a penalty. The vast fortunes extracted from India during the British Raj and the British East India Company from the 1700s left India impoverished by the time of Indian Independence. The stripping of assets by the British East India Company was preceded by the Dutch, the French and the Portuguese.

CJM: What does this painting have to do with your mother?

SB: I'm interested in the female narrative. Within Britain, the constant stereotyping of South Asian women as passive objects alongside our devaluation as citizens through state legislation has been brutal, with laws such as the 'virginity test' introduced by the British Home Office functioning as forms of gendered and racialised violence.[1] These are subjects of essays by Hazel V. Carby and Pratibha Parmar in Paul Gilroy's 1982 anthology *The Empire Strikes Back*, which I read in 1983 alongside Edward Said's seminal book *Orientalism*.[2] Both books were influential for *Housewives with Steak-knives* and the video-performance *Kali* (pls. V–X). My painting *Housewives* placed the narratives of Afro-Asian women at its centre in response to the systemic racist and patriarchal violations that we faced daily as Black women.

1. On 3 February 1979, when *The Guardian* published 'Airport Virginity Tests Banned by Rees', it was the first major news outlet to report on the 'gynecological tests', more commonly called 'virginity tests', conducted on Indian women entering Heathrow airport.

2. Centre for Contemporary Cultural Studies (ed.), *The Empire Strikes Back: Race and Racism in 70s Britain*, London: Routledge, 1982, and Edward Said, *Orientalism*, Abingdon and London: Routledge & Kegan Paul, 1978.

CJM: Your Kali figure is noticeably dark. When was the first time that you were called Black?

SB: When applying for our UK citizenship and first passports, you had to tick one of two boxes available to us at the time to describe one's 'ethnicity': (a) 'Are you white?' or (b) 'Are you black?' That was it. The state identified us as Black, and identifying ourselves as Black was important to forming critical allegiances between those of us who were 'Othered' by the state and who shared histories of being oppressed by colonialism.

The word Kali literally translates as 'black'. The deity Kali is therefore traditionally represented as being Black. Considered beautiful, she embodies the eternal Shakti that is both a 'feminine' and 'masculine' force. Calling this work *Housewives with Steak-knives* was a homage to the powerful voices of South Asian women I had grown up with, who were my heroines. My father and I had a strong relationship, but I wanted to create an image that engaged with Black women's subjective space and to subvert stereotypical and dominant Western patriarchal images of Black women. Growing up in the UK we rarely saw positive representations of Black people on television or generally in the media. Racist tropes were commonplace, so occasionally catching glimpses of Angela Davis, Muhammad Ali, Jayaben Desai, Martin Luther King or Malcolm X on television or in newspapers were gifts to me and my family. These were people whom we looked up to and who gave us hope and voice and space. The title *Housewives with Steak-knives* was intended to situate our experience within the everyday context; a call to collective resistance against a patriarchal and imperialist order.

CJM: How were you introduced to Kali?

SB: In 1986, after completing *Housewives with Steak-knives*, I travelled to India for the first time in twenty years, discovering that my grandmother — who had adopted my father after his natural parents had died at an early age — had been the first to introduce me to Kali. We were close because I spent a lot of time with her. Relatives took me to what had once been her room. There on a mantlepiece was a small print of the goddess Kali she had left to me. In this image Kali is depicted wearing more or less the same ikat design that I had painted in *Housewives*. A widowed woman, I learned that my grandmother was a prototype feminist, educating herself, becoming a teacher, and a strong devotee of Kali, for which she was well known in this Indian district.

CJM: Did your mother see your work?

SB: Yes, she saw *Housewives* at the ICA. In 1987, returning from India, I recall saying to her, 'You didn't tell me about the picture, or about Kali; you didn't tell me that my grandmother was this extraordinary devotee and prototypical feminist.' To which my mother responded 'Well, when I saw *Housewives with Steak-knives* I thought you must know!'

This experience led to my becoming more interested in psychoanalytic theory and how memories are buried. The tunic design represented in *Housewives* was based on a Miss Selfridge top that I found in the local high-street store in my early twenties. I must have gravitated towards it because there was something about it that had subconsciously triggered this memory from early childhood. I had also been studying Op Art in Fred Orton's lecture series at the University of Leeds and was drawn to the formal optical aspects of the design, which to me resembled mouths or eyes protecting the body against a hateful gaze. The design had symbolic presence in a number of subsequent works.

CJM: In what other paintings does the top appear?

SB: It also appears in a work called *The Only Good Indian...* (1985) (fig. 9), and in my diptych *As I Stood, Listened and Watched, My Feelings Were This Woman Is Not for Burning*, (1985–6, pl. II). The title *The Only Good Indian* was drawn from cowboy films. I encountered the phrase — 'The only good Indian is a dead Indian' — endlessly as a child. That experience coincided with my perception of the way in which the media in the UK treated South Asian women and men. Anybody who was deemed to belong to a Black community was portrayed as worth less than their 'white' counterpart. We were collectively treated as though we were expendable.

CJM: Those Westerns are American and the target of their hatred is indigenous Americans, but the sentiment is the same.

SB: Yes, racial slurs have historically been interchangeable as shown in images relating to the British Raj in India held in the Yale Center for British Art archives. In the context of the film genre of Westerns I always identified with the Indians. American culture being persistently screened on television in the UK, at school in a group of children that were White and Black, I would be put into that position of being cast as 'the Indian'. I didn't have a problem with taking on that role, but I did have an issue with the concept that in Westerns the Indians were portrayed as barbarians and were expendable. These encounters of growing up in England were formative and I became interested in subversion early in my life. Resistance to racism was also instilled in me from a very early age by my father, who himself had been part of the resistance movement against British colonialism in India.

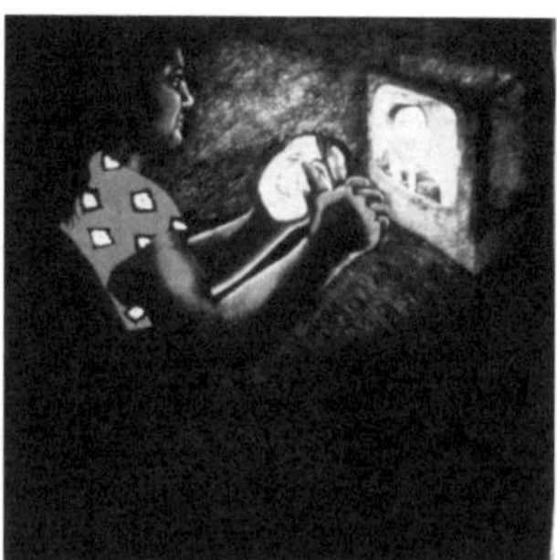

Figure 9
The Only Good Indian..., 1985

II

CJM: *Housewives with Steak-knives* is a mixed-media composition comprising paint, pastel, paper and collaged photocopied elements. Do you call it a painting?

SB: I absolutely call it a painting. In fact, others have tried to dispute its status as a painting.

I started this work in 1983. While an undergraduate and conducting research in the University of Leeds library at a regular spot, on one occasion I noticed that someone had inscribed into the surface of the desk 'I like to fuck black girls'. It was devastating to read, but again, it was symptomatic of the position we women of colour occupied at that particular moment in British history. My work grew out of this in resistance. The white background represented in *Housewives* is a metaphor for white space, the institution of Whiteness and a direct reference to Robert Rauschenberg's *White Paintings.*[3]

CJM: What substances did you use?

SB: I used a combination of acrylics, house paint, pastel, pencil and photocopy collage on paper mounted onto canvas. The paper is inexpensive; whatever was affordable and available, probably Fabriano. It started with just a head...

CJM: Kali's head or another head?

SB: Kali's head. The work expanded beyond the width of paper I had initially begun with. To accommodate the central figure's growth I added sheets of paper to it, joining each additional section with white masking tape. It was an interesting process because it felt like stitching sections of material together in the way that a sail is made.

I was aware that using a combination of acrylic paint and pastel would create surface wrinkles on the paper. This was important to me because on reading a review of Rauschenberg's *White Paintings* when they were first exhibited, I was struck by the fact that they were critiqued in terms of their poetic spatio-temporal, formal qualities. In other words, interpretations nuanced by the ways in which sunlight hit the flat painted surface to create shadows only visible at a given moment in time before disappearing. This spatio-temporality stayed with me, and I applied this to how I made *Housewives.*

CJM: Had you seen one of his paintings in real life at that point?

SB: No. So it was an imagined painting in some senses. But I was bowled over by its concept and still am.

CJM: The painting is leaning away from the wall. She's coming out at you. Can you describe the elements of the composition? Her tongue is out because in the story of Kali she sticks out her tongue in a moment of disgust and rage following the death of her husband. It's a reaction, right?

SB: *Housewives*, when installed, is positioned at an angle sitting forward of the wall

3. In 1951 Robert Rauschenberg created a series of panel paintings using white latex house paint. The *White Paintings* are notable for the absence of brushwork or marks. Almost from their inception, he enlisted others (Brice Marden, Darryl Pottorf, David Prentice, Cy Twombly and Lawrence Voytek, among others) to repaint them to maintain their pristine surface quality.

by 330mm, activating the painting and lending a sense of movement in the way that a sail does. Compositionally, it is significant that the machete is angled as if it moves beyond the framing. The central figure is portrayed as gesturing with her tongue out. We call this 'paap'. It is an active acknowledgment of a wrongdoing — a spontaneous reaction, a little bit like a tic.

CJM: Why is she holding a machete and not the titular sneak knife?

SB: The painting is a play on concepts, words and forms. It is a machete because within the traditional iconographic representation of Kali as a warrior goddess, she's portrayed wielding a weapon. According to mythology, the deity Kali was created on earth in order to destroy evil in the form of mankind — a beast born out of bestial relations. Each time Kali killed an incarnation of evil manifested in its human form, another would rise up from the blood spilled. She was thus engaged in an endless war that drove her to a state of near madness. Kali's lover, witnessing her plight, throws himself in front of her in self-sacrifice to end the violence. In stepping on her lover's body, Kali recentres herself, sticking out her tongue. Her existence is both Yin and Yang, the bringer of peace and war. The title's reference to 'steak' was to deliberately undermine any associations of my painting with Hinduvata fascism.

CJM: Is the facing-right side the violent warrior goddess side?

SB: Yes.

CJM: The facing-left side is the balanced Yin and Yang side.

SB: Yes. The bringer of peace, hence her hand is held upwards.

CJM: The mudra?

SB: Yes. She is also holding a rose-like flower intended to look as if it had thorns and referencing the 'English rose'.

CJM: Is there blood on the machete?

SB: It's ambiguous. It represents altha or sindoor, a red pigment worn by women as a symbol of power and fertility.

The painting's emphasis is the power of matriarchy in the context of the South Asian community, bringing together the housewife with references to Kali, accentuated by the altha on her hands, and the redness of her tongue. It counters passive representations of women, for example the media aggression towards Jayaben Desai and the Grunwick strikers, whose protests ignited national support among workers in their fight for equal pay and fair working conditions, resulting in changes to union laws that allowed previously excluded Black workers to become members. Initially supportive of the Grunwick strike, the unions subsequently succumbed to pressure from the then Labour government to withdraw support for the strikers.[4] Media coverage of the strike directed vitriol towards South Asian women who led the strike. Countering this, *Housewives*

4. The Grunwick dispute was a significant industrial dispute concerning trade union recognition the Grunwick Film Processing Unit in South London. Jayaben Desai led the strike that followed between 1976 and 1978, protesting the mistreatment of the primarily South Asian workforce by the factory management. More information about the dispute and Desai can be found here: https://www.bl.uk/womens-rights/articles/remembering-the-grunwick-dispute.

created a space that was a positive force for Black women against the dominant culture's demonisation of us.

CJM: Whose is the severed head in her right hand?

SB: It's an archetypal character, but by the time I had finished making this work, it was representative of the British Raj. Many say it resembles the British Conservative politician and former Home Secretary Willie Whitelaw.

CJM: I always wondered if it was Mountbatten (Louis Mountbatten, 1st Earl Mountbatten of Burma), since his assassination in 1979 by the Provisional Irish Republican Army (IRA) was still a contentious issue in the 1980s. Whose are the other heads in the painting?

SB: Hitler is on our far right. The head immediately below was one of the last I painted onto the garland and represents an archetypal art collector as referenced in Gavin Jantjes' painting *Frightful Knowledge* (1982) that I saw in late summer in 1984 at the exhibition *Into The Open*, although many people have said it resembles Edward Heath.

CJM: Absolutely. Whose is this head next to the Edward Heath-looking head?

SB: He was supposed to be Leon Trotsky. Trotsky is represented but Rosa Luxemburg, who is one of my heroines, is not. There are no women here.

CJM: Who is next to Trotsky?

SB: He's an archetypal figure representing the colonial British Raj and the East India Company. Hence, he's wearing a monocle.

CJM: Every few years I re-examine the painting and the heads seem different to me. Why did you include the quotations of Artemisia Gentileschi's painting, *Judith Beheading Holofernes* (c. 1620) (fig. 10)?

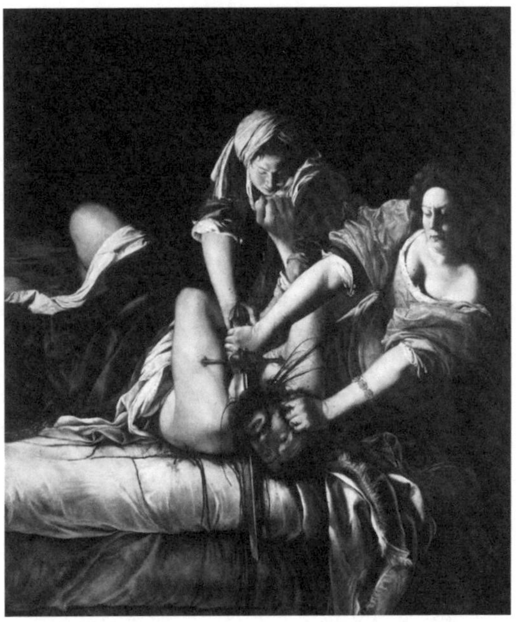

Figure 10
Artemisia Gentileschi, *Judith Beheading Holofernes*, c. 1620

SB: Many artists have painted this narrative, but Gentileschi's portrayal in my view is the most powerful; palpable in the way that representations of Kali are.

But it is of significance to me that they are Xeroxed images from Griselda Pollock and Rozsika Parker's very famous book, *Old Mistresses: Women, Art and Ideology.*[5] Pollock was my undergraduate university tutor. During this time from 1981, we developed an important intellectual relationship beginning with my challenging her about the absence of readings of art history from a postcolonial perspective. It was important for me to take a page out of that book and to incorporate it into this work in order to situate what was missing from feminist critiques of art history. In juxtaposing Gentileschi's work with iconography from outside Eurocentric references, I was calling for a feminist resistance to patriarchal violence against women's bodies that was anti-colonial. Secondly, it was a call for collective organisation and unity among women and across geographical spaces and cultures, against imperialism. It was also a way of saying to Pollock 'Where am I in your narrative of *Old Mistresses*?'

CJM: Because there aren't any Black women in *Old Mistresses*, are there?

SB: Not really, no.

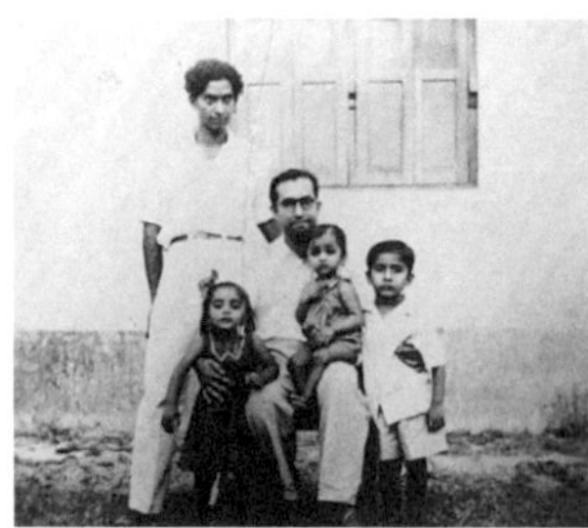

Figure 11
Photograph of Debidas Biswas, carrying his second daughter, accompanied by two other Biswas children and his colleague, Visva-Bharati University, Tagore Institute, Santiniketan, India, c. 1960. Photographer unknown

III

CJM: How did *Housewives with Steak-knives* get from your degree show in Leeds to the ICA?

SB: While I was undertaking research for my thesis on the work of Black women artists — it was later titled *'One Hell of a Big Subject': Contemporary Black Women Artists in Britain* — by chance I found some information about the exhibition *Into the Open.*[6] I then attended the associated symposium in summer 1984, where Lubaina Himid, among other artists, was speaking. I introduced myself to Himid, asking her if I could interview her for my thesis. She also kindly read the chapter on her work, according to the acknowledgments. In 1985 I invited both Himid and Sonia Boyce to come and speak at Leeds University. During the visit they saw *Kali* and *Housewives with Steak-knives*, both of which I had started making in 1983; *Kali* was completed and *Housewives* almost complete. Thereafter, Himid included both these artworks in the ICA exhibition she curated.

CJM: This is the first time the painting has been shown outside of the degree show? In your degree show it did not have a backing.

SB: Yes. In my degree show, *Housewives* was exhibited on a stretcher, installed at an angle. The idea was that every time *Housewives* was taken off display, it would be rolled up, increasing its surface texture over time.

CJM: You wanted the paper to crease?

5. Rozsika Parker and Griselda Pollock, *Old Mistresses: Women, Art and Ideology*, London: Pandora, 1981.

6. Curated by Lubaina Himid and Pogus Caesar, the survey *Into the Open: New Paintings, Prints and Sculptures by Contemporary Black Artists* toured to Mappin Art Gallery, Sheffield; Castle Museum, Nottingham; and the Newcastle Media Workshops, Newcastle upon Tyne, throughout 1984.

SB: Yes, prompted by my interest in spatio-temporality from Rauschenberg and other artists associated with Fluxus. I loved both the concept and the beauty of the resulting creases and shadows this created on the surface of my painting because it challenged ideas of fixity and the longevity of art. It is supposed to be unrolled for exhibition display and to last, but the idea was that it gains creases, and that you might have to repair it a little bit every time along the way.[7] It received its permanent backing when it was accessioned by Cartwright Hall in Bradford in the mid-1990s.

CJM: How does the image spill out from the paper onto what's now the canvas?

SB: These were formal concerns that were significant to me. It was important that the paper was not cut neatly so that it spills over onto the canvas. It defies traditional painting conventions.

CJM: It does, and it happens at the edge of the blade.

SB: I was very interested in breaking containment and transgressing the formal space. Seeing Artemisia Gentileschi's painting for the first time in Florence in 2006, I was blown away by the formal parallels.[8]

CJM: Is it all done with house paint?

SB: No, acrylic is used but some of it was house paint. Acrylics were expensive so I limited myself to using them mostly for the central figure, where the pigments in acrylic paint lent themselves to achieving a luminescence not possible with normal house paint.

CJM: Even at the level of material, there is economic critique in this painting.

SB: Yes. House paint is cheaper than acrylic paint and the paper used was relatively inexpensive. The pastels were of a high quality though. In terms of my interest in the economies of difference, this stems from my interest in the histories of European colonialism — especially relating to India. Basically, India was Britain's bank. Enslavement, looting and extortionate taxation exhausted the country's resources. There was a lot of anger from my parents towards the British, which was only heightened after arriving in England, where they were treated in a very, very hard way.

CJM: How do you reconcile the anger against the British with moving to Britain?

SB: Not with any ease. But we did. Though some may assume that the independence of a nation would be triumphant, after four hundred years of brutal European colonialism and the partition of a land mass that left millions dead, this was not the case. My father left India because he had no choice; as an academic he was very vocal about the impact government policy was having on the indigenous, nomadic communities and was more or less held under house arrest. A relative shared with us that had my father not left when he'd left, most likely he would have been shot. He had a cousin who worked for the Indian High Commission, who helped him get papers to travel to

7. See Ian Baucom, 'Two Places at Once, of the Same Place Twice: The Art of Sutapa Biswas', *Sutapa Biswas*, ed. Sarah Campbell, London and Portland: inIVA and Reed College, 2004, pp.58–65, 59.

8. Artemisia Gentileschi's, *Judith Beheading Holofernes*, (c. 1620) is in the collection of the Uffizi Gallery, Florence, Italy.

England and find a job. In some ways, England was random and not random. In 1964 he received a scholarship to undertake a doctoral study at Chicago University; we almost made the move, but he was convinced otherwise by family worried about his political investments and the violence towards civil rights protesters in the US, who they felt sure my father would become involved in supporting. I have often wondered what our lives would have been like had we gone to the US instead of England. But it also says something about the affinities of struggle in terms of the civil rights movement more broadly, right across the globe from India to the United States to what was happening in the UK. Civil rights remain a pressing issue.

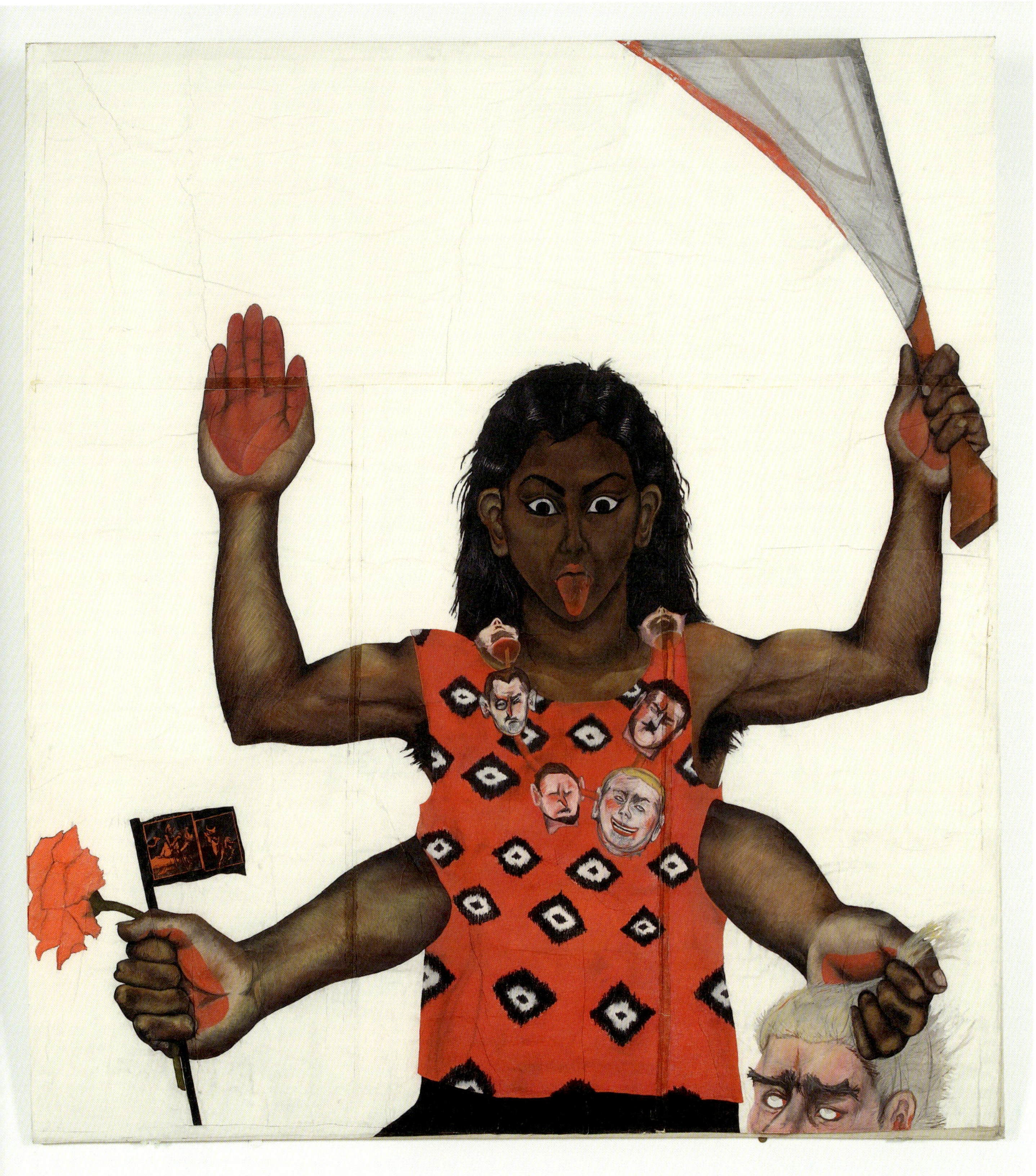

Plate I
***Housewives with Steak-knives*, 1983–5**

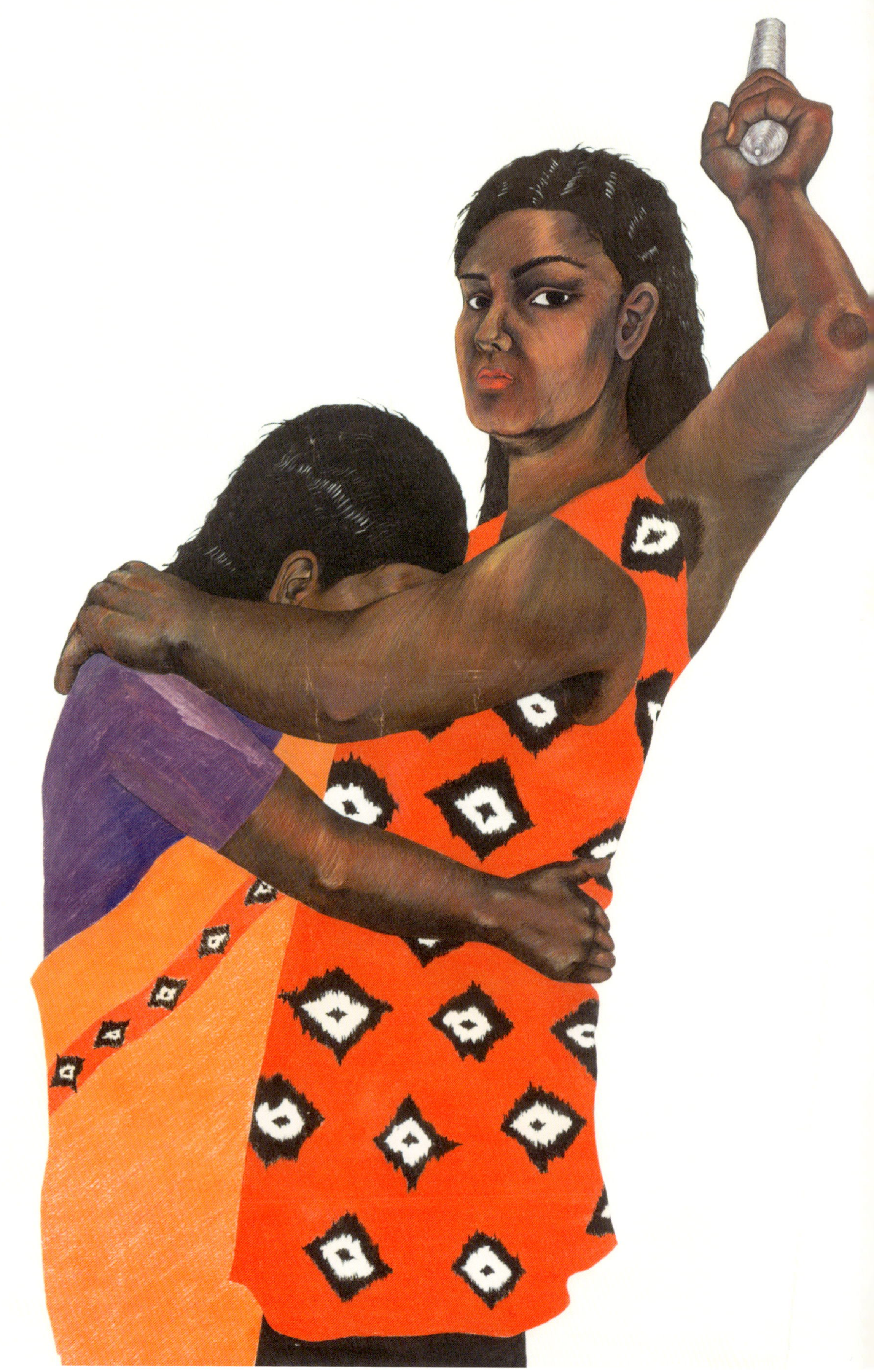

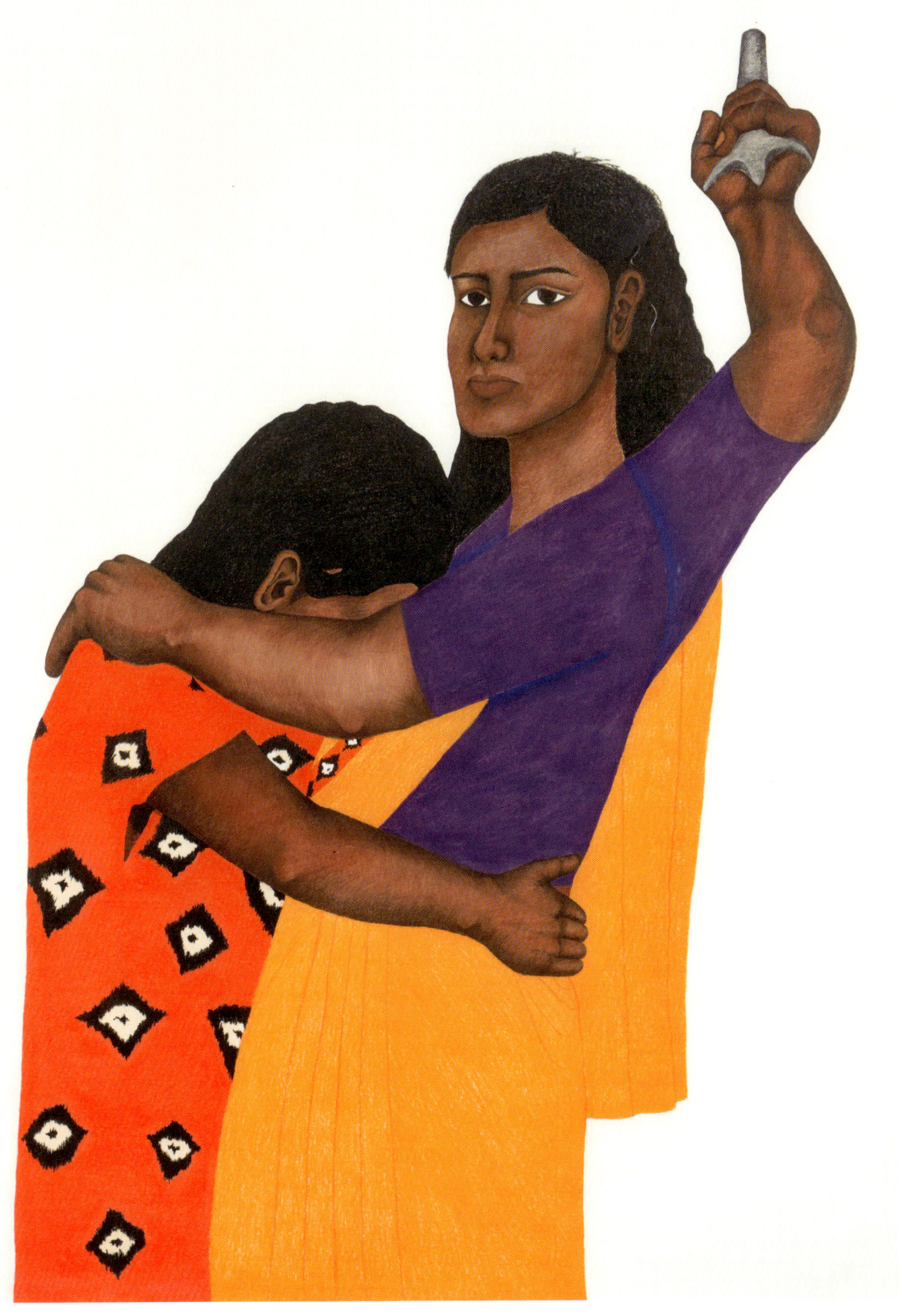

Plate II
***As I Stood, Listened and Watched, My Feelings Were This Woman Is Not For Burning*, 1985–6**

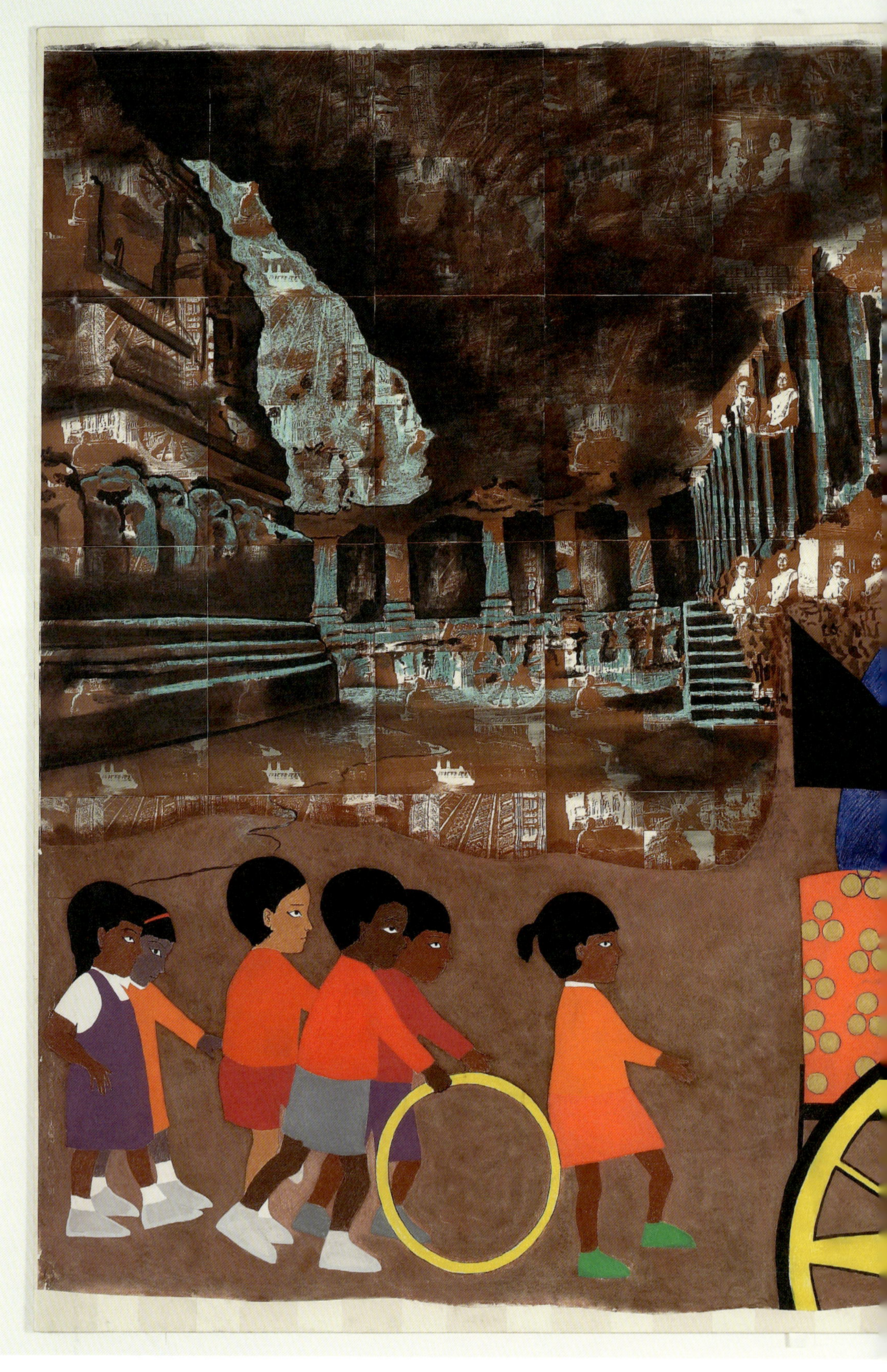

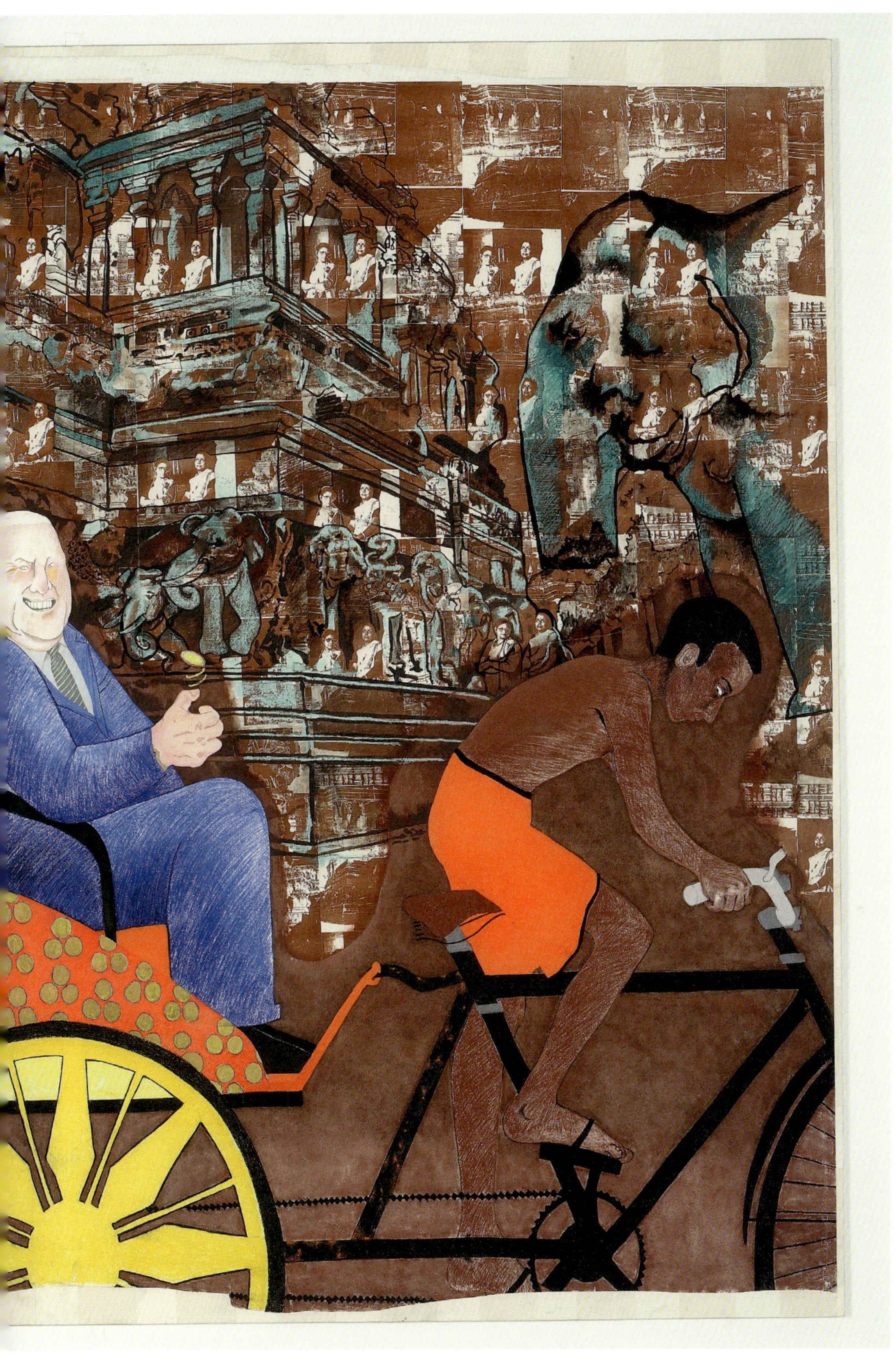

Plate III
***The Pied Piper of Hamlyn – Put Your Money Where Your Mouth Is*, 1987**

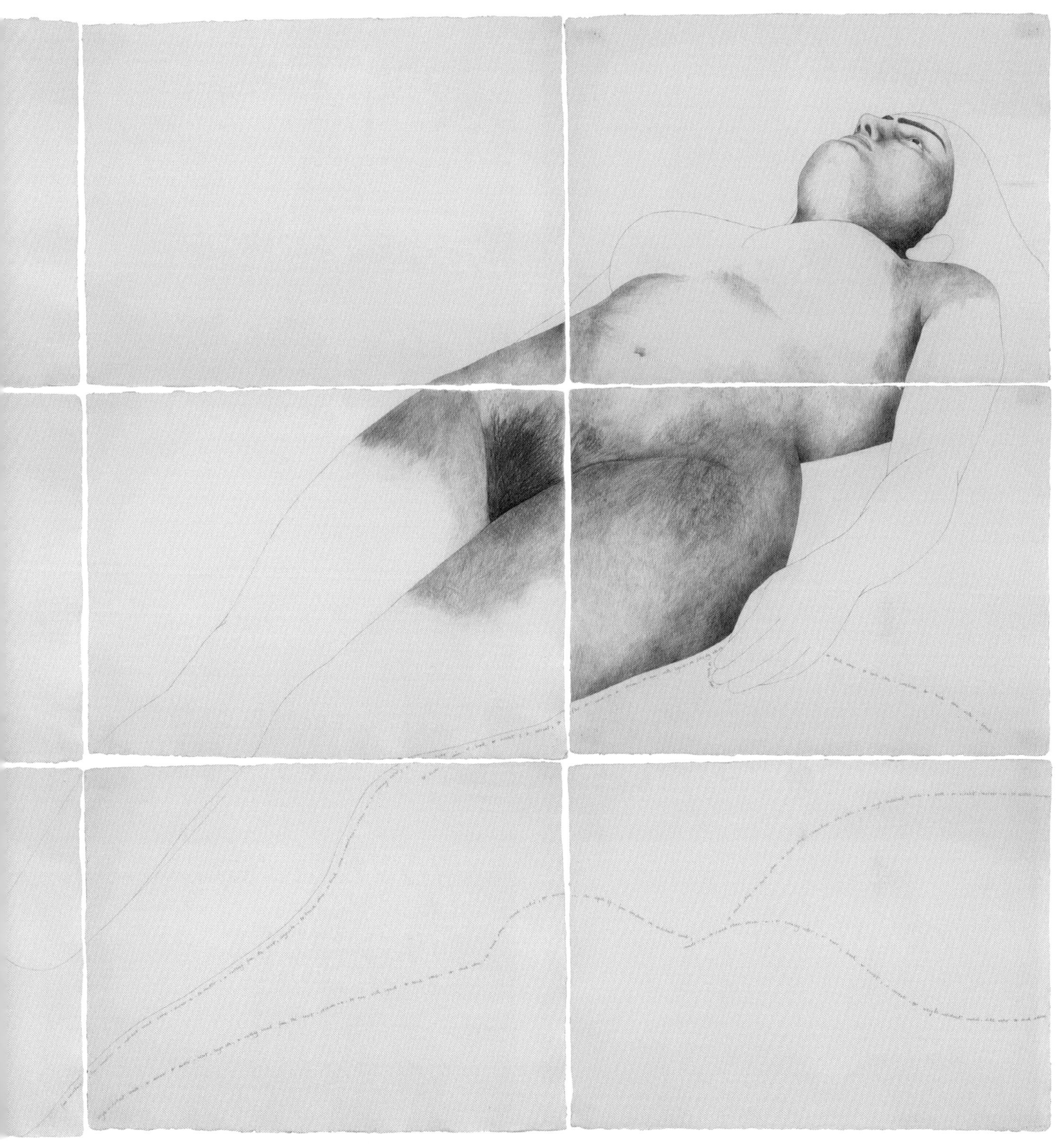

Plate IV
***To Touch Stone*, 1989–90**

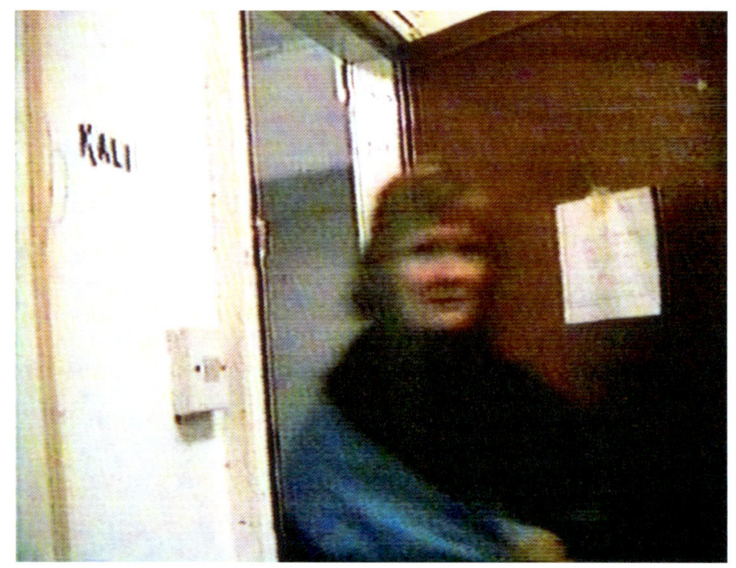

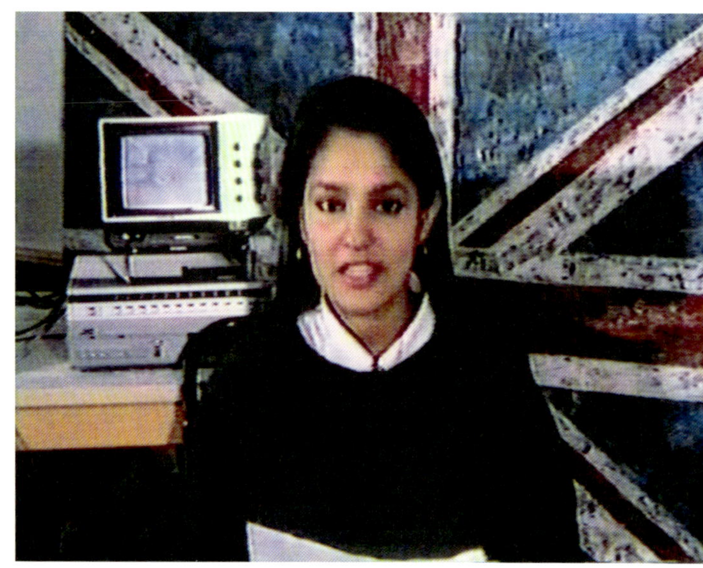
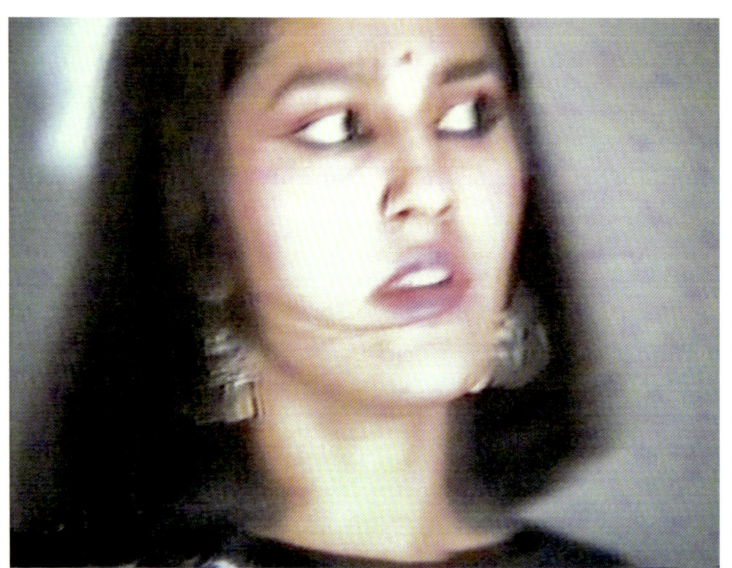
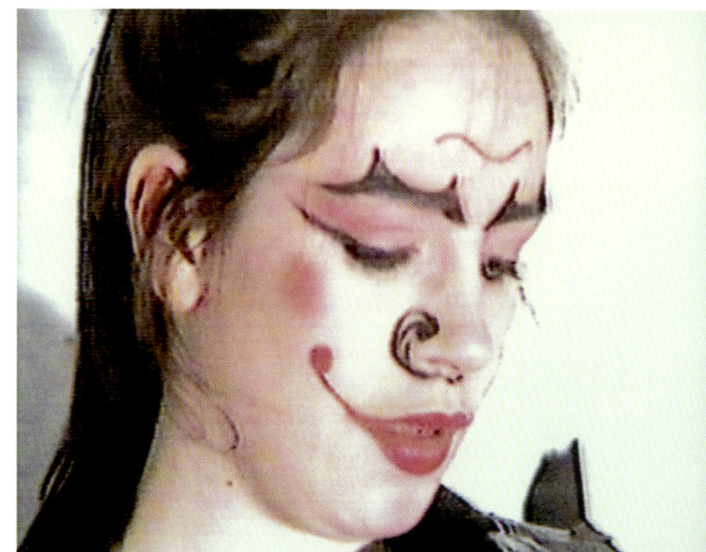
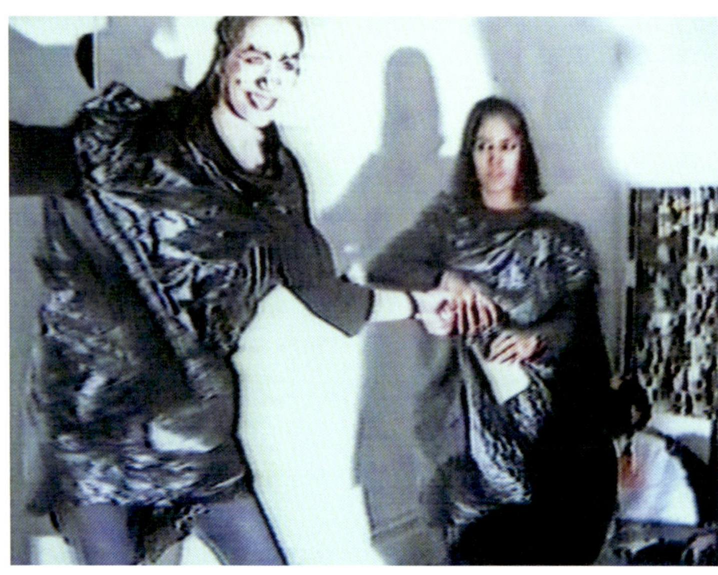
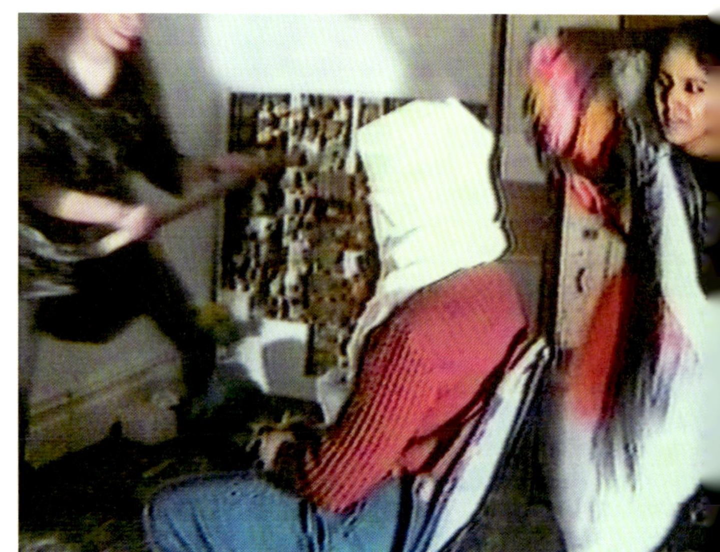

Plates V–X
***Kali*, 1983–5**

Reading between the Texts: **on Kali**

Alina Khakoo

Kali (1983–5) (pls. V–X) is a multi-part artwork produced during Sutapa Biswas's third year as an undergraduate in the Department of Fine Art, Leeds University. It began as an undocumented performance in front of Biswas's tutor, the art theorist John Tagg, in November 1983, which was repeated in January 1984 with another of her tutors, the art historian Griselda Pollock. The artist filmed this iteration of the performance, and made two 25-minute and 36-minute videos, both of which now reside in the Tate's collection.[1] The longer video consists of raw performance footage — beginning with preparations in the artist's student residence — whereas the shorter video artwork comprises edited performance footage, post-performance cutaway shots, and an accompanying soundtrack, bookended by an 'Introduction' by Biswas and end credits. At once a performance that derived from a performance, and a video that derived from a video from a performance, *Kali* demands to be read intertextually: 'in the light of its relation to other texts'.[2]

A literary critical term — though by no means confined to the written word — intertextuality punctures the hermetic seal around a work, opening it up to an unbounded tissue of connections, paraphrases, fragments, texts and contexts. Thinking intertextually about *Kali* accommodates the overlap between the multiple performances and videos, as well as inviting more speculative associations. It is also in step with

1. In this essay I only discuss the shorter *Kali* video, which was accessible at the time of writing during the COVID-19 pandemic.

   For discussion of the longer video, see Andrew Wilson, 'Kali', https://www.tate.org.uk/art/artworks/biswas-kali-t14278, (accessed 5 December 2020).

2. 'intertextual, adj.', OED Online, https://www.oed.com/view/Entry/240985?redirectedFrom=intertextual, (accessed 5 December 2020).

Biswas's personal history in the Indian diaspora in Britain: having edges to an artwork — an aesthetic world 'inside' the frame, and a separate social world 'outside' — is not a privilege afforded to artists whose everyday reality has always been shaped by racialised and gendered forms of representation.[3]

Cutting into the canon

Kali is replete with art historical references. The documented performance began when Pollock entered Biswas's studio, having been invited to what she assumed would be a conventional crit for a performance she would attend. The artist then asked her tutor to take off her shoes, wear a hood fashioned from a pillowcase, and take a seat in the centre of the room. Biswas and her fellow fine art student Isabelle Tracy proceeded to perform semi-improvised sequences around Pollock, comprising Kathak dancing, a pre-recorded monologue by Biswas in Bengali, and a puppet show in which the eponymous Tantric goddess Kali battled the demon Raban, among other elements. Fashioning the costumes and props from everyday materials — the puppets, for example, were made from pillows, rubber gloves, and paper doilies — quoted the avant-garde turn to found objects. Meanwhile, the semi-impromptu performance styled itself as a Happening — which Biswas encountered in Fred Orton's lectures on 1950s American culture and society at Leeds — as well as catching up with recent feminist experimentation with performance and video, which Pollock taught on her Theories and Institutions course.

Biswas not only invoked these intertexts, but also collaged them, leaving traces of the artist's hand in the delicately handcrafted puppets, and Tracy's crudely painted face, thereby making obvious the manual labour of cutting and reassembling.[4] In some instances, her collage clashed quotations: at the start of the performance, Biswas painted a fluorescent orange circle around the base of Pollock's chair, invoking both Jackson Pollock's drip paintings and Indian Rangoli floor painting. At other moments she carried references across media: painting, dancing, percussively shaking them, or playing them through a ghetto blaster in the corner of the room. *Kali* can be thought of in its entirety as an expanded, multi-dimensional collage.

3. Kobena Mercer, *Travel and See: Black Diaspora Art Practices since the 1980s*, Durham: Duke University Press, 2016, p.10.

4. Thank you to Iman Khakoo for pointing this out.

Biswas's contemporaries in the Black Arts Movement — which she formed links with later in 1984, upon interviewing Black feminist artists Lubaina Himid and Sonia Boyce for her undergraduate dissertation — were similarly turning to collage. For example, the Blk Art Group's 'cut-and-mix aesthetic' entailed selecting, excising and reconstructing image and text fragments from art history, popular imagery and vernacular visual cultures, such as protest banners, to create polemical assemblages.[5] Later in the 1980s, the cultural theorist Stuart Hall borrowed the musicological phrase 'cut-and-mix' from Dick Hebdige to describe young Black and Asian cultural practitioners' tendency to 'mix', 'blend' and 'cross over'.[6] A 'diasporic aesthetic' in its hybridity, cut-and-mix also drew upon the postcolonial strategy 'which critically appropriates elements from the master-codes of the dominant culture and "creolises" them'.[7] Tearing discourses apart, and repurposing the pieces for Black and Asian expression, presented a way out of the construction of Whiteness and Otherness through representation, which Biswas had experienced at Leeds.

'I loved being a student [...] because of the exposure to visual imagery [...] it was luxury actually', Biswas remembers of her course, which included art practice and history in equal parts.[8] At the same time, however, she was forced to notice 'I'm not there', as the canon was White and Eurocentric, and made no mention of colonial history, which Biswas had lived through when her family was displaced from West Bengal to Britain in the aftermath of India's partition and independence. At Leeds Biswas recognised the role of cultural forms in reproducing colonial and racialised ideologies: an art historical canon that hosts only White Europeans absents everyone else, declaring them abject, while papering over colonial violence. As her Black Arts contemporaries were experimenting with cut-and-mix and experiencing their own marginalisation at other art schools in the UK, Biswas was developing a distinctive collage technique informed by Fluxus, Jasper Johns, Mary Kelly and other references from her art history lectures, as well as punk bands that she saw perform live in Leeds.[9] Working in collage was a way of cutting into dominant discourses, at once deconstructing them and opening out new critical space.

Through multi-dimensional collage, *Kali* collided art historical intertexts from Orton's and Pollock's courses at Leeds with

5. See Kobena Mercer, 'Perforations: Mapping the Blk Art Group into a Diasporic Model of Art History by Looking at "Translations" of the US Black Arts Movement Ideas and the Prevalence of a Cut-and-Mix Aesthetic', paper presented at *Reframing the Moment: Legacies of the 1982 Blk Art Group Conference*, University of Wolverhampton, 27 October 2012, http://www.blkartgroup.info/conferencevid.html (last accessed 5 December 2020). See also Elizabeth Robles, 'Collage and Recollection in the 1970s and 1980s', *Wasafiri* 34, no. 4, (2019), pp.52–63.

6. Stuart Hall, 'Cultural Identity and Diaspora', *Identity: Community, Culture, Difference*, ed. Jonathan Rutherford, London: Lawrence and Wishart, 1990, pp.222–37.

7. *Ibid.*

8. Sutapa Biswas, artist talk presented at *A Feminist Space at Leeds: Looking Back to Think Forward*, University of Leeds, 16–17 December 2017.

9. See Eddie Chambers, *Things Done Change*, Amsterdam: Rodopi, 2012, pp.xxi–xxii.

imagery outside their orbit, for example family photographs of Saraswati Puja and Kali Puja ceremonies, which Biswas mounted on a board and propped against a wall in her studio during the performance. As well as staging an encounter between visual cultural registers, the artist reinvested art historical quotations with new meanings: during the Kathak sequence, Biswas and Tracy taunted one another with a can of Heinz lentil soup and a jar of Nescafé coffee, as well as scattering desiccated coconut — which also resembled salt or sugar — around the room, and shaking an Alpen muesli box filled with beans. By combining an iconic, if anglicised, Andy Warhol reference with plantation crops and foods that had been subjected to colonial taxation, Biswas enmeshed histories of colonial extraction in Pop Art's ironic celebration of consumerism. Nevertheless, the artist never cemented these alternative meanings: she offered them momentarily, before throwing them into disarray, or directing the viewer's attention elsewhere.

This tactic is apparent throughout the *Kali* video, not least in the music score composed by Biswas with Andrew Rodgers. This layers diegetic sounds from the performance — including rustling costumes, shuffling feet and music — with extra-diegetic audio such as white noise, and a composition of drum machine, harmonica, bass and slide guitar, which mimics a spaghetti western soundtrack. The listener momentarily picks up on meanings, such as solidarity with the anti-apartheid movement via music by The Bahumutsi Theatre Company, before these are folded back into a cacophony. Analogously, Biswas splices lucid, visual intertextual sequences with abstract, out-of-focus shots of mesmeric light, shadow, colour and movement, captured by cameraman Raj Batra.[10] Tending towards ambivalence rather than the articulation of coherent new meanings, *Kali* intervenes in representation by using multi-dimensional collage to cut these discourses open and leave them unsealed.

Refractions

Another critical use of intertextuality in *Kali* is the artist's citation of herself. The work is titled after the goddess Kali, with whom Biswas felt a particular affinity, partly because Kali represents both fearsomeness and protection — thereby troubling Western gender paradigms[11] — but also because

10. Though the video's end credits list the camera crew as: Andrew Rodgers (interview sequence), Kulvinder Bhatra [Raj Batra], Symruth Patti [Symrath Patti], Pat Forbes (performance sequence), Biswas has since stated that Rodgers shot the interview sequence and post-performance cutaway shots, as well as working with her on the video edit. Meanwhile, Batra filmed the performance, Forbes was the sound assistant, and Patti was absent from the performance, but credited as a member of Biswas's circle in 1983–4. Rodgers was her partner, and Batra, Patti, and Forbes were fellow fine art students at Leeds Polytechnic. Biswas, correspondence with the author, 9 April 2021; Eva Bentcheva, 'The Cultural Politics of British South Asian Performance Art, 1960s to the Present', PhD thesis, SOAS, 2017, p.135.

11. Gilane Tawadros, 'Beyond the Boundary: The Work of Three Black Women Artists in Britain', *Third Text* 3, no. 8–9 (1989), pp.121–50, p.145.

of an unconscious pull towards her grandmother, who had been a devotee of Kali.[12] *Housewives with Steak-knives* (1983–5) (pl. I) is a monumental self-portrait of Biswas as Kali, which was executed alongside *Kali*, where the artist likewise took on the goddess's role, while Tracy performed as her adversary, Raban. If Kali is Biswas's avatar, then the title of *Kali* calls attention to self-reflexivity within the work. In the video introduction, for example, Biswas is shown seated in front of her now lost painting *Flag* (1983–5) and a set of recording equipment, resembling a newscaster in a smart costume of black sweater and exposed white shirt collar, speaking directly to camera in a mid-range close-up shot. In this sequence, Biswas prefaces the performance footage in Brechtian style as a 'struggle between the East and the imperial West', thereby auto-referentially becoming a critic of her own work.

Not only does Biswas make the performance her own intertext in the video, but she also quotes other works from her oeuvre: *Flag* in the background was an encaustic painting that switched the stars and stripes in Jasper Johns's *Flag* (1954–5) to the Union Jack. Moreover, invoking the second-wave and Black feminist affirmation that personal experience, as political experience, was legitimate source material for artmaking, Biswas ends the introduction by quoting her experiences as the only person of colour in the Department of Fine Art at Leeds. This includes an anecdote of her tutor Marie Yates's projection of White feminist anxieties about the reproduction of patriarchal iconography onto Biswas's work, stating 'categorically' that she could not produce figurative representations of women, as in *Housewives with Steak-knives*.

In 'Black Diaspora Artists in Britain: Three "Moments" in Post-war History', Hall observed that the wave of artists to which Biswas belonged foregrounded Black and Asian bodies and selves in the frame, as done emphatically in *Kali*. Again, this was an intervention into dominant cultural forms that fixed the Black or Asian body as stereotypes.[13] News broadcasts, for instance, which Biswas alludes to in her introduction, routinely represented Asian women as 'mute and oppressed wives and mothers', breeding 'Asians flooding the country in their millions and scrounging off the state'.[14] In response, artists such as Biswas experimented with staging those bodies on their own terms, often in

12. Moira Roth, 'Reading between the Lines: the Imprinted Spaces of Sutapa Biswas', *New Feminist Art Criticism*, ed. Katy Deepwell, Manchester: Manchester University Press, 1995, pp.31–43, p.37.

13. Stuart Hall, 'Black Diaspora Artists in Britain: Three "Moments" in Post-war History', *History Workshop Journal* 61, no. 1 (2006), pp.1–24.

14. Pratibha Parmar, 'Hateful Contraries: Media Images of Asian Women', *Ten.8*, no. 16 (1984). Republished in *Looking On*, ed. Rosemary Betterton, London: Pandora Press, 1987, pp.93–104, p.99, p.95.

portraits or self-portraits. This was not a celebration of some essential Black or Asian self — which would only reverse the stereotype rather than discarding it — but rather 'the staking of a claim, a wager'.[15] Biswas's artist contemporaries devised formal tactics to subvert the conventions of racialised representation, such as cropping, captioning, and fracturing. Claudette Johnson's pastel portraits overturned conventions of scale and background, while Rotimi Fani-Kayode's photographs intersected planes of difference along lines of race, gender and sexuality. Together these triggered 'a kaleidoscopic proliferation of meanings around Blackness', as well as Brownness, which colonial and racist representational regimes had sought to establish as monolithic.[16]

In *Kali*, Biswas explores the disruptive possibilities of *mise en abyme*: the insertion of self-reflexive references in artworks, often to suggest a recurring sequence. If the work is named after the artist's avatar, then the entire work is a kind of expanded self-portrait. Therein, Biswas insists on her presence in the frame in both the performance and video versions, as well as using her own oeuvre and experiences as artistic material, and taking on a meta-role as critic, glossing her work. Not only does she insert the Brown body into the artwork, but she does so many times over: creating frames surrounding frames surrounding frames, and so on, adopting the logic of Russian dolls. This is encapsulated in the introduction, where the monitor connected to the camera is not in front of the artist — as in much second-wave feminist video — but behind her, creating an image within an image, like an infinity mirror. Here and throughout *Kali*, Biswas uses *mise en abyme* in a similar mode to transfigurations of Black and Brown bodies across the Black Arts Movement, even before she had formally met any artists associated with it: to refract the body that had long been presented as total, stable evidence of negative stereotype.

Conclusion: Invoking *Kali*

Kali has become an object of invocation, notably by Pollock. In the essay 'Tracing Figures of Presence, Naming Ciphers of Absence'[17], Pollock interprets her role in *Kali* as imperial spectatorship. She describes how she was thrust, unwittingly and hooded, into the centre of the room, while Biswas and Tracy performed disorienting vignettes around her, thereby exorcising her symbolic power.[18] Pollock's

15. Hall, 'Black Diaspora', p.20.

16. *Ibid.*

17. Reprinted in this volume, pp.49–73.

18. Griselda Pollock, 'Tracing Figures of Presence, Naming Ciphers of Absence', *With Other Eyes*, ed. Lisa Bloom, Minneapolis: University of Minnesota Press, 1999, pp.213–36. See also Eva Bentcheva, 'Who Belongs in the New Art History?', *The SOAS Journal of Postgraduate Research* 6 (Summer 2014).

essay is a testament to *Kali*'s transformative impact beyond the diegetic worlds of the performance and video. Sara Ahmed has argued that citations can be 'critically sexist or racist' — by upholding a dominant, White cis male history of ideas — or critically feminist or anti-racist by invoking womxn of colour forebears.[19] In this vein, the citations in 'Tracing Figures' — encompassing Valerie Amos, Homi Bhabha, Frantz Fanon, bell hooks, Chandra Talpade Mohanty, Pratibha Parmar, Edward Said and Gayatri Spivak — demonstrate Pollock's dedication to thinking postcolonially since encountering Biswas, who she credits for pointing out the racial blind spots in her feminist critique of art history. In her essay, Pollock weaves the footnoted theories into her argument at the level of the sentence. For instance, where Amos, Mohanty, Parmar and Spivak contend that White feminists speak ignorantly for all women — or worse, define themselves in opposition to a homogenous collective of oppressed Third World women — Pollock refuses to speak in undifferentiated terms, attending closely to cultural, political and historical specificity. Elsewhere in her body of work, Pollock maintains an intolerance for *indifference*: both the universal White subject's blasé attitude towards complexity and plurality, as well as the grouping of heterogenous individuals into a singular category such as 'woman'. Throughout, Pollock invokes *Kali* as a subtle intertext, a trace of this occasion when Pollock experienced imperial dynamics acutely, affectively.

Finally, the *Kali* video has circulated in feminist safe spaces since its initial screening at Biswas's degree show in 1985. It was included in the events programme that accompanied the seminal Black feminist exhibition *The Thin Black Line* (1985–6) at the ICA, as well as *A Feminist Space at Leeds* (2017) at Leeds University. In these contexts, *Kali* can be read as a latent intertext, a 'letter sent, waiting to be received'. This phrase is the title of Catherine Grant's 2019 essay about letters published by queer feminist Black British artists, partly for a 'counterpublic' that may comprise their loved ones, friends, contemporaries and future readers.[20] Grant's letters are from books and journals, yet Biswas's monologue in the introduction to *Kali* could be read along similar lines: as a spoken letter addressed to other feminists of colour to 'make our links very strong, so that we can act as a kind of support mechanism'.[21] Biswas's work continues to offer this to artists and curators who must survive racial and other

19. Sara Ahmed, *Living a Feminist Life*, Durham: Duke University Press, 2017, pp.15–16.

20. Catherine Grant, 'A Letter Sent, Waiting to be Received: Queer Correspondence, Feminism and Black British Art', *Women: A Cultural Review* 30, no. 3 (2019), pp.297–318.

21. Sutapa Biswas cited in Yasmin Kureishi, 'Reworking Myths: Sutapa Biswas', *Spare Rib* 173 (December 1986). Republished in *Visibly Female: Feminism and Art, An Anthology*, ed. Hilary Robinson, London: Camden Press, 1987, p.37.

injustices in the art world. For instance, the QTIPOC artist group Collective Creativity included Biswas in its imagined peer group and historical continuum mapped in *Surviving the Art School: An Artist of Colour Toolkit* (2016). In these circles, *Kali* is a call-out to artists seeking solidarity. Belying the work's throwaway aesthetic — Biswas's and Tracy's costumes are fashioned from black bin bags — it persists, awaiting a response.

Tracing Figures of Presence, Naming Ciphers of Absence

Feminism, Imperialism and Postmodernity in the Work of Sutapa Biswas

Griselda Pollock

* Kindly reprinted in this volume with the permission of the author. This version originally published in 1998.

It is one of the privileges of teaching fine art degree courses that I work in the presence of artistic practice. The challenging relations between art making and theoretical or historical reflection on and research in art history, when not kept in strictly segregated time zones, allow for a dialogue that can creatively alter each side. This article is a product of one such moment of exchange in which the relations between teacher and student, artist and art historian, structured and then recast two women's engagement with their practice, its politics and the question of art.

I begin my writing on Sutapa Biswas with some memories. These are not mere nostalgia for those simpler days when we had just about gotten used to the idea that modernism was in for some serious critical revision and before postmodernism had begun to empty all our gestures of their intensity and hope. If, as a teacher at a formative moment of a young artist's education, I had any impact on Biswas, an articulate young artist of Indian birth, taking on the possibilities and blind spots of a particular art department proud of its socialism and feminism but hardly self-conscious about its racism, she has had a profound impact on me and my work. The opportunity to write about Biswas's work is not only the outcome of an intellectual relationship forged in moments of becoming and difference; it is a product of a moment in the history of feminism, postcolonial discourse and the artistic gesture. This moment has changed how I think and write, indeed has made these practices visible, susceptible to a creative and often critical self-consciousness, which abjures the possibility of remastering the shattered hegemonies challenged in the name of those they excluded. Instead, there is a double movement in which we have to find the positions allotted to us, the positions adopted by us, and the movements that can be made to create other relations of difference not premised on the phallocentric One/other models. Feminism of the class- and race-limited kind alerted us to the tropes of masculine imperialism before yet another more powerful internal complaint shattered the false unity of feminism, recasting it as a perpetual process of self-provocation and dialogic covenant between the specific, singular, situated particularity of each of us who nonetheless uses this place, space, and discourse, rudely named 'feminist', to grapple with the structures of power and position, desire and language, possibility and determination, in a world that by being called postcolonial or postmodern only makes us more alert to the perpetuated force of modernity and coloniality.

Beginning where something started

Sutapa Biswas completed her undergraduate degree at the Department of Fine Art at the University of Leeds, England (1981–5). For some readers, this statement will immediately signify something quite significant. For others, it may indicate no more than educational background. The Department of Fine Art was one of the few in a British university to have the practice of fine art within its regimes of academic study.[1] After the appointment in 1975, and brief tenure of the Chair of Fine Art by social historian of art T.J. Clark, the faculty attempted to create a distinctive programme for the study of fine art

1. This has changed with the reorganisation of higher education in Britain, which is no longer divided between 'old' universities and 'new' polytechnics. These latter institutions had absorbed the independent art schools and provided the majority of sites for the undergraduate programmes leading to a BA in fine art. Until the early 1990s, when this binary system was abolished and all polytechnics became universities, there were only seven traditional universities that offered degrees in fine art, varying according to the origins of these departments in their balance between studio practice and academic study. At the University of Leeds, BA students in the fine art course were required to have high academic grades for entry and devoted half their time to art history/theory and half their time to studio practice in a programme that aimed to integrate them into a self-critical artistic practice.

with art history by creating a course evenly divided between history/theory and practice/theory. By acknowledging the modernist legacy that had created a breach between practice and theory, the department undertook a historically and critically informed realignment that would as much challenge the shibboleths of modernist studio practice as it would demand the production of a new discourse in art history attuned to the problematics of artistic production.

The join between two sides of the course was created by the common interests shared by artists and art historians in the context of a politicised and increasingly theorised critique of modernism. Terry Atkinson, Fred Orton, John Tagg, Tim Clark and I forged links through seminars, 'crits' (studio-based discussion of students' work in progress) and lectures that bridged hitherto separated domains whose boundaries had been systematically policed as the condition of making ambitious modernist art.

Art history, itself being reshaped according to an emerging programme for social and feminist histories of art, worked to provide a critical genealogy of the formation (1850s–60s) and disintegration (1950s–60s) of modernism. Artists in the studios explored these complex legacies and manufactured a critical practice that, while it was chronologically post-modernist, was not theoretically entirely symptomatic of those fashions now chaotically packaged as postmodernism. The critical difference between the two can simply be defined by the words *history* and *politics*. From several points of view, history — predominantly theorised through the tradition of historical materialism — ensured that theoretical revision was grounded in an understanding of interests, power, domination, exploitation. Such a conception of history stresses that there are important and concrete issues at stake in the challenges mounted to modernism's suspension of the social in favour of a formally isolated aesthetic domain. This engaged sense of the historical became a means to articulate a politically diversifying project, a naming of interests and an investment in concrete change rather than a fashionable substitution of ideas.

Feminism played a vital part in both the historical and political discourses that were developing at Leeds. As a historical perspective, feminism aimed to revise the canonical histories of art in order to acknowledge the presence and persistence of women artists over the ages. The realisation, through such reclaimed histories, that femininity and creativity were not, as ideologically presented, incompatible, forced revision of the very practices of art history and criticism in order to understand the specificity and meaning of women's inscriptions on the texts of culture. Feminism necessitated a critique of modernist art and art history as much as of the critical revisions to it that were becoming the hallmark of the Leeds Department of Fine Art.

There can be no doubt that this academic environment — or, rather, this informal and still emergent conversational community, productively located in an art department that was considered marginal and provincial despite its prestigious past professors (Quentin Bell, Lawrence Gowing, Arnold Noach, Arnold Hauser) — influenced the development of Biswas away from the immensely skilful and professionally accomplished figurative painting she had been producing as a student. Biswas was encouraged toward an ambitious and critical intervention in contemporary art by means of multimedia presentations in the field of dominant representations, both local to Leeds and on a world scale.

Biswas's presence in the course, however, was itself a factor in the evolution of the Leeds project. It was she who defined the absences in these seemingly radical discourses deriving from Marxism and feminism. It was she who named the imperialism that still structured analyses speaking in undifferentiated terms of class and gender, never acknowledging the issues of race and colonialism. It was her critique that forced us all to acknowledge the Eurocentric limits of the discourses within which we, the staff, practised. Her challenge was mounted face to face, not at the level of abstract taunts. She directly engaged in dialogue with people sharing an intellectual and artistic space. We were thus assumed, by her political generosity, to be able and willing to enlarge the critical discourse we were developing to accommodate the subjects of class, gender and race in their intricate and painful configurations between us and within us.

She demanded change. Response was made, and the course then altered. No longer repressing the question of imperialism and its racist practices, the space of the studio

2. Sutapa Biswas and Moira Roth, 'Sutapa Biswas: A Narrative Chronology', in *Synapse*, London: The Photographers' Gallery, 1991, p.23.

3. The phallic mother refers to an infantile, masculine fantasy that retrospectively endows the mother with the attribute of omnipotence; in fact, she is endowed with what the child attributes to himself.

and the lecture theatre had to articulate the pressure of the social and psychic relations that imperialism as a still powerful structure installed in us all. Instead of binary oppositions, Biswas's practice as student and as producer of artworks systematically eroded the pairing of accusation and guilt to release the critical problem from defensive denial or mere liberal tolerance.

This is visible in the work she produced as a conclusion to her degree, *Housewives with Steak-knives* (1983–5) (pl. I). This vast tableau uses several pieces of paper mapped together with masking tape: 'I sought to find a language that deliberately brought together components that were both of a Western and Eastern aesthetic and ideology. For me, the phenomena did not present such distinct borders, but in fact there were similarities and parallels in both camps.'[2] This extended and hybrid space was constructed to house the collision of images, systems, meanings. At a formal level, the piece knowingly sets White against Black, by imaging the Hindu goddess Kali, which means black, on white paper. Within Hindu thought, however, Kali represents the destroyer of evil, and the signification of this mission through blackness directly assaults the Eurocentric colour symbolism that has been used in the imposition of the whitened, Christianised Europe's self-legitimating morality. The scale of the Kali figure and her adornment with both knives and flowers, with one of several hands raised in the Hindu gesture of peace, make this representation of she who pursues and punishes evil dominate the space of the picture and the space of the viewer. A centralised and frontal figure of a female goddess is not merely a signifier of power, which is, therefore, threatening. It is also a signifier of power and, therefore, comforting, because it is an allegorical figure of empowered femininity — the mother, who is too often misrecognised in Western patriarchal psychology as only the phallic mother.[3] Her power precedes the slightest intimation that the phallus might signify. The evocation of the maternal as a force of *both* order and power, of *both* anger and peace, reminds us of a measure of meaning other than that which European phallocentricism erects with its perpetual divisiveness. The binary opposition and hierarchical ordering of male and female, characteristic of the Western imaginary, are dislocated by this grand image of activity and moral purpose in the feminine. She sports a necklace of decapitated but still identifiable men's heads, which form a recognisably contemporary cast of political miscreants. These masculine trophies representing capitalism as well as communism, imperialism, and colonialism symbolise the evil that must be purged, in contradistinction to the Hellenic-Christian West's projection of evil onto women through the allegorical figures of Eve and Pandora, for whose apparent crimes all women must be punished. Hindu mythology provided Biswas with a vocabulary with which to localise and reduce Western mythologies that, in permitted ignorance of other cultural systems, mistake their local stories and sexual mythologies for narratives of universal truth.

Hanging in one hand of Biswas's *Kali* is a photocopy of another image of an active woman punishing male evil and threat, Artemisia Gentileschi's *Judith and Holofernes* (1625, Detroit Institute of Arts)*. This apocryphal story itself has a colonial dimension since a Jewish narrative was appropriated by Christian culture and reworked to convey completely refigured metaphoric meanings that erase the historical and ideological resonance of the story in its own national context. It thus becomes difficult to define what the considerable popularity of this imagery of a woman decapitating a man meant at the time a seventeenth-century woman painter, Gentileschi, began a series of repeated engagements with it. As part of Biswas's image, the photocopy of a Gentileschi image further functions as a metonymic sign for contemporary Western feminist art history: for the photocopy is from *Old Mistresses*, a text used in the lecture series Theories and Institutions at the University of Leeds that Biswas attended and critiqued.[4] Within feminist art history, still intoxicated in the early 1980s with recovering a 'hidden heritage',[5] Artemisia Gentileschi and her Judith paintings were celebrated as *exceptional* because, by creating a murderous political heroine, the painted image seemed to disrupt and to counter prevailing assumptions about the inevitable passivity of women. Set in diminished proportions against Hindu culture's major deity, Kali, the counter but still Western femininity, signified by Judith as heroine/Gentileschi as artist, was relativised by Biswas's picture. The powerful image of an active, divine, and politically insurgent femininity from Hindu culture functioned equally to displace racist stereotypes that currently represent Asian women as passive. The engagement with a culture's mythic sign in relation to lived sociohistorical femininities also addressed the complexity and contradiction

* Editor's note: Note there are two reproductions on the flag in *Housewives*. One, on the right, is Artemsia Gentileschi's *Judith and Her Maidservant with the Head of Holofernes* (1623–5, Detroit) as Pollock suggests here, the other, on the left, is Gentileschi's *Judith Beheading Holofernes* (c. 1620, Uffizi) as mentioned in Biswas's interview with Courtney J. Martin in this volume, pp.23–32.

4. Rozsika Parker and Griselda Pollock, *Old Mistresses: Women, Art and Ideology*, London: Pandora Books, 1981 (rev. ed., 1995).

5. Eleanor Tufts, *Our Hidden Heritage: Five Centuries of Women Artists*, New York: Paddington Press, 1974.

within modern Indian culture itself, as well as between cultures brought by history into both confrontation and potentially creative exchange.

Tropes and theories: centres and circles

Writing on 'Imperialism and Sexual Difference', Gayatri Chakravorty Spivak has argued that feminism functions to expose the truth claims of the discourse of the privileged male of the White race, that is, to challenge their monopolistic claims on truth, defined according to their own interests.[6] Feminism, however, has often failed by the same token to acknowledge its own complicity in imperialist discourse. Spivak argues for the necessary development from mere *oppositional* feminism, directed against patriarchal power, toward what she names a *critical* feminism that constantly examines its own complex imbrication in institutions and ideologies. Spivak exemplifies her point by noting, from within literature studies, the different degrees of individuality ascribed to Western and non-Western women. Thus feminist literary criticism (and art history does much the same with its artist-heroines) struggles to create and legitimate for its women writers the very individuality that is the hallmark of Western bourgeois identity. Jane Austen, Charlotte Brontë and Virginia Woolf are named in their complex subjectivities and ambivalent negotiations of identity and social place and become, as the effect of this attention, major icons of feminist discourse. By contrast, Western feminist scholars continue to produce studies on the undifferentiated collectivity of 'Third World women'. African, Asian or Arab women are not endowed with a comparable privilege of either subjective particularity and complexity or of the capacity for resistance and negotiation of their sociopolitical situations. Thus if spoken of at all, African, Asian or Arab women constitute a featureless collectivity, Third World women, the very icons of oppression.

Biswas's use of Kali as housewife deploys an image from Hindu culture precisely to overwhelm that objectification of Asian women, and its implied inequality in relation to modernity measured precisely by degrees of individuation. Equally, by setting this image in both a relation and a contrast to a figure from a Western mythology (Judith/Gentileschi), Biswas retains the allegorical potential of the female deity to be a sign of a dense cultural and political freight that

6. Gayatri Chakravorty Spivak, 'Imperialism and Sexual Difference', *Oxford Literary Review* 8 (1986), pp.225–40. See also the critique of this tendency in sociological writing by Chandra Mohanty, 'Under Western Eyes: Feminist Scholarship and Colonial Discourses', *Feminist Review* 30 (1988), pp.61–88.

bespeaks the complexity of any cultural engagement with issues of power and sexual difference. She does not, however, flip back only to Westernise the Asian woman by creating for her a compromised, that is, imperial and bourgeois, individuality, even though the features may be based on her own, giving the figure animation and immediacy. Finally, by naming such a figure, redolent with its place in high cultural discourses, a 'housewife', Biswas refutes a false exoticism. The woman is, after all, ordinary, working with her knives in the daily processes of domestic duty and familial transmission of language, culture and its embodied stories. The artist thereby pays a certain debt to her own mother, to the place of domestic work, confusing and refuting the binaries that diminish the particular meanings of women unnamed by history, though influential through personal and familial networks in particular individuals' histories.

This major piece of 'history painting' was produced in tandem with a remarkable performance, recorded and exhibited as a video, titled *Kali* (1983–5) (pls. V–X). At the time, I had felt privileged and trusted to be invited to witness, so I thought, a performance Biswas was preparing in order to explore her double vision.[7] Her feminism was larger, broader and more finely calibrated to the questions of difference and power than that within which I had been allowed ignorantly to remain. When I arrived to watch the performance, I was kept inexplicably waiting in the corridor while preparations continued inside the room. At last I was ushered in to find myself not a spectator at the margins but part of the spectacle. The centre, British imperialism, was to be put on discomforted display, and made to figure as part of the created ritual contesting its postcolonial hegemony. Obliged to sit in the centre of a circle, hooded, though I could just see through the slits at eye level, I was made to function as an icon of imperialism around which Biswas's enactments of resistance would be performed. Physically central by my actual positioning in the real space of the room, I was positioned as 'I', the figured subject of imperial colonialism. Yet that position was exposed and made vulnerable by being deprived of the privilege of being a protected observer, or a surveilling eye of power. The tropes of imperial power involve the excessive and objectifying visibility of the Other who consolidates the coloniser's subjectivity in its place of empowerment through the screen of the gaze. In

7. The phrase derives from the work of the American feminist historian Joan Kelly, 'The Doubled Vision of Feminist Theory', originally published in 1979 and reprinted in Joan Kelly, *Women, History and Theory*, Chicago: University of Chicago, 1984. Kelly identifies *double vision* as that which embraces both the private and public spheres of Western bourgeois society. I am using it here for Biswas's project, which creates two centres in conflict and dialogue, each having to acknowledge that the other is always already a part of the other, because they are both lived by the subjects – women subjects, colonial subjects (this phrase implies both coloniser and colonised and, in doing so, acknowledges the colonised as also a subject of the process, and not merely the passive object of Europe's Othering).

the physical enactment and positionings created by the performance, these historical relations of power and visibility were reversed. The figure of imperial power was indeed secreted behind its hood; but its vision was impoverished, signifying the utterly partial and disfiguring nature of a disassociated understanding/ignorance of the culture and people it observed. Yet being placed in the ring, as actor in the drama, the assumed invisibility of the imperial as merely panoptical gaze from above or elsewhere was crudely exposed to everyone else's view. (The performance was also being filmed by a group of Indian students from both the department and other local art schools, so there were plenty of other viewers to witness this.) As bearer of this bared look, 'I'/I could not distance myself from the mythological representation of a historically conditioned struggle that was concretised in Biswas's experience as an Indian student in a British university art department. The performance's play between the larger histories that tied India and Britain and the local experience she was having at Leeds thwarted the processes by which colonialism seems to happen 'elsewhere', over there, and not at home, and by which colonised peoples are displaced backward in time as if they belonged to a past, or a timeless zone, statically captured by religions and cultures that are ethnographically recorded as being stuck in time immemorial, before history. The physical proximity of real persons in a room that performance rewrote as the space of history, power and resistance became the signifying device for piercing the temporal ellipsis of colonialist discourse.

Because I was participant yet target, forced to hear and struggle to see meanings that silenced me, and to which I must react, an emotional register was activated to lend its intensities to the structural relations of colonisation, which was the topic of the performance. I was made witness to the representational making of another configuration of subjectivities around the now-eroded binaries of coloniser/colonised. The performance exploded the oppositions Black/White, Indian/English to demand recognition based on the experiencing of what might otherwise only be known abstractly, theoretically — namely, the radical interdependency of subjectivities and conditional nature of meaning within oppressive, oppressed or resistant languages. Imperialism functions in its colonial as well as classed and gendered forms as the privilege of neutrality.

The imperial subject is made to feel itself the norm, without colour, sex, difference. Difference and its injuries are projected out, to be carried and signified by that which is othered in terms of class, race, gender, ability and so forth. Purely positive endorsement of the Other's Otherness — any form of essentialist and uncritical celebration of ethnicity, class culture, femaleness — may offer momentary solidarity and necessary affirmation. Nonetheless, it confirms the mythic structure of the opposition, leaving it in place while, more often than not, merely and ineffectually reversing the evaluation of its terms. People who are the products of imperialism cannot sustain this binary opposition and its use of distance, for we carry the imbrication of world cultures within us. Whiteness, Europeanness, maleness, and so forth depend for their meanings on that which they Other, even while they use the Othered to exnominate and disguise themselves. In the global movements of peoples and the circulation of goods and cultures characteristic of colonial and international capitalism, there are no more discrete cultures and radically fixed differences. Some see the present situation as a kind of postmodern hybridity that is to be embraced. Others stress the ambivalence that underlies our inevitable complexity as postcolonial subjects. Biswas's work operates in these mutually contaminated spaces through which she can explore this historically specific subjectivity that cannot be one and cannot be assumed, fixed, possessed or simply affirming. The very use of performance as a media, utilising the complex relations between actual persons in real space as an alphabet for a postcolonial script, enacted the pain, violence and necessary hope that pulse across the hitherto masked interconnections of 'the colonial subject'.[8]

Spaces and places

Since that performance, Biswas has travelled literally and metaphorically to other spaces, and her work now retains the imprint of this concern with space and the positioning of the viewer in relation to an experience of the work that is not contained by sight. Standard spectatorship allows the viewer a distance from the object. It renders what is seen an object, objectifying in turn the subject who has produced the work. Biswas seeks ways to undermine this metaphorically imperialist spectatorship. Initially, this interest revealed itself in the way she used the spaces of the two-dimensional

8. This analysis leans on the work of Homi K. Bhabha, 'The Other Question: The Stereotype and Colonial Discourse,' *Screen 24*, no. 6 (1983), pp.18–36. Bhabha's critique of Edward Said's *Orientalism*, London: Routledge & Kegan Paul, 1978, involves redefining the 'colonial subject' as the ambivalent figure where colonising and colonised are structurally inseparable. Said's analysis revealed how the European self was produced by its Othering of the Oriental, subjected in a Foucauldian manner, to the discourse of its own Othering. Bhabha uses a psychoanalytical model of the economy of the subject shaped in desire in conjunction with Foucauldian governmentality to paint a more complex picture of the psychic investments and effects of the colonial encounter in which both coloniser and colonised are constituted relatively. Thus the colonial subject signifies the ambivalent space of that complex constitution of subjectivity in the colonial/postcolonial field.

surfaces of drawings and pastels. Scale is important. To be confronted with very large pictures alters the spectator's own sense of importance in relation to the figured presences of the images. But Biswas also uses the blank, unworked spaces of the paper. These read in several ways.

On the one hand, they imply a sophisticated engagement with the problematics of modernism, which specified the particularity of painting as the flatness of the support in opposition to the illusion of three dimensionality achieved by the use of perspective devices. Biswas's figures elaborate that flatness while stressing it. Pastel is used to indicate the rounded forms of well-muscled arms, yet its own materiality insistently draws attention to its placing on and creation of the surface. Areas of dense colour, which always threaten to advance or recede, are held in check by her use of a pattern shaped both like an eye and a mouth, which, for instance, appears on the garments of Kali and the figures in *As I Stood, Listened and Watched, My Feelings Were This Woman Is Not For Burning* (1985–6) (pl. II). Such devices, which so affirmatively define the surface of the paper on which she works, yield yet another semantic dimension. In refusing the eye the fascinations of the female body that are so adamantly not offered in Biswas's densely worked pastel surfaces, modernist fidelity to flatness is made unexpectedly to serve feminist concerns. The saturation of the skin of colour stands in, as signifier of modernist respect for medium and flat surface, for the body that masculine fantasy nonetheless desires to see. Her dramatic and uncompromising use of the female body by these reappropriated modernist moves, moreover, also bypassed the quarantine into which feminist artists and filmmakers had in the 1970s placed the representation of the female body.

On the other hand, the empty parts of her surfaces also engage with modernist concerns, critically rather than sycophantically. Biswas refers to the impact of Robert Rauschenberg's *White Paintings*, encountered perhaps in Fred Orton's lecture course on American culture and society in the 1950s. Entirely blank canvases, ironically the epitome of modernism's purity, nonetheless, were full of incident, caused by their interaction with an environment and the spectators whose own presence is inevitably registered, however remotely, on the never entirely pristine surface. Biswas used this insight in her own work quite differently at first. Large areas of unworked surface create not a blank space of nothing, but a counterpoint to what is so energetically worked in the areas she has drawn. Using modernist notions of flatness and surface, she can make the figured and the as-yet-unmarked, the full, and the seemingly empty work in tension — a creative incongruity that makes the viewer recognise that what seems empty may still signify, and may still be active in contributing to the impact and meaning of the whole. This notion of other space, space off, brought into play, continues to be explored in a variety of practices that ultimately led Biswas back toward the spaces of interaction so specific to performance, without abandoning the spaces of representation or, indeed, represented space.

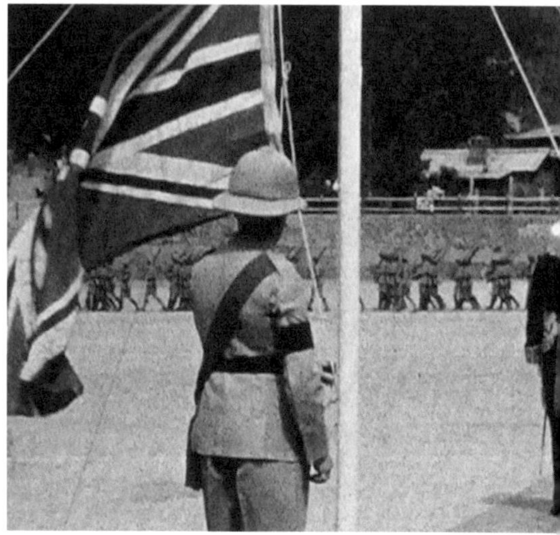

Figure 12
from *Lumen*, 2021

Speaking of her own work, Biswas has described the impact of a journey to India in 1986–7, the first in twenty years, a journey that involved going back both to the times and spaces of a remembered childhood and to the times and spaces of a historical India, one of the cultural compass points from which she had been working to negotiate her specific position as an Indian/British artist within contemporary British culture. She visited the cave temples of Ajanta and Ellora, the temples of Orissa and Khajuraha. She recorded the significance of the encounters with these architectural realisations of her interest in the interactions of individuals with physical space. What she found in these sites was a space that leads away from the fetishising spectatorship typical of Western art to the multilayered semiotic experience characteristic of ritual or ceremonial architecture. With its varied uses of sculpture and painted imageries within a spatial totality, these great ensembles act on the participant through the sculptural figuration of the body that invites a corporeal empathy to create the channel of experience of the space and its mythological inscriptions.

These discoveries did not serve only formal purposes. The relation of Biswas herself to these places was not merely antiquarian or scholarly. She came to them not only through space, from England back to India, but through time, from professional art practice in adulthood to childhood, memory, and family. What the discoveries in India offered, and why these places meant so much, were determined within a specific subject's configuration of a widespread contemporary condition of displacement, with its freight of loss, memory

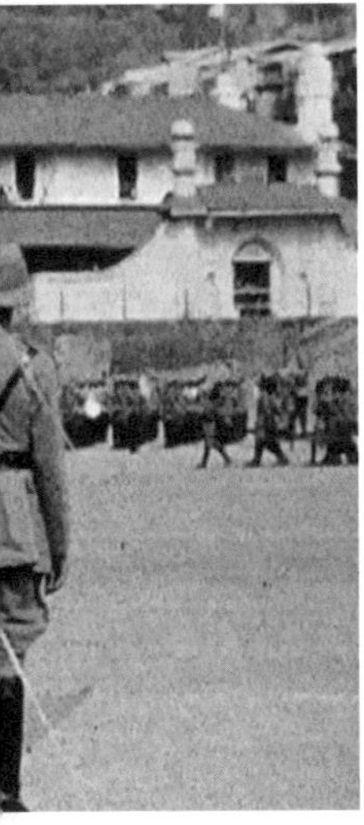

9. Edward Said, *Orientalism*.

10. Gayatri Chakravorty Spivak, 'The Rani of Sirmur: An Essay in Reading the Archives', *History and Theory* 8 (1985), p.251. Spivak derives her concept of worlding from the philosopher Martin Heidegger, who used it to define the origins of the work of art as resulting from the gap between earth and world, a gap filled by the texture and substance of the artwork.

and desire. Indeed, this condition may be one of the major decisive formations of the postmodern subjectivity that those writers and artists who do not merely straddle two cultures but embody the pain and pleasures of a historically shaped multiplicity are now finding forms to signify.

That this is a post- or anti-Orientalist programme cannot be doubted. It is significant that Biswas's art historical studies at Leeds involved a critique of what Edward Said called 'Orientalism' in Western painting, particularly of the nineteenth century.[9] *Orientalism* refers to the array of political, scholarly and aesthetic discourses that turned a Western gaze on the Islamic world and constructed an 'Orient', an 'East' as the cipher of difference by which a European selfhood and identity were constructed as both superior and dominant. Orientalism is the form of domination constructed by a variety of strategies and devices. Orientalism is a projection of both fear of the Other and fascination with difference whose interactions create its characteristic myths of Oriental backwardness, laziness, sensuality, cruelty, luxury and indifference. Orientalism, furthermore, creates a temporal ellipsis, which projects that which is named as the Orient as belonging to a permanent past so that the European colonial invasion is represented merely as the inevitable rescue of dying cultures that will be brought into the present by becoming subjected to Europe, thus made synonymous with modernity. Domination thus reads as historically determined progress.

Orientalism is, in the words of Gayatri Chakravorty Spivak, a process of 'worlding'. The actual interventions of the European colonisers as soldiers, traders, scholars, artists, and governors involved a process of moving from ignorance about the societies and cultures that were illegible to them, treating India as a kind of uninscribed earth, toward the imposition of their own maps of 'knowledge', the projection of their own schemes of meaning through which the colonised were then invited to recognise themselves. This metaphor of cartography, which marks the blank inert earth with the colonisers' meaning, thus making it a world that can be navigated and used, yielding meanings for its subjects, Spivak calls the 'epistemic violence of the imperialist project'.[10] It once again involves notions of space, for imperialist worlding is a political semiotics of space. Such cartography has to be engaged with and rewritten, and the field of experience must be reworlded by the artist who wishes to explore the ambivalence and multivalence of that history. Yet the return must also avoid the mythologising of East, Orient and Otherness, which by virtue of evacuating history remains in the imaginary spaces of Orientalism and imperialism.

Biswas has written of her project as attempting to *demythologise* Otherness. This term, *demythologise*, takes us back to the critical work of Roland Barthes, whose study 'Myth Today' was written at the height of France's Orientalist crisis, the Algerian struggles for liberation from France's colonial domination in the later 1950s. For his example of myth as the prevailing semiotic form of bourgeois representation, Barthes analysed a provocative image from the magazine *Paris Match*. The cover showed an African soldier in French military uniform saluting the French tricolour. Barthes names myth a depoliticised form of speech. Myth works by appropriating one level of meaning or fully constituted signs, such as results from our decoding the colour photograph as the picture of an African man in a French uniform saluting a French flag, then emptying these of their historical specificity — the agonising struggle of the Algerian people for liberation — so that they can be filled up with a more dispersed, yet globalising meaning, the natural acceptance of French imperiality. Barthes uses a number of terms to describe this complex process of ideological colonisation of signs. Myth appropriates the first level of meaning, denotation, making it then the accomplice of the mythic sense. Myth deforms, distances, distorts. But it never completely obliterates:

> What French imperiality obscures is also a primary language, a factual discourse which was telling me about the salute of the African in uniform. But this distortion is not an obliteration: the ... African remains here, the concept needs them; they are half amputated, they are deprived of memory, not of existence; they are at once stubborn, silently rooted there, and garrulous, a speech wholly at the service of the concept. The concept, literally, deforms, but does not abolish the meaning; a word can perfectly render this contradiction: it alienates it.[11]

11. Roland Barthes, 'Myth Today,' in *Mythologies*, trans. Annette Lavers, London: Paladin, 1973, pp.122–23, originally published in 1957.

12. This idea is powerfully explored in Frantz Fanon, *Black Skin, White Masks*, London: Pluto Press, 1986, originally published in 1952.

13. Sunil Gupta, *Fabled Territories: New Asian Photography in Britain*, Leeds: City Art Gallery, 1989.

Alienate has several meanings. It is about rendering something alien, making it other and foreign. It also means separating what belongs to someone from them, in the sense of alienating affections, or property, or in Marxist terms, the rights to the product of a person's own labour. In psychological parlance, it refers to the subjective experience of not feeling at one with oneself, or feeling cut off from those with whom we should or would like to feel close. *Alienate* is a promiscuous and labile word. Nonetheless, it captures the condition of the imperialised subject: made Other, thus cut off from her/his own centre and made to feel separate from what should be close, affirmative, comfortable. It also contains the sense of being deprived of the products of one's own culture and labour, which is represented back as no longer available for use in the present. To demythologise is thus to undermine and resist that alienation, that being made to feel alien in one's own land, time, family and person.[12] The myth produced by imperialism/Orientalism is that there are other lands, somewhere else and in another time. It obscures the fact that these are geopolitical spaces of interaction. To contest that myth is to refuse being constructed as 'belonging elsewhere'. In the 1980s there was a critical project to articulate this demythologised, de-alienated space, and it was undertaken by Indian artists born in India but growing up in Britain, and by those intellectuals who actively see themselves living across the geopolitical realities of a postcolonial world, through the accidents of birth and professional work or through growing up in the West as part of an Asian culture, refusing in their persons to confirm the mythic absoluteness of the division. The articulation of demythology can be achieved precisely in the spaces of representation, in 'fabled territories', as the title of a touring exhibition of Asian photography in Britain, named it.[13]

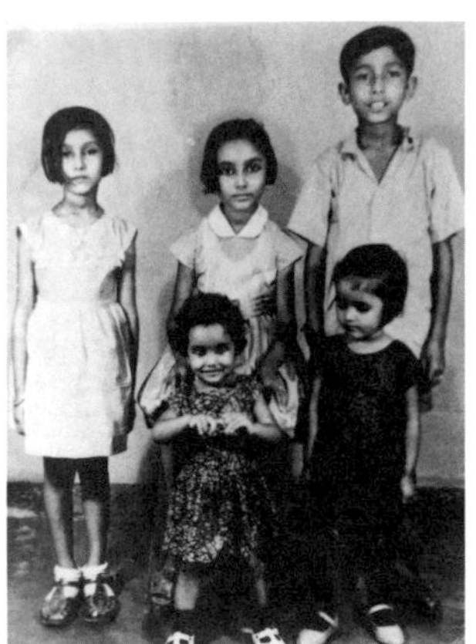

Figure 13
Biswas children, West Bengal, India, c. 1966. Photographer unknown

Photography is a specifically cogent form of representation within which to work through this problematic. Biswas has used it in her *Infestations of the Aorta — Shrine to a Distant Relative* (1989) (figs. 6–7) and other works. Photographic space simultaneously contains fact and fantasy. It can make things seem concrete because we are led to believe in the existence of what we are shown photographically. Yet photography has always been a fantastic medium, a medium of fantasy, for it stills time, freezing the moment into a perpetual past that can uncannily still be held and looked at in the present. It can record, yet it also is the means of representing entirely fabricated scenarios that access memory and nourish desire. Barthes defines myth as depriving the image of memory while appropriating its existence. Biswas's work demythologises in precisely activating memory at the site of the now-ambivalent image. In a literal, autobiographical sense, she makes use of the memories that she reactivated on her trip to India to revisit the places associated with her childhood (see *Blue Skies and Sunday Lunch*, 1989). But her installations also aim to create the space of memory, which is also historical and cultural. The personal can become a mythic signifier because it can be used to absent the historical context in which we are produced as subjects. The Othered, colonised subject is alienated from history and memory, made into a static fetish of its exoticism. To insist on subjectivity, through play of memory and desire, is to return time, history and society as the context of our experience, our mediated relation to the structural determinations that made us subjects of time, place and desire.

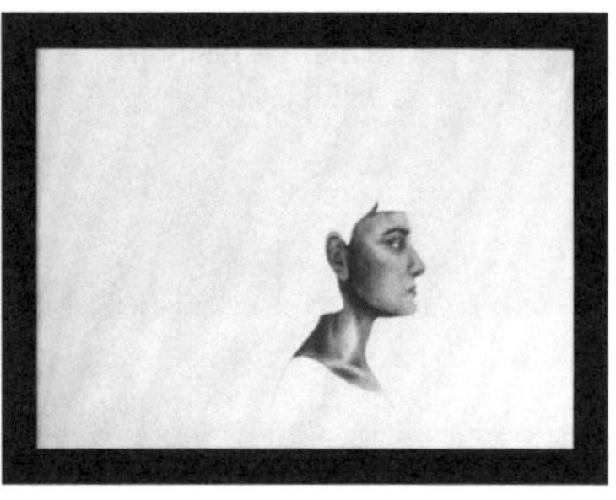

Figure 14
Sacred Space
1989–90

How can that be managed in an art practice? Biswas orchestrates the space of her exhibitions so that she is the author of an entire installation. This was most marked in the piece/event/installation *Sacred Space* (1989–90) (fig. 14). She used a room in the Slade School of Art, London University, a building that neighbours the Orientalist foundation, the London University School of Oriental and African Studies, established in 1909. Her presence in this room, hinged to its surroundings, forced into view the architecture of Orientalism. Edward Said quotes arch-Orientalist politician Lord Cromer, advocating in the British Parliament the foundation of this school: 'The Creation of a school [of Oriental studies later to become the London University School of Oriental and African Studies] like this in London is *part of the furniture of Empire*'.[14]

Biswas carefully restored the room so that its pristine whiteness marked the division between its created and aesthetically charged space and that of the decaying building itself. Using lights installed outside the windows, the room became one vast white painting constantly reworked by the play of natural and artificial light in ways that Biswas affirms were suggested by the paintings of rooms by American painter Edward Hopper. Mounted on the walls

14. Said, *Orientalism*, p.213.

behind non-reflective glass were three large framed images, pastel, line drawing and acrylic. Again these images were placed on large white surfaces whose edges were hard to discern against the surrounding whiteness of the walls. The subtle erosion of the boundaries between picture and space almost suggested that the images were directly drawn on the walls, and the viewer was incited then to move in for closer inspection. At that distance, the hanging of the piece and its size emphasised an architectural space, in which the viewer cannot imagine him/herself merely the mastering eye but is forced to know him/herself as a body in space.

On another wall were mounted, at a top eye level of six feet, a series of black-and-white photographic images. Printed on litho film and mounted as transparencies pressed between glass, they were further textured by the wall behind. Yet they were framed, holding the flow of space so that the viewer, coming close to read the images, constantly being eroded by light reflecting on them from outside, and the texts, had to work to see and read. Participant, engaged, worked on, the viewer becomes visitor to the installation, which put Biswas's world, that which she as artist has 'worlded' and thus inscribed with her meanings, into a special kind of encounter with that visitor. Like my own experience as decentred witness/participant object in her earlier performance, *Sacred Space* offered an invitation, drawing the viewer closer and making her work to read the signs within the mapped space of the installation. Paradoxically, it also challenged the viewer because the work so insistently embodied the subjectivity of the artist who made this space 'sacred':

> Of memory, we change
> From one conversation to the next
> Always in search of
> The edge of the surface
> And of textures
> There is pleasure
> and sometimes none
> So thinking back to our space
> Marked only by fallen clay
> There is both absence and presence

Of violated territories —
You, whose spirit is dull
Brought me here
To the great mountain
Whereupon, I died in the thinness of its air
From violated territories
Its boundaries,
With fierce eyes
I watch
This sacred space.

— **Sutapa Biswas** (1990)

The images in the sequence of photographs are those of a bare foot stepping in footsteps imprinted in the sand. For some this will conjure up both Sigmund Freud's reflections on Jensen's *Gradiva* and Victor Burgin's photowork of the same title, reflecting on Freud's essay, using the fetish of the beautiful and lost girl's unsandalled foot glimpsed at Pompeii.[15] Such formal parallels serve to give this work its sense of belonging, here and now, to a world that includes Freud and a critical semiotic art practice itself invoking psychoanalysis precisely to insist on questions of subjectivity in the production and consumption of art. Not nostalgia for some lost homeland but the complexities of desire are the animating terms of Biswas's use of memory, image and space. Psychoanalysis argues that in our formation as human subjects we become human only as we are marked by loss and lack. This condition results in the specific configuration of our subjectivity as split between conscious and unconscious. Each side of the division has its own characteristic modes of producing and connecting meaning. Between both, however, there is a regular, if displaced, traffic, by means of which the psychic journey we undertook to become a subject is perpetually recorded and reworked. Subjectivity is, therefore, not to be understood only as a developmental, organic achievement of simply living over time and growing up. Within the psychoanalytical model, the human subject is viewed as an archaeological site created out of a layering of experience through time and shifting and reframing of meanings because of both the accumulation and the division into conscious and unconscious that fracture our self-understanding and repress much of what nonetheless determines our ways of being. Every stage in this journey into subjectivity is sedimented within us. Its forms of survival or persistence, however, are affected by its configuration

15. Sigmund Freud, 'Delusions and Dreams in Jensen's *Gradiva*' (1907), in Sigmund Freud, *On Art and Literature,* Pelican Freud Library, vol. 14, Harmondsworth: Penguin Books, 1985.

with all other stages and their related traumas, fantasies and knowledges. The multilayered spaces of the subject can be evoked and addressed in the multiplaned spaces of an artistic installation, where image, surface, space, figure, body and sign are put into orchestrated tension and play, overlapping, reconfiguring and allowing meanings to be donated to sense in the gaps between.

The body in space — viewer in gallery and figured image on drawn page or canvas — functions as a literal sign for real subjects in a concrete history that is the territory on which we must engage in dialogue about the epistemic violence of imperialism and the violated territories that are its subjects. The acknowledgment of such a freight is neither comfortable nor painless for any of those caught in its historic webs. But there is no other space, utopic or nostalgic, that will heal the rifts, in our persons, as human subjects, in our social beings, as products of real histories. There is no essential mother India to salve the wounds of displacement and separation, but, in Biswas's work, we experience a confrontation with loss and grief for an actual grandmother who was the beloved figure of territorially and culturally distanced childhood. There is no universal space called art or being human that can relieve the pain of learning about Whiteness and Western power by attending to the articulation of the specificity of someone's experience, which is not Other but particular, distinct from, yet shaped by Whiteness and its West, while also sustained by other memories, themselves historically contaminated but also resistant.

Historical subjects: subjects in history

In Biswas's complex aesthetic fashioning of the spaces of contiguity for India and Britain, these two poles of postcolonial formation are made contemporaries — thus signally a de-Orientalising and demythicising strategy — and while the particular interaction of the two is particular to Biswas precisely because she makes their imbrication the condition of her practice, its historical hybridity and cultural opportunity become part of the viewer's world, too. The body in space functions thus as an allegory for the problems and disjunctions of communication: connection and disconnection, hearing and distortion, projection and confrontation. Made present by participating in Biswas's work is the subject of history.

But even as I write this I realise that it once again inscribes a Western worlding. There is no subject, but we must always speak of subjects; there is no history, but always histories. I have stressed the issues of imperialism in subjectivities and histories so far because it is the condition of Biswas's work. In our conversations at Leeds, it was its legacy of racism that rendered my feminism both local and imperial. Feminism is not displaced by the politics of race. For just as there has always been Black women's creativity, there has also always been Black feminism. Yet to qualify women's creativity and feminism with a signifier of colour is to become enmeshed in the ideological constructions of racism. Biswas's feminism challenged the ideological limits of what Valerie Amos and Pratibha Parmar call 'imperial feminism'.[16] Amos and Parmar quote bell hooks's argument about the racism inside the women's movement evidenced by the way that feminist scholarship is written as if Black women were not a part of the collectivity, women.[17] Thus a feminism that perpetuates its own ethnocentricity actively sustains racism. Amos and Parmar critically examine some of the key theoretical concepts of White feminist literature. They examine their pertinence for Black feminist theory. Difference, family, sexuality all are qualified by being considered in relation to the specificity of the experiences of Asian women and women of African descent. There is an important link here with *Housewives with Steak-knives*. It is also a powerful text about femininity, setting in conflict and tension Western ideologies of Western and Asian femininity (stereotypes of passivity) with the interruption of both by the fact of Biswas's active creativity and her use of an image of female power, Kali. Writing of Biswas's work in the context of the politics of modernism and postmodernism, Gilane Tawadros calls this painting the 'clearest enunciation of Black women's creativity as a form of creative resistance':

> Here, Hindu mythology is invoked to serve a political content which is quintessentially modern. The image of the goddess, Kali ... has been appropriated by Biswas as a means of dissolving the absolute distinction and binary oppositions which characterised European thought. In opposition to these false and essentialist categories, the precepts of Hindu culture reflect the ascendance of ambivalence. Thus, the Western notion of 'femininity' as essentially fragile and passive is contested by the ambivalent status of Kali who is at once goddess of both

16. See Valerie Amos and Pratibha Parmar, 'Challenging Imperial Feminism', *Feminist Review* 17, no. 1 (1984), pp.3–19.

17. bell hooks, *Ain't I a Woman? Black Women and Feminism*, London: Pluto Press, 1982.

> peace and war. In adapting the Hindu iconography of Kali, Biswas asserts the ambivalence of femininity, both pacifist (as opposed to passive) and aggressive, both 'feminine' in a traditional sense and strong. She also affirms the existence, in terms of the Hindu system of knowledge, of a 'zone of indiscernability', to borrow Gilles Deleuze's phrase, between myth and reality. Thus, Biswas implies, there is an element of the real in the mythologisation of 'femininity', and equally an element of myth in the reality of black womanhood.[18]

18. Gilane Tawadros, 'Beyond the Boundary: The Work of Three Black Women Artists in Britain', *Third Text* 3, no. 8–9 (1989), p.145.

Tawadros also suggests that by using icons and myths (from Indian and Western art and culture) Biswas suggests a fusion between past and present, a way in which history is activated for the present, while also acknowledging other temporalities embodied in myth and religious thought. Finally, Tawadros points out the corruption of the key Western distinction between public and private, which is a gendering of social as well as psychic space, associating the feminine with the domestic and the private in opposition to the supposedly masculine domains of politics, power, and action. In this work, and later drawings from the same period, the housewife and her domestic tools, knife here, potato peeler in *The Only Good Indian...* (1985) (fig. 9), become tools of aggressive defiance because domestic spaces are perceived as equally penetrated by the politics of gender power and race power, both equally the site of resistance. Indeed, the family space is a critical space for Asian women in the struggle with White and Black patriarchs, with the imperial state and its racist immigration and employment policies. The complexity of the mutually inflected struggles requires the production of artworks that are not ambivalent in a typically postmodern avoidance of accountability, politics or ethics. They are cogently ambivalent in order to invent through the cultural inscriptions of a British Asian woman artist multiple registers of meaning that are activated in the spatial encounter between subjects, with bodies and histories.

Not so much beyond the boundary, this project works as a perpetual crossing, eroding and unfixing of the frontiers where we must engage in dialogue, self-recognition, acknowledgment of difference within the realisation of complexity and ambivalence. Through the use of many media, formats and installations in space, Biswas orchestrates a highly *affective* aesthetic staging for a non-hierarchical worlding—where desire, fascination, pleasure and pain are inscribed and evoked. Footprints in the sand are fragile and transitory, yet their pressure leaves the trace of an Other's journey or pathway that we—any spectator—are invited to follow. Biswas's materials increasingly invoke the notion of the trace, the fragile imprint in the historical and cultural archive of people's bodies, memories and experiences. If we can all invest these traces with the full though not undivided subjectivity that they signify, we can begin to resist the alienation created by mythology (in Barthes's sense, the making foreign, the depriving of what is of or belongs to oneself), and in particular the West's destructive use of foreignness and its fear of ambivalence.[19] The binary oppositions of Western culture—White/Black, self/Other, here/there, man/woman, to name but a few—are very local yet destructively hegemonic. Positioning her work as a historical practice, dialectical, full of interaction and mutual determination, while fashioning its poetics at the level of the intimate, tactile, personally charged, Biswas produces a powerful, empowering and critically feminist text that enlarges the world by overlaying and thus mutually redefining these oppositions, of which yet one more is that of centre/periphery. Tawadros again:

> The constellation of voices and the plurality of meanings which are postulated by post modernity serve to obscure its continuities with cultural modernism, and suggests, perhaps, that this may not be a fissure or a 'new dawn' in European consciousness but merely a transformation of the grand narratives of the West. In this context the 'populist modernism' of black cultural practice, I would argue, signals a critical reappropriation of modernity which stems from an assertion of history and historical processes. Black women's creativity in particular expresses the ambivalence of identity and redundancy of exclusive and unambiguous absolutes. It dissolves fixed boundaries between past and present, public and private, personal and political.[20]

The cultural practice of Biswas, she argues, is the space of the diaspora, which is not predicated, according to Tawadros, on the primacy of difference and dispersion; rather, 'the cultural expression of the margins and the periphery represents an aesthetic and political project which is predicated on resistance and change'.[21]

19. Both themes have been treated by two important Western thinkers, Zygmunt Bauman, *Modernity and Ambivalence,* Cambridge: Polity Press, 1991, and Julia Kristeva, *Strangers to Ourselves*, trans. Leon Roudiez, Brighton: Harvester Wheatsheaf Press, 1991.

20. Tawadros, 'Beyond the Boundary', p.150.

21. *Ibid.*

22. Sutapa Biswas, *Synapse*, Leeds: City Art Gallery, 1992, p.27.

23. *Ibid.*, p.13.

Postscript 1998

This essay was originally written on commission and in advance of the exhibition of Sutapa Biswas's *Synapse*, which first took place in Vancouver in 1992 (fig. 1, pls. XI–XVI). It was penned in ignorance of what that work would be. Yet some of the conclusions drawn from the analysis of her whole project to date sympathetically anticipated the new realisation of these continuing concerns in the installation *Synapse*. The artist has written:

> Synapse is a metaphor for many things, but most recurringly, echoes that point of exchange between two or more components. That between the viewer, and the work of art, the artist and the critic. A relationship in which through the work, each individual is able to situate themself. The focus has been a concern for boundaries — a psycho-geographic journey between people, places, language, culture. As an artist, it is the journey to which I am constantly drawn.[22]

In medical terms, synapse refers to connections that permit transmission of coded information from one nerve cell to another. Degrees of expansion or shrinkage condition the number and quality of impulses transmitted through this branching network of possible connections. It thus becomes for her 'symbolic of an undefined territory or space. Memory itself is of a shifting nature, vivid in places, with blind spots'.[23] What conditions the degree of transmission, at this extended level, may be called Desire, which itself is the force that springs across the gaps and ties us into both a world of objects and an imaginary field of fantasy.

The project *Synapse* was largely photographic, although it included light-box pieces and a particular installation of boxes with memorabilia and other uncanny objects. Dominating the exhibition were nine very large photographs, which had been made by projecting slides, taken on the artist's 1986–7 trip to India, onto her own unclothed body. In this project, the process of making the work returned the artist to the arena of performance where the body of the artist works within the art, which is thus indexed to a lived, existential social body that is also the productive body at work. Unwitnessed but recorded, these images signify the artist's curious, wondering, desiring, intellectually motivated, and aesthetically responsive gaze on, for instance, the Khajuraha temples. At the same tune, the artist is literally trapped in the beam of light from the projector and captured by the photographic gaze, which is not where she is. Reminiscent of Jacques Lacan's later theory of the subject as 'photo-graphed', that is to say, found by the gaze, instituted by desire at the point of being in the field of the desire of the Other, *Synapse* opens poetically on this complex field of subjectivity as a dream landscape in which 'I' am seen, 'I' am a picture.[24] Thus the body in social space that made the work by performing it undoes itself to allow the body to signify as the support for a field of fantasy signified by projected images, themselves the captured memories of the artist negotiating her own relations as an artist to cultural legacies from both Hindu and Islamic components of the subcontinent's ancient and modern histories. In one sequence of these photographs, the velvety darkness is pierced by an image—a photograph of a piece of sculpture, a building wrapped in scaffolding, a holiday snapshot of children at the seaside—that seems to float unanchored. When we look more closely, the curve of a woman's breast or the interlaced fingers of two hands resting on a female abdomen, almost cradling the image, make us realise the intimacy of memory trace and body.

Just as the artist devised a means to create a forceful representation of an embodied femininity in *Housewives with Steak-knives*, here she has also risked the issue in order to keep the tension between poststructuralist insistence on the psychic and discursive levels of our constitution as subjects and the materialist attention to socially constituted persons in concrete histories. The use of a medical term as metaphor for memory and desire itself encodes this rebellious refusal to be policed into a 'correct' position on what must remain an undecidable and impossible distinction. Even at the heart of psychoanalysis, in the early work of Freud and now again in the important work of Julia Kristeva and the later work of Lacan, the question of the body, or, rather, of the corporeal as both image and uncharted site of drives, asserts itself as an always necessary dimension of thinking about subjectivity and desire. Biswas's *Synapse* aesthetically connects more intimately than her previous work with this debate and offers a form within which the viewer can encounter not the argued terms and theories of that debate, but the substantive and affective material it tries to hook into analysis. The

24. Jacques Lacan, 'The Gaze as *objet a*', *Four Fundamental Concepts of Psychoanalysis* (1973), London: Penguin Books, 1979.

artwork, the product of a performance within the artist's studio, becomes a performance experienced by the viewer because of the precarious intimacy these photographs evoke for us between the inside and the outside, the body and the imaginary, the past and the present. One of the key crossovers is the recurrence of the image of a goddess figure set between two columns. In one photograph, she is carried on the body of the artist, crossed fingers echoing the formal patterning of the seated goddess's crossed legs. In another, the slide of the same sculpture is projected large, on a curving surface and the body of the artist appears to lie on the sculpture, swathed in dark shadow, with only the soles of her feet and the tips of her fingers illuminated. All the time the lighting and the composition oblige the viewer to examine her own curiosity, perception, attention. Nothing is obvious and explicit, while the scale and quality of the photographic prints provide the iconic frame for a series of reflections on the permeability of borderlines, the transmission of meaning, and their site: the subject in history, an embodied subject and an inscribed history. The interchange between the artist's body and the historical monument stage another kind of 'sacred space', offer another kind of postcolonial mapping, question the representations of femininity, trouble the boundaries between present and past. These are the questions that Sutapa Biswas has been pursuing across several continents, in varied media, and always with revealing effects.

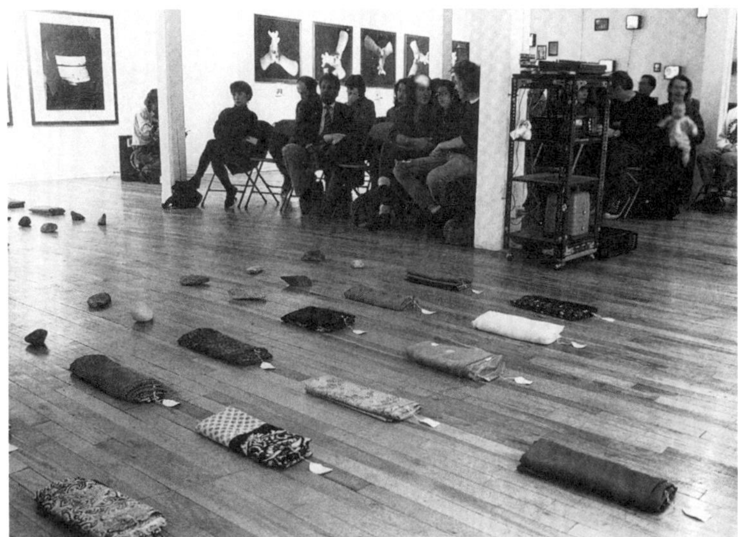

Figure 15
***To Kill Two Birds with One Stone*, 1994**

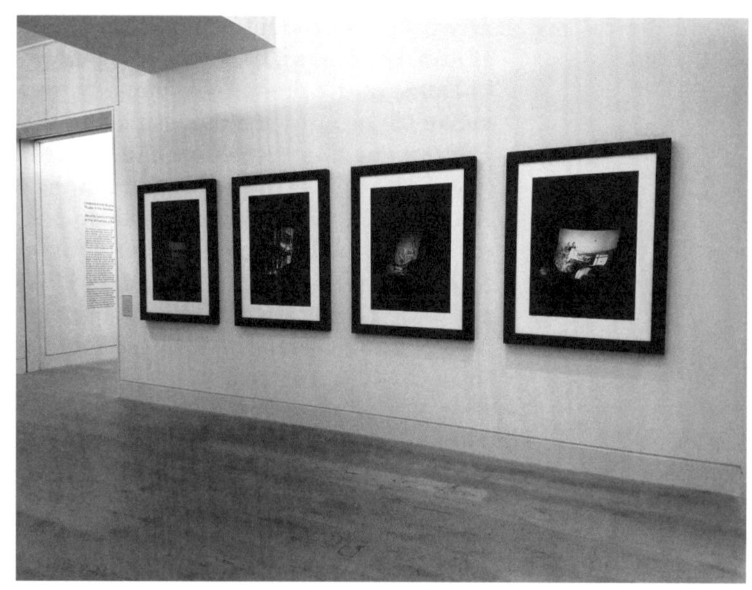

Figure 16
Synapse I **(1987–92) in *Lessons in the Studio: Studio in the Seminar: Seventy Years of Fine Art at Leeds* at The Stanley & Audrey Burton Gallery and Project Space, University of Leeds, 2019**

A **Postface,** and a Continued Conversation

Griselda Pollock

I have watched in admiration the continuing evolution of the artistic practice of Sutapa Biswas since I wrote this essay for the exhibition catalogue *Synapse* in 1992. In 2019 I co-curated an exhibition with the artist Sam Belinfante at the University of Leeds titled *Lessons in the Studio: Studio in the Seminar: Seventy Years of Fine Art at Leeds.*[1] We included Biswas's photographic series *Synapse I* (1987–92) (fig. 16, pls. XI–XIV) in that exhibition along with her film *Birdsong* (2004) (fig. 2, pls. XXIII–XXV), works that were made more than ten years apart, but that engaged with the legacies of Biswas's education at Leeds.

In our exhibition, Belinfante and I aimed to showcase the work of former students from the Fine Art Department at Leeds as a way to chart legacies of a vision for university-based fine art education advocated by the British art historian and writer Herbert Read in 1949 and the artist and art historian Maurice de Sausmarez, who was appointed in 1949 as the first lecturer in a fledgling department. Both believed artists would benefit from immersion in the full range of the multi-disciplinary university environment and from the double challenge of historical-theoretical and aesthetic-practical investigation of art. Biswas's two works were shown alongside work by our first Fine Art

1. *Lessons in the Studio: Studio in the Seminar: Seventy Years of Fine Art at Leeds* took place at The Stanley & Audrey Burton Gallery and the Project Space in the Fine Art Building, 4 December 2019–31 October 2020. The exhibition is available online here: https://artsandculture.google.com/story/oAIyv6jWaqXIKA.

PhD students such as Nicky Bird, Elizabeth Price, Hayley Newman, Judith Tucker, Janis Rafa, as well as artists/writers with long and active careers artists such as Jacky Fleming, Nicky Bird, Sue Wilks, Steve Bell, Peter Morgan, John Hyatt, Kerry Harker, Sam Belinfante and the infamous Leeds 13. As an internationally recognised artist, she was also part of conversations — actual (recorded) and virtual (via artworks) — with influential teaching presences such as Terry Atkinson, T.J. Clark, Vanalyne Green, Lubaina Himid, Wild Pansy Press and myself. Each space (The Stanley & Audrey Burton Gallery and the Project Space in the Fine Art Building) also had a 'library', a sculptural installation that visually represented the doubled project of the title *Lessons in the Studio: Studio in the Seminar.* The University Collection has since acquired Biswas's work *Synapse I* that was on display.

These works were created in response to the artist's first return to India since her childhood, an encounter of profound significance for the artist who had for so long challenged the absence of art from the world beyond Europe in the conventional Western art historical curriculum while playing an active role in establishing the presence of Black artists on the British scene. This sense of imaginatively belonging to migratory spaces and cultures both 'here and there' — remembered and transmitted, silenced but reclaimed, effaced and now explored, shamed and now proudly honoured — became the dynamic of both critical and creative postcoloniality of which Biswas was such an early artist and thinker. Postcoloniality signifies critical resistance to the legacies of racist imperialism while its creative activity engendered aesthetically the excitement of a worlded consciousness of many possibilities provided by the multiple worlds these heritages delivered, precisely through the throwing off of the burden of the colonial not merely politically but through the imaginative and transformative practices of art intercontinentally and transculturally.

In *Synapse*, Biswas embodied this double work of lost memory and regained contact and aesthetic travel between several worlds. She daringly made her own female body a presence: as so much more than a screen for the projection of images of the places, memories and sculptural languages she 're-found' by travelling to India to discover with delight the dynamic figuration of male and female forms in both Hindu and Buddhist sculptural and architectural histories.

2. *Migratory Aesthetics* took place at University Gallery, University of Leeds, 11 January–15 March 2006. More information about the exhibition is available at: https://www.leeds.ac.uk/cath/ahrc/events/2006/0111/intro.html.

Her arms encircle the fragile play of projected light, holding close to her body the ungraspable immaterial deposits on her belly. The work appears to lodge the photographic memory trace of past and recent encounters with other bodies on her skin, as itself a newly located skin and a window to a past of India's many cultures and their imaginaries, emerging from within her body.

The second work we exhibited was *Birdsong* (2004) (pls. XXIII–XXV), which had also been shown in an exhibition in 2006 that I curated titled *Migratory Aesthetics*.[2] This exhibition brought together Jewish and postcolonial African, Caribbean and Subcontinental artistic inscriptions of personal and familial migration and the migration of the aesthetic forms of the cultures they carried or reclaimed. The artists included Martine Atille, Mieke Bal, Sutapa Biswas, Bracha Ettinger, Lubaina Himid, Isaac Julien, Lily Markiewicz, Fanozi Chickenman Mhlize, Roger Palmer, Ingrid Pollard and Judith Tucker. The show brought together complex negotiations of difference and specificity within shared experiences of the effects of colonial and genocidally racist modernity. *Birdsong* is a lyrical and mesmerising work that juxtaposes a folded silver paper horse, suspended in space, with the face of a young boy, seated and watching in fascination tinged with apprehension and uncertainty, as a dark, enigmatic but living form enters his own space. Only as we arrive at the six-minute mark, does the camera draw back to reveal the entire scene: a well-appointed but not over-luxurious British interior, with a full-grown, saddled and bridled horse standing patiently before the small boy.

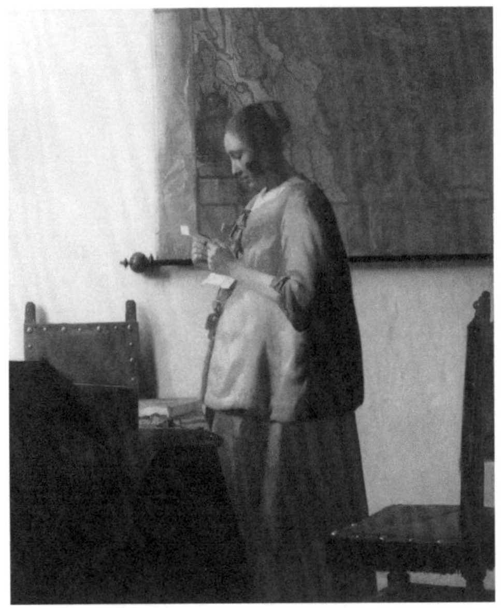

Figure 17
Johannes Vermeer
Woman in Blue Reading a Letter, c. 1633

Another critically important feature to be drawn from this work, and indeed works such as *Untitled* (*The Trials and Tribulations of Mickey Baker*) (1997) (pl. XIX), is that it enacts a particular dimension of the postcolonial artist that Biswas powerfully establishes in relation to the paradox of the politics of identity and the specificity of the artist's belonging to an unboundaried world of art. While in *Birdsong* she speaks back to English painter, George Stubbs (1724–1806), in *Untitled* she reflects her sustained admiration for the paintings of interiors with figures by the Dutch artist Johannes Vermeer (1632–75) and the American painter Edward Hopper (1882–1967) in terms of the shared exploration of stillness and time as she moves between the still and the moving image. The looped video reveals a portly, naked White man standing in a sun-filled room before a window, surrounded by the ordinary features of a domestic space — a bookcase, a comfortable armchair, abandoned shoes. The walls are painted a duck-egg blue, evoking but not replicating Vermeer's recurring palette of yellows and blues. There is no sound but the man rocks slightly on his feet, redrawing the shadows his feet create in the sunlight as he does so. The movement introduces time and movement — the properties of the moving image — into the stillness of painting that engenders time by the solicitation of prolonged, unfolding gaze. Hopper and Vermeer focused their gazes upon the women in their families; Biswas reverses the normality of the invisible gaze of a masculine artist and the visible object of his fascination, longing, desire, or fear. She, a woman and an Indian artist, takes up their place and reformulates it as a compassionate gaze extended towards an other, a man made vulnerable in his ageing nakedness while remaining a named individual. He is not a type, a condition or a position in a nexus of Oedipal familial or erotic relations such as nude, wife, daughter, lover. Speaking to Guy Brett, Biswas explained: 'in one sense film rediscovers the condition of painting, but there is still all the difference in the world between the film of a subject that keeps still and a still painting or photograph. The difference lies in a way of conveying "life".'[3] Conversing with Vermeer and Hopper, and indeed with Andy Warhol's six-hour filmwork *Empire State Building* (1964), Biswas reminds us that while self-identification as a Black artist in the context of the contestation of British racism and colonialism was a strategic imperative in her early work, in her mature work she also defines herself as an artist and as such the entire history of art is hers to inhabit, to contest and to speak beside.

All art is, thus, an unlimited, open resource for all artists in defiance of the tendency to impose geo-ethnic and gender labelling only on artists who are not White, European or male. Politically and strategically, faced with effacement because of institutional racism that ignored, failed equably to collect and sustain British artists of Asian and African, African-Caribbean cultural and geopolitical heritage, geo-ethnic self-identification functioned, therefore as a collective necessity as well as the affirmation of the creative resources and expansion of each artist's own imagination through such intercultural access. At the same time, the singularity of each artist's contribution to the world of art is to be

3. Guy Brett, 'Spaces inside Time', in *Sutapa Biswas*, exh. cat., London and Portland: inIVA and Reed College, 2004, pp.42–43.

treasured because of each artist's unique entanglement of place, history, desire, social class, family history, religious or cultural affirmation or legacy, age, ableness and because of each artist's aesthetic formulation of those possibilities as art addressed to the entire world. This is the paradox of the moment of the postcolonial artist. Labelled and categorised positively or negatively by the notion of identity, there is a danger of fixity and even geo-ethnic essentialising of artists as 'other' on the part of the dominant, White art world. Yet to deny the specificity of both inherited pain and cultural brilliance of the diverse societies and cultures these migratory artists carried, is to impoverish the entire world of art to which each artist speaks for her or him or their selves. Collectively, in the 1980s, a diversity of artists in Britain took action as the Black Arts Movement at a time of deadly racisms, anti-immigration violence, xenophobia and cruel discrimination. Yet within that movement were many different worlds, whether it concerned which island of the Caribbean communities, which continent, or even which British city and which class, gender and sexual orientation had formed the artist's imagination and personal history.

Sutapa Biswas was born in Santiniketan, 100 miles or 158 kilometres north of Kolkata, now a World Heritage site founded by the spiritual universalist, Debendranath Tagore (1817–1905), father of the poet and artist Rabindranath Tagore (1861–1941), the leading figure of the cultural renaissance in an India under Britain's formal colonial (1858) and imperial (1877) rule. This locates her origins in one of the great centres of modern Indian thought and art. Culturally, Santiniketan — the abode of peace — represents a historical experiment in humanism, internationalism, gender equality and the protection of the environment through rural reconstruction, all based on shared values from different cultures and faiths. Santiniketan is world renowned now both for the architectural expression of these aims and for its philosophy. Biswas's restored connections to this unique place of birth and its history carries the modernist, internationalist aesthetics and vision of inclusion into later twentieth-century Britain to join conversations with a diverse community of new voices seeking to make comparable radical changes in the West.

Yet it must be noted that while Blackness became an elective and political identity of resistance to British racist society in the later twentieth century, it united artists from many, and yet also very specific, historical cultures. It created a complex community, diverse in itself along all axes of class, gender, sexuality, training, as well as in relation to distinctive histories. This group shared the postcolonial and the migratory conditions their artistic practices sought to understand by developing aesthetics that bridged the worlds of parents and ancestors and their place as part of an incompletely postcolonial Britain.

Biswas's work stands out as a prolonged and deeply theorised and aesthetically fashioned meditation on being an artist in the world, on being an artist of the world, on being an artist carrying the heritage of her worlds in Britain and in an India reworlded by colonisation and migration. She is an artist at home in every form of art the world's artists have created.

I have written about these two works — made over a decade apart — and of Biswas's long and productive career as one of Britain's most probing postcolonial artists, to remind myself of what is remarkable about the ambition and scope of her life of artmaking and art thinking in relation to the immensity of the challenge the migratory and postcolonial artists have faced working and creating in Britain. Recognition has come to Biswas in Canada, a society that constantly confronts its own complexities as a nation formed in colonialism and challenged by its own incomplete postcoloniality. In Britain such recognition has been subtle and constant, but official institutions have perpetuated their indifference, belatedly choosing only few from that great upheaval of the Black Arts Movement to be embraced as brilliant British artists of our own time. Study the dates of accession of their works to the keepers of our cultural memory such as the Tate. Selectivity on grounds of gender is as evident there as is their failure to find a way to see the works that emerge from and aesthetically transform Britain's colonial imprint on the continents of the globe. I welcome this exhibition and commend the new generation of curators and scholars who have here given us an opportunity to experience a major show of one of the most brilliant, challenging, artistically and theoretically intelligent artists that we at Leeds are so proud to be able to claim as part of our history and to celebrate in these major exhibitions.

Plates XI–XIV
***Synapse I* (1–4), 1987–92**

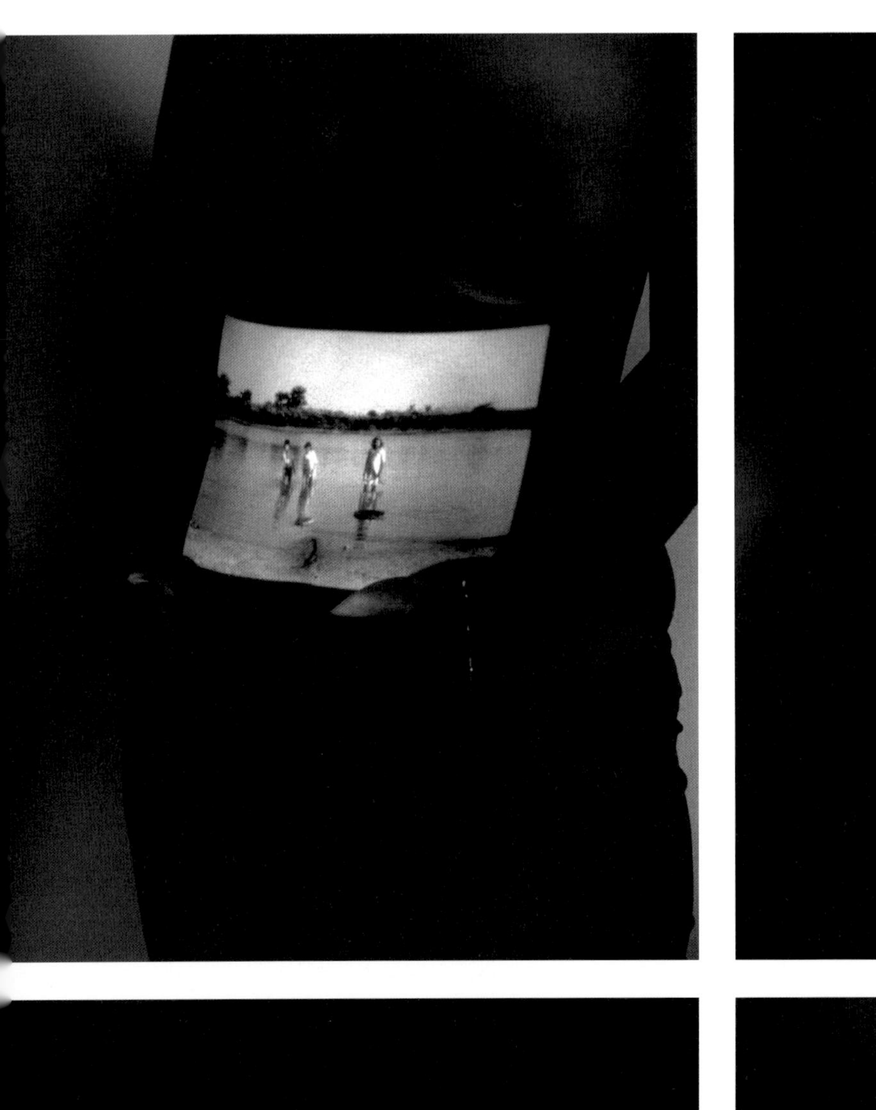
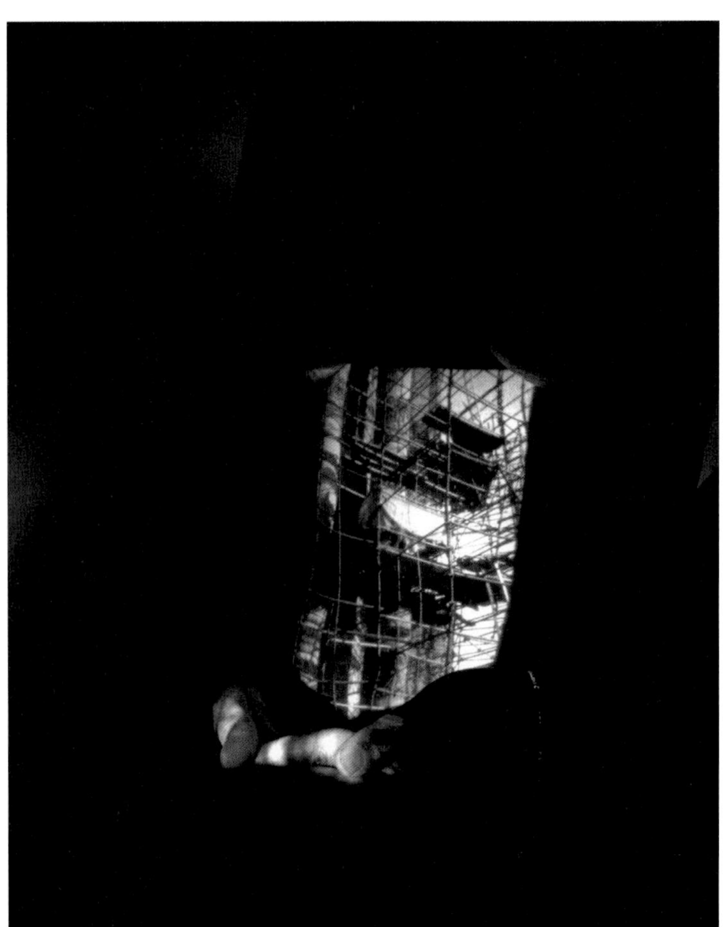
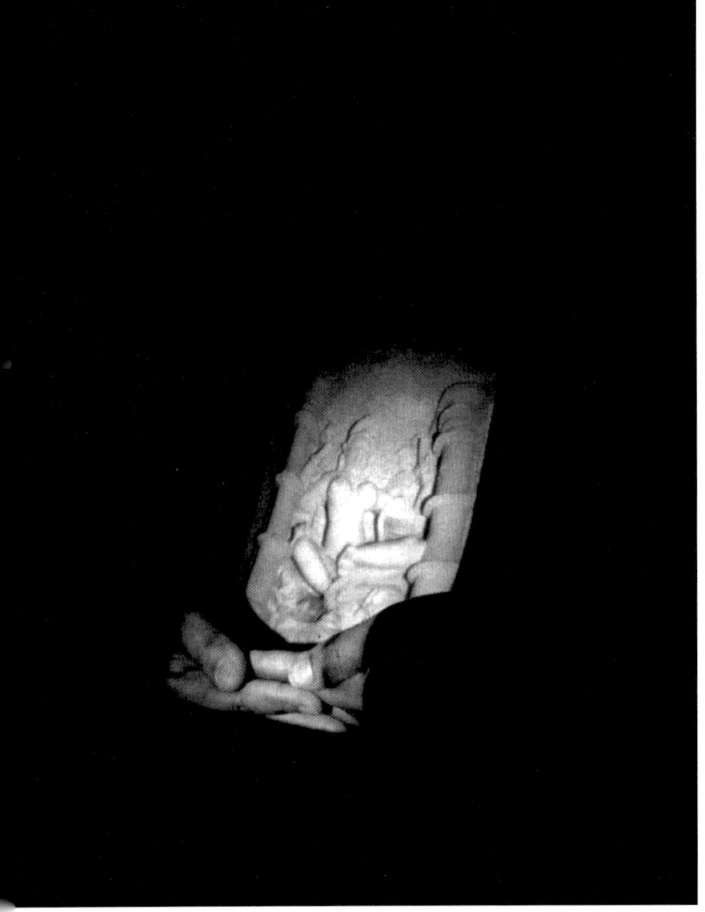
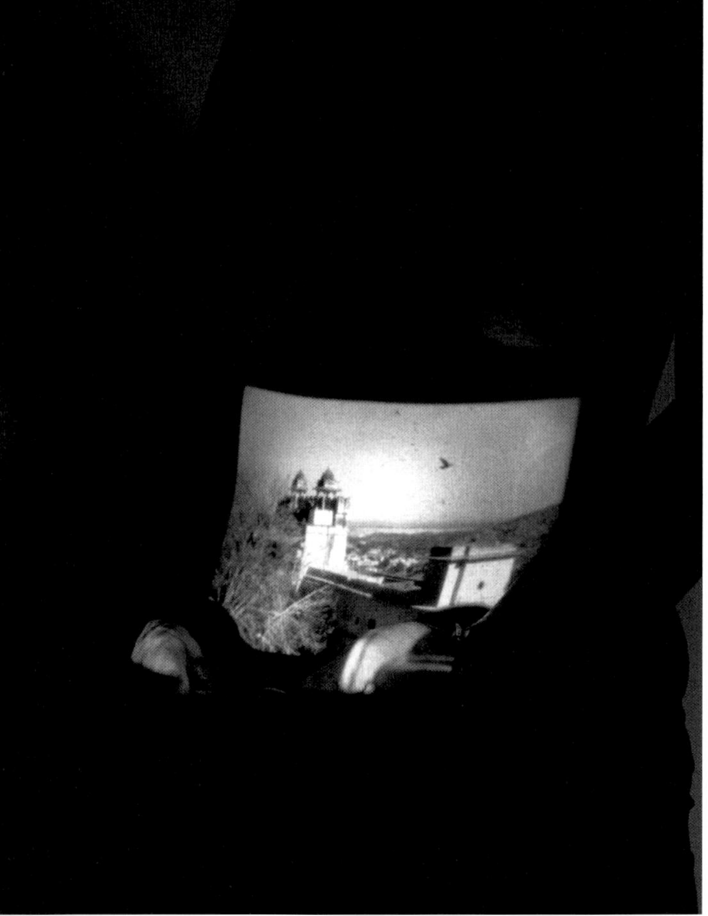

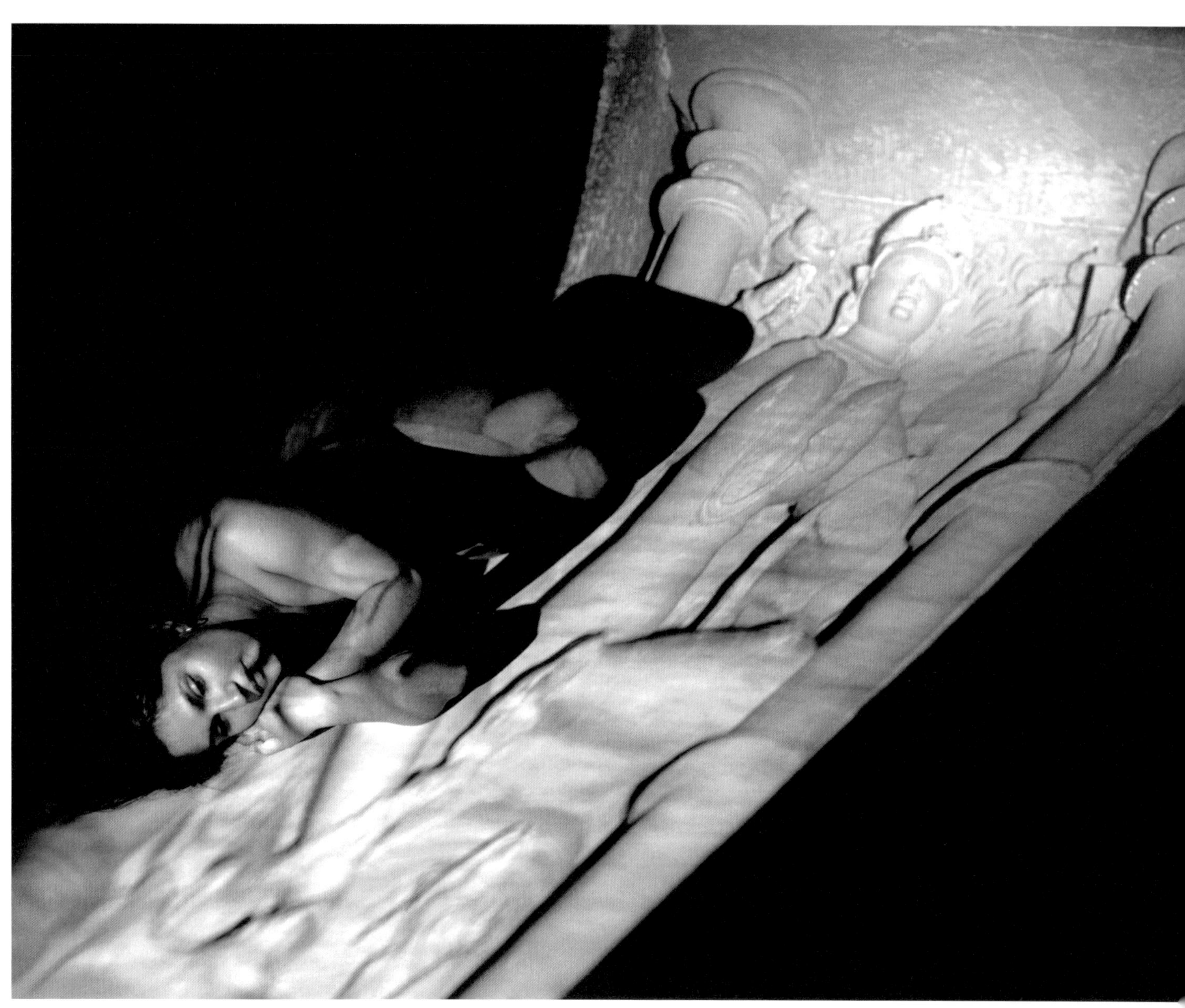

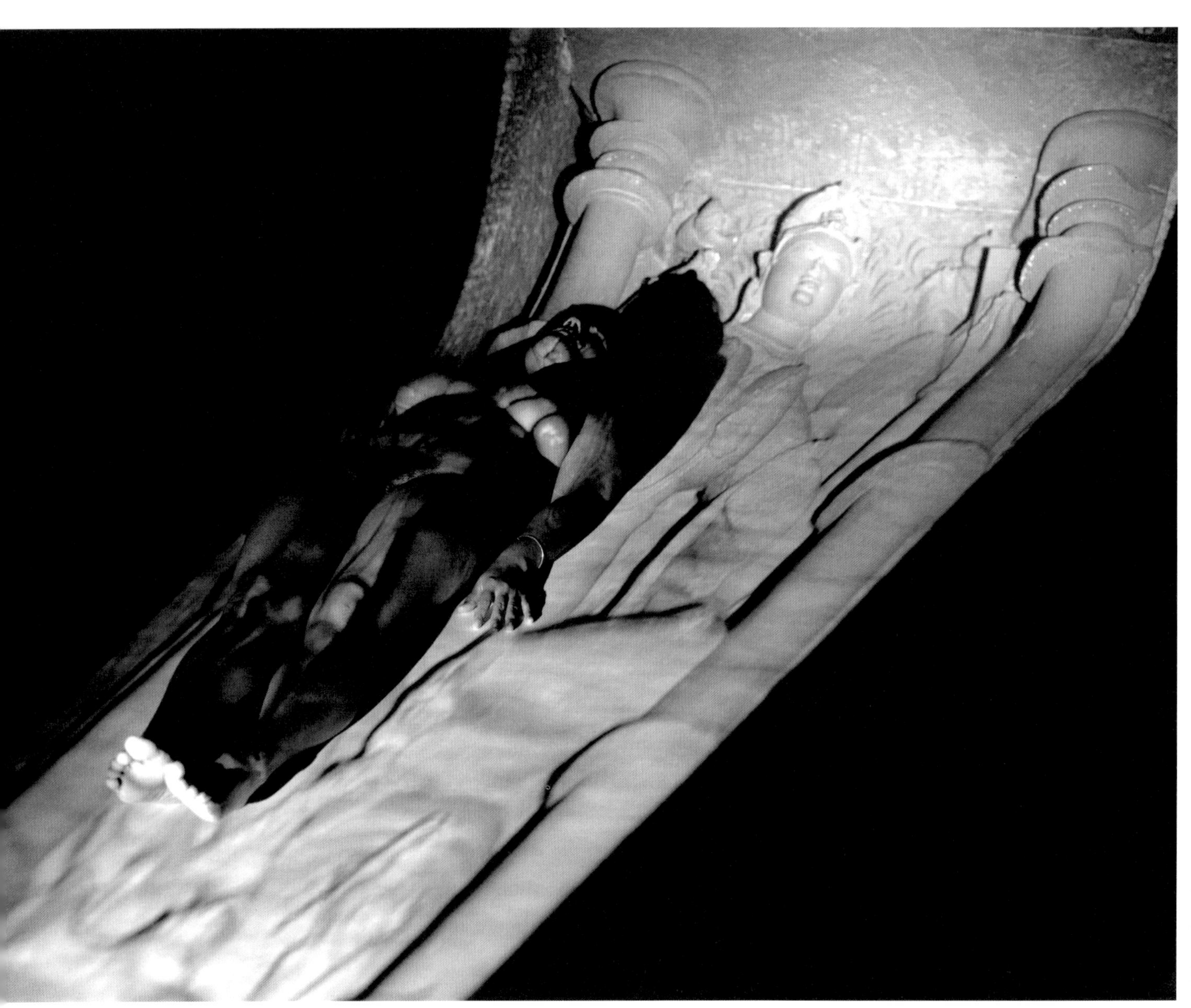

Plates XV–XVI
***Synapse II*, 1987–92**

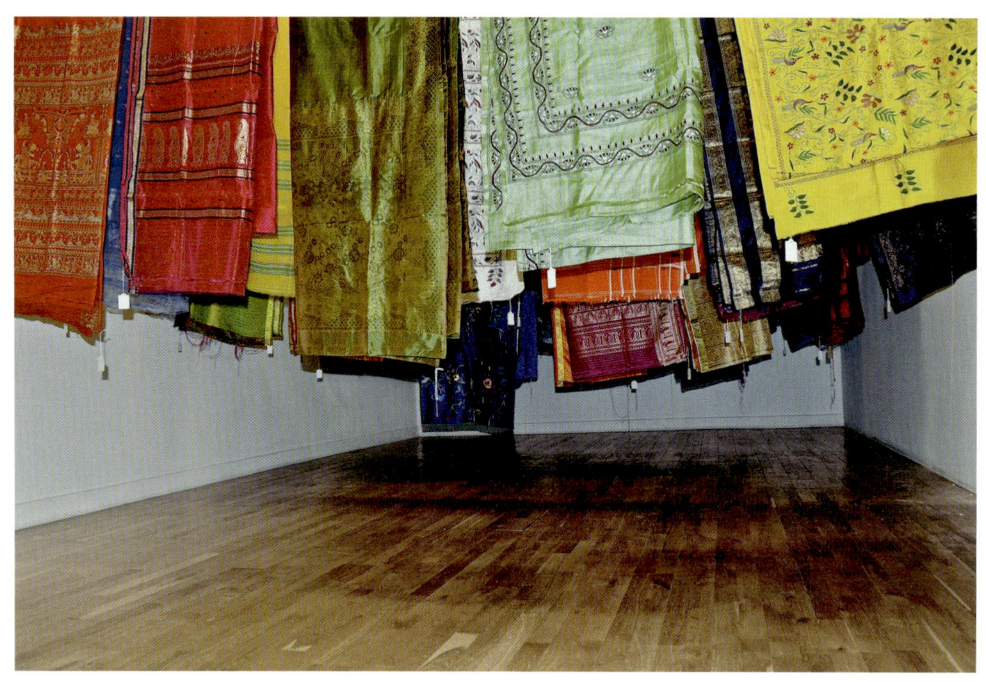

Plate XVII
***Flights of Passage*, 2014–15**

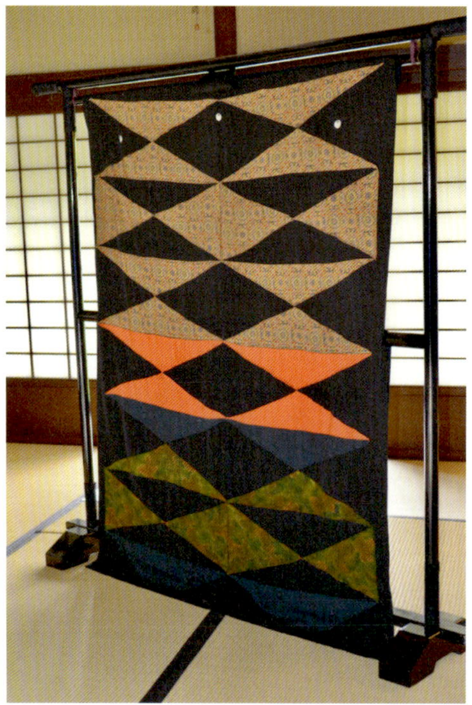

Plate XVIII
***Stitch by Stitch*, 2015**

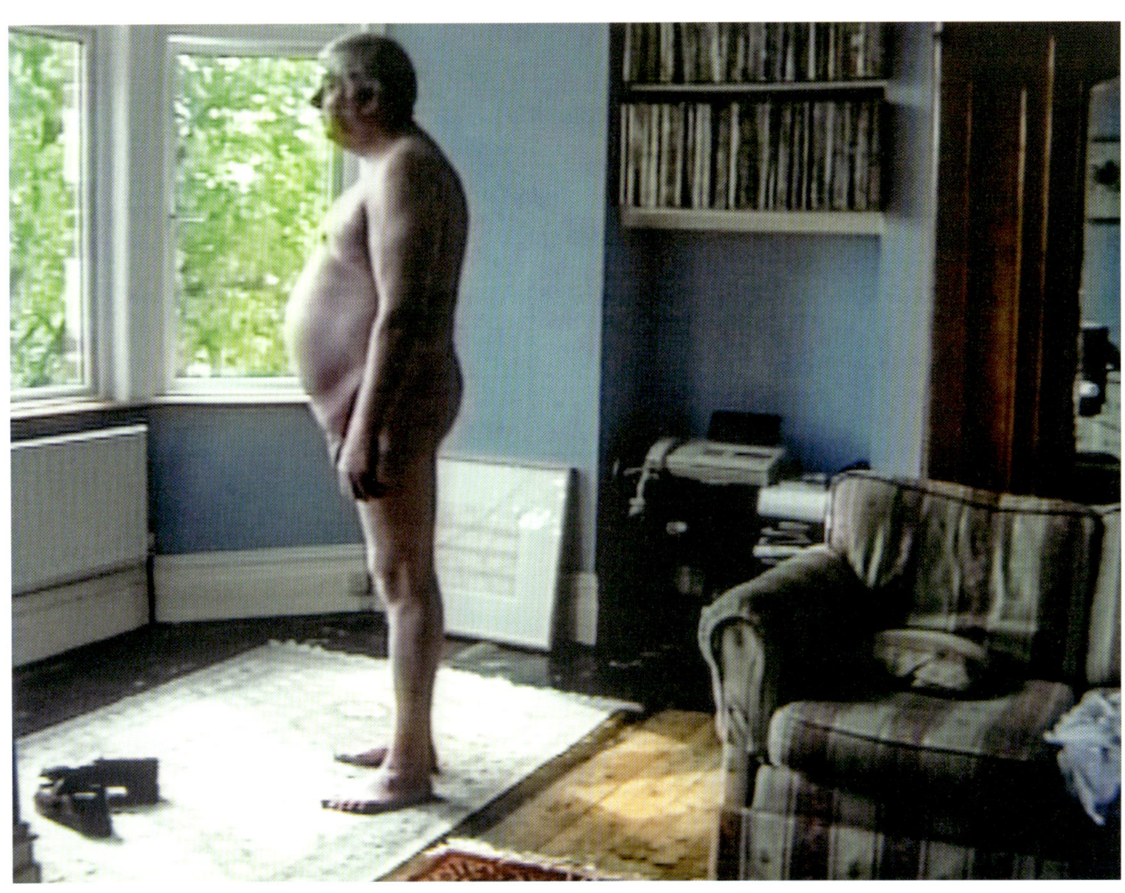

Plate XIX
***Untitled (The Trials and Tribulations of Mickey Baker)*, 1997**

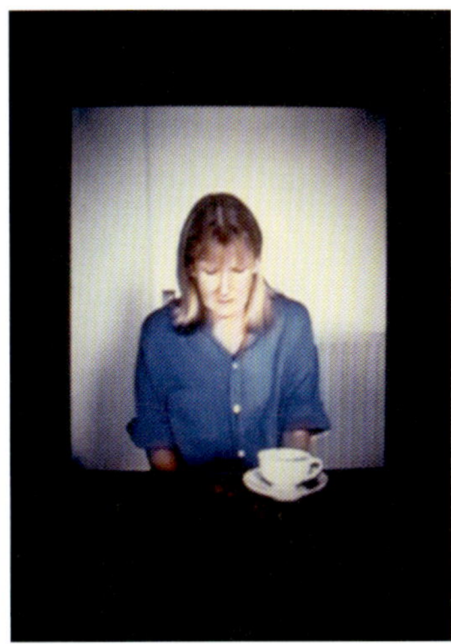

Plate XX
***Untitled (Woman in Blue Weeping)*, 1996**

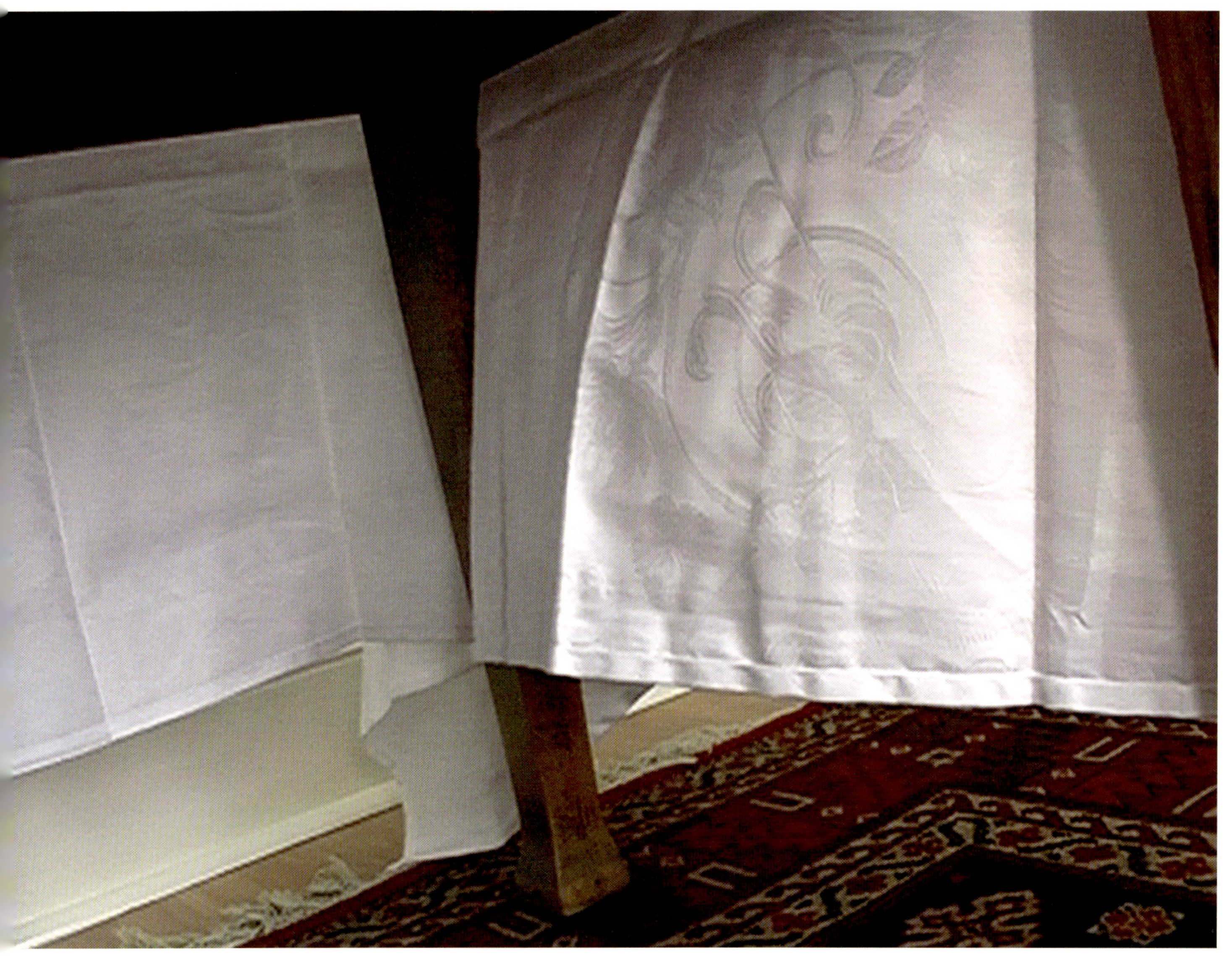

Plate XXI
***Under my table*, 2006**

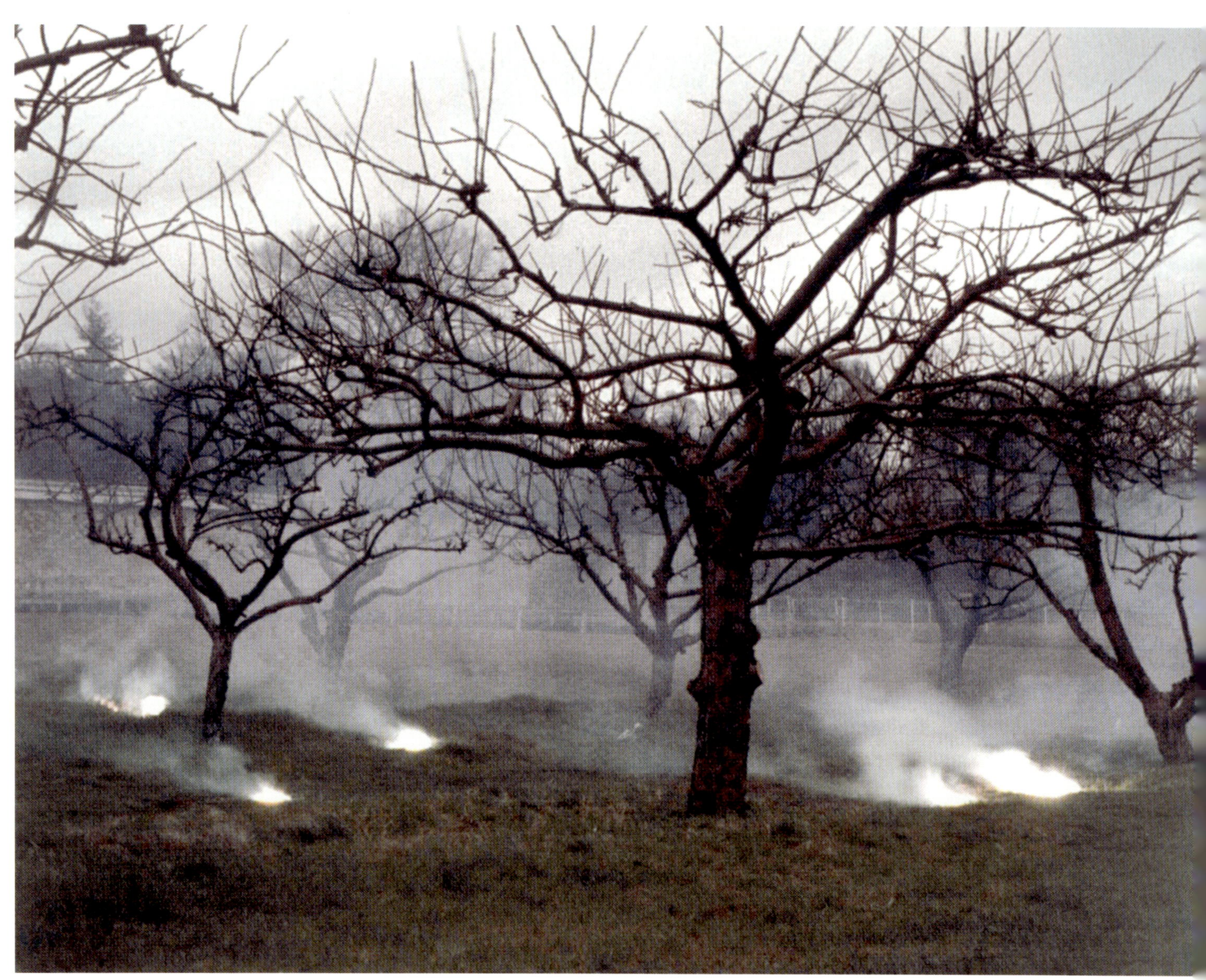

Plate XXII
***Magnesium Bird*, 2004**

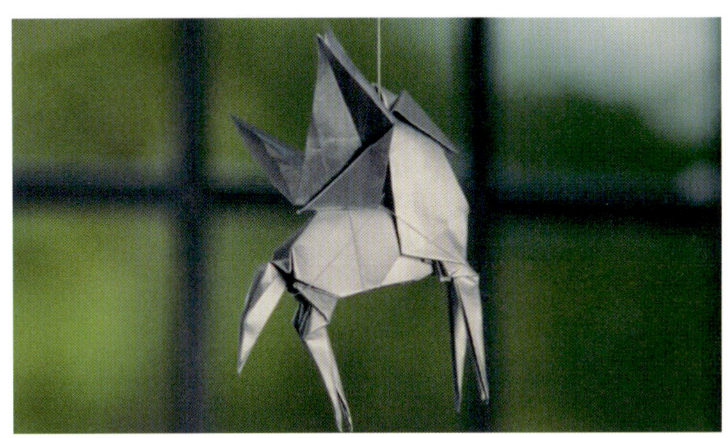

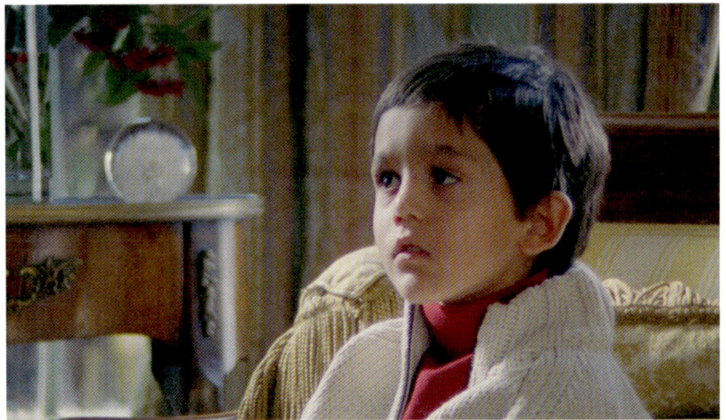

Plates XXIII–XXIV
***Birdsong*, 2004**

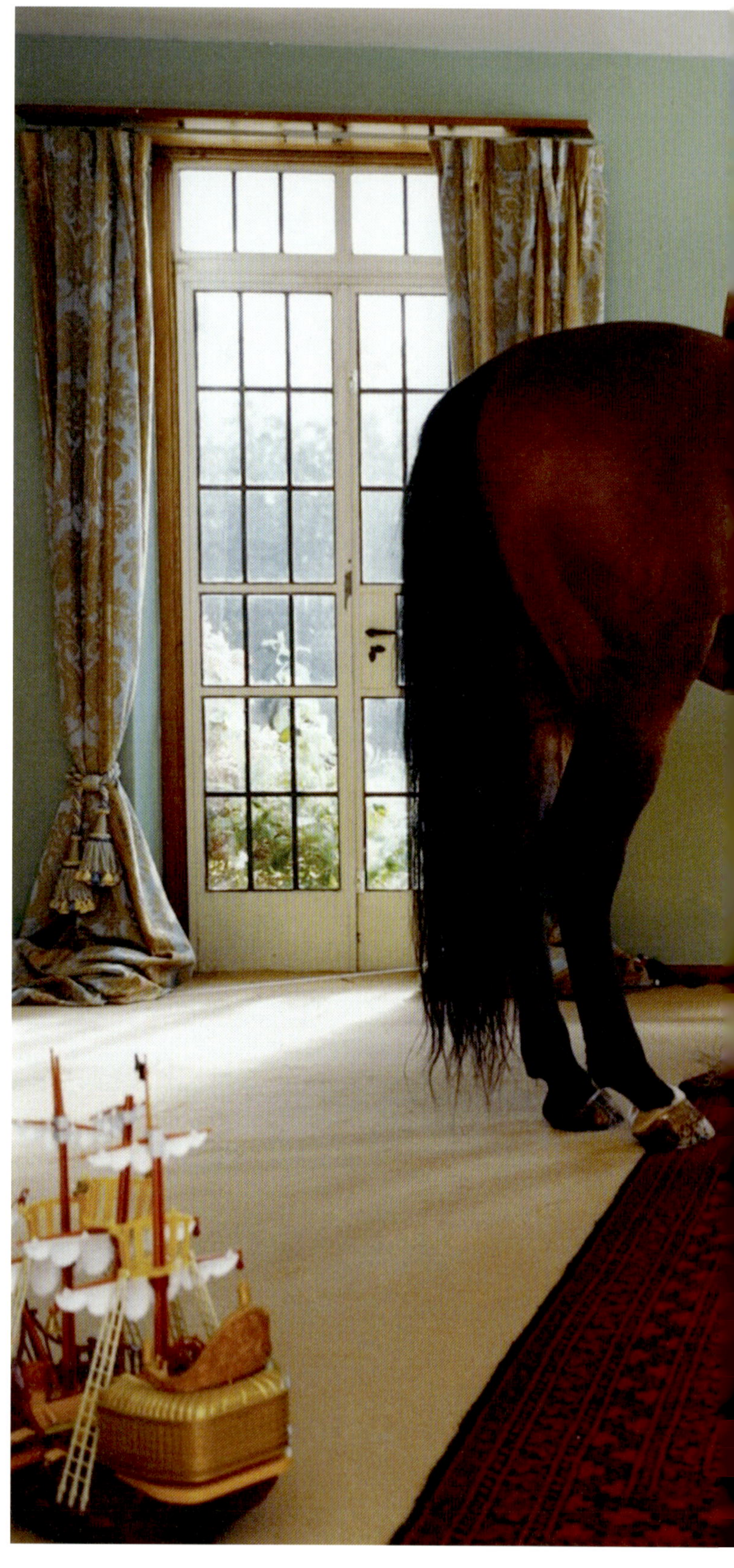

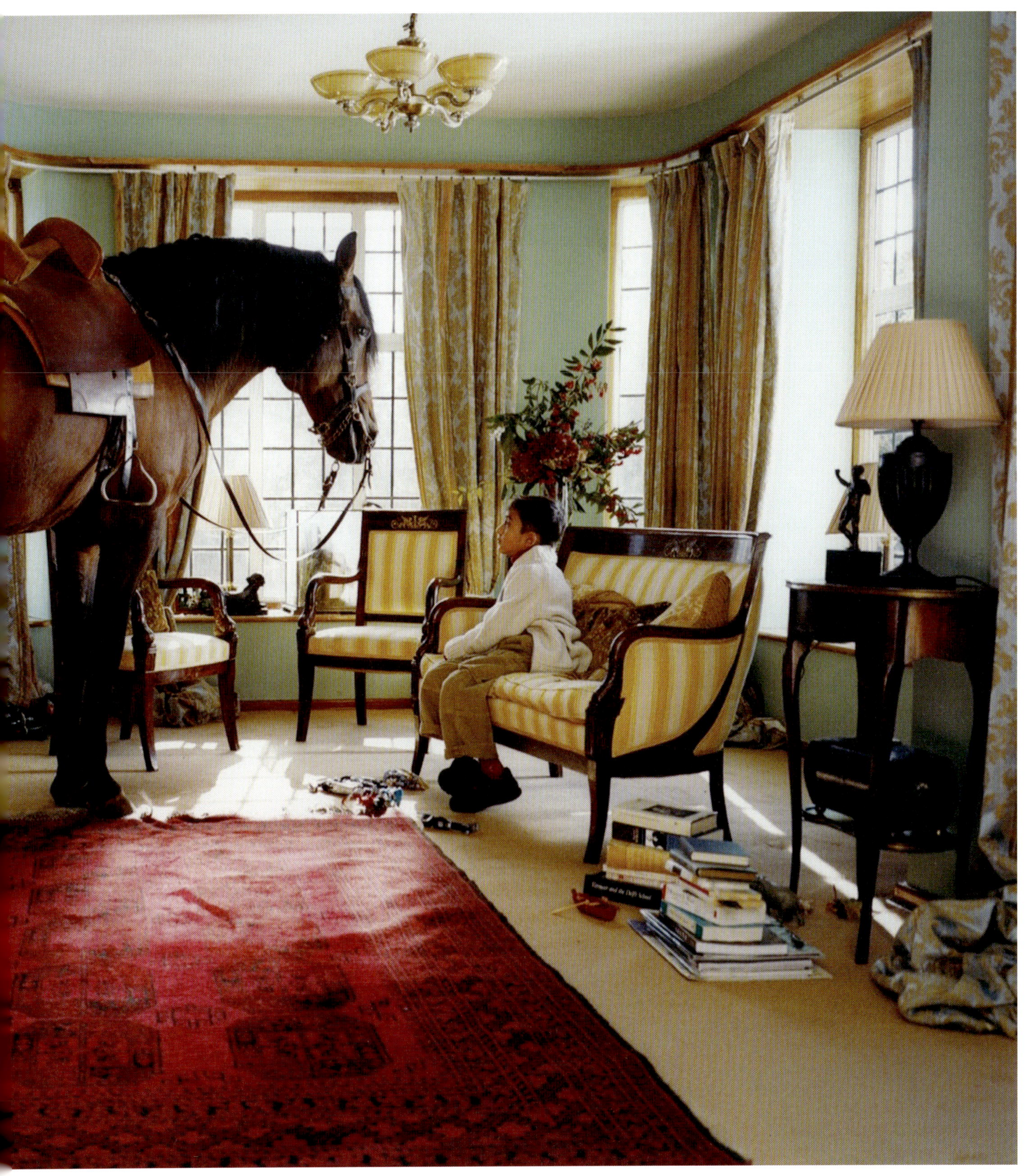

Plate XXV
***Birdsong*, 2004**

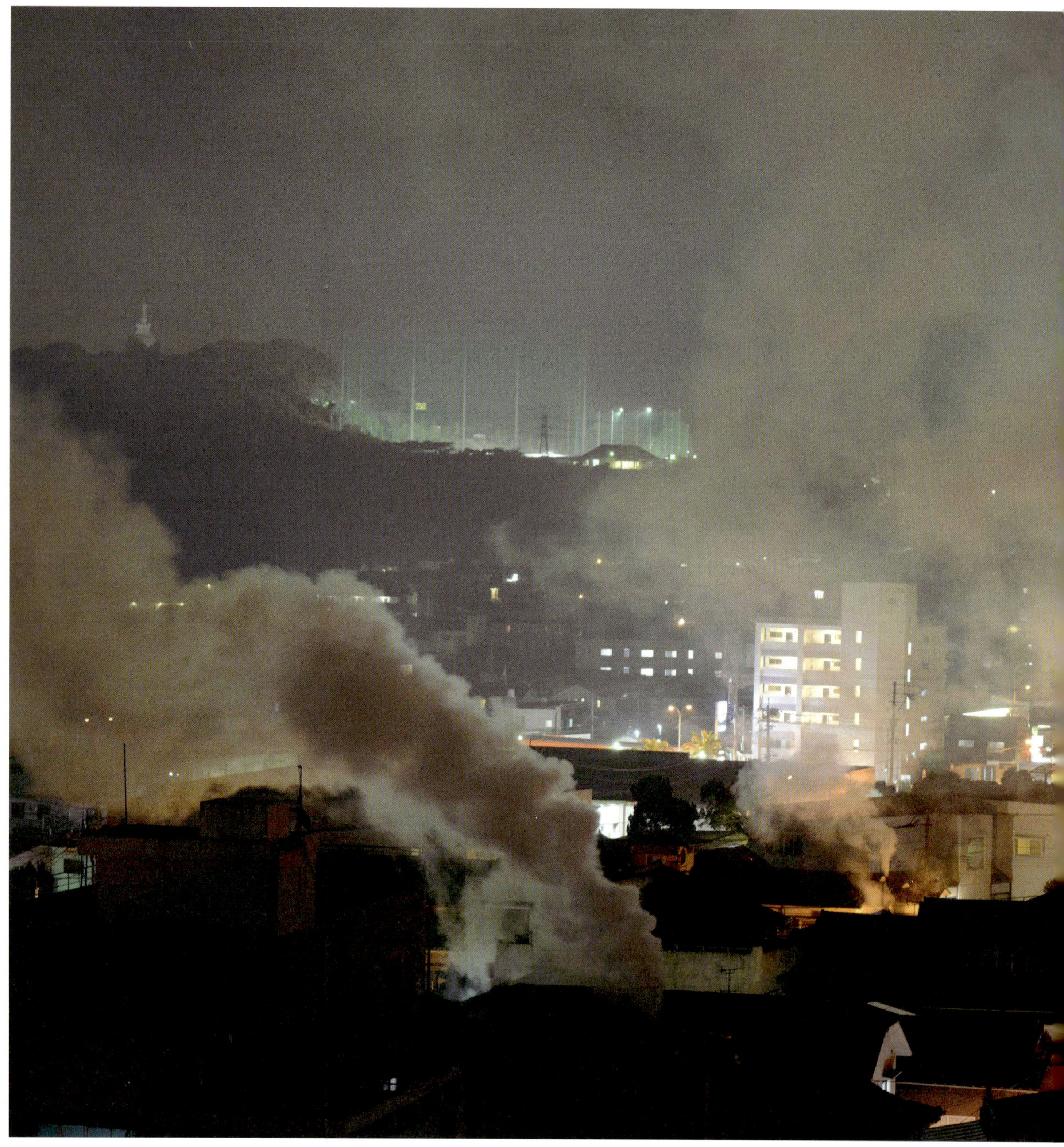

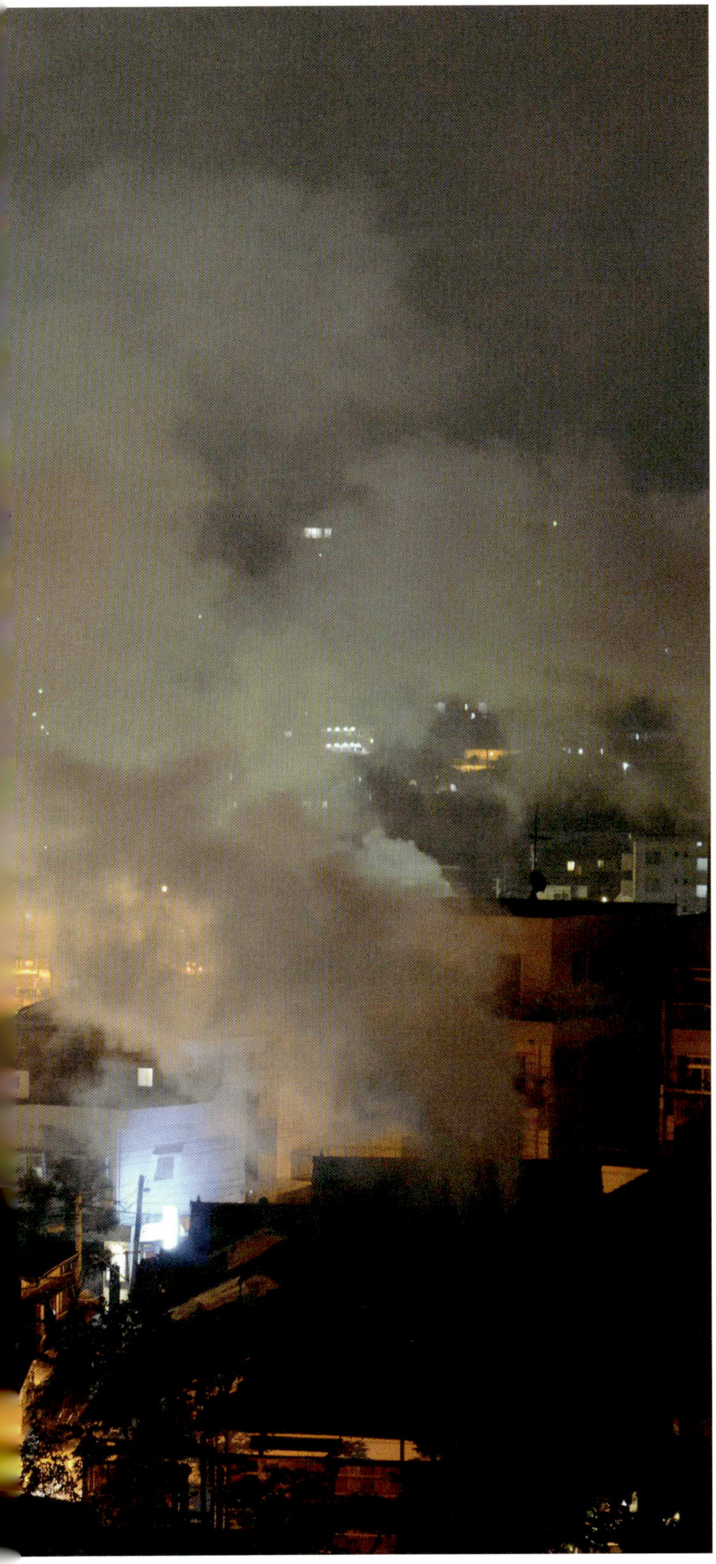

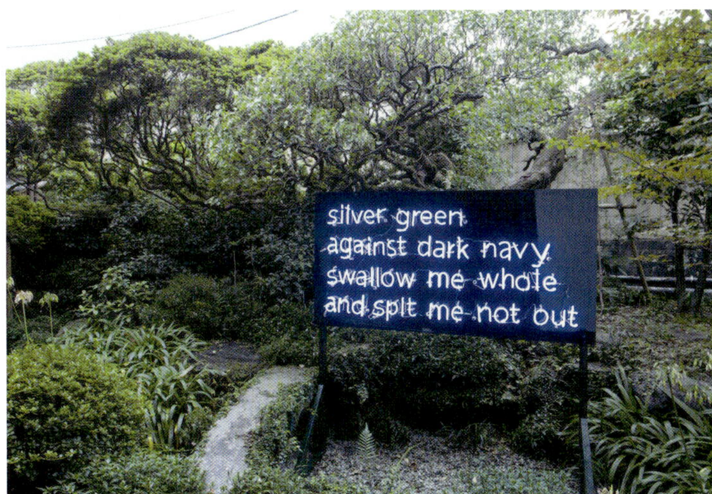

Plate XXVII
***silver green against dark navy*, 2015**

Plate XXVI
***Light rain*, 2015–21**

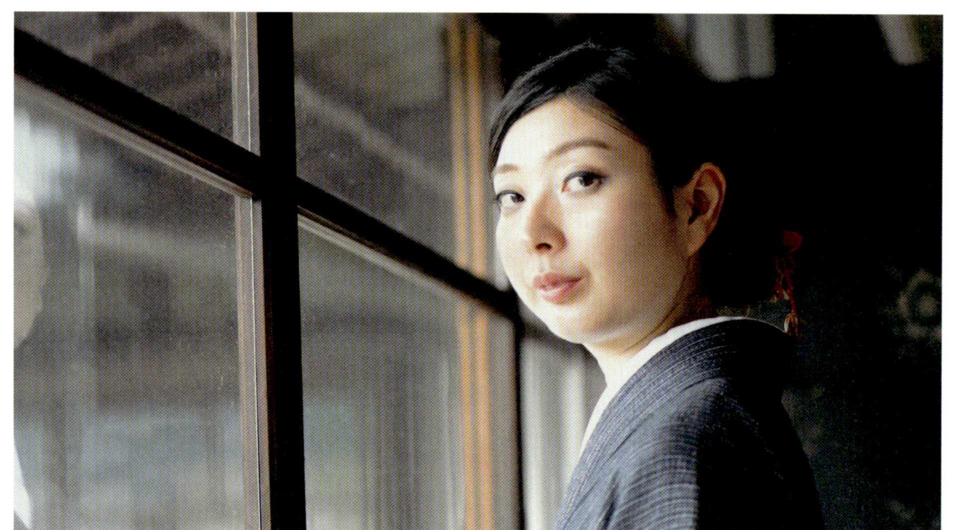

Plate XXVIII
***mata ne*, 2015–21 (detail)**

Plate XXIX
***mata ne*, 2015–21**

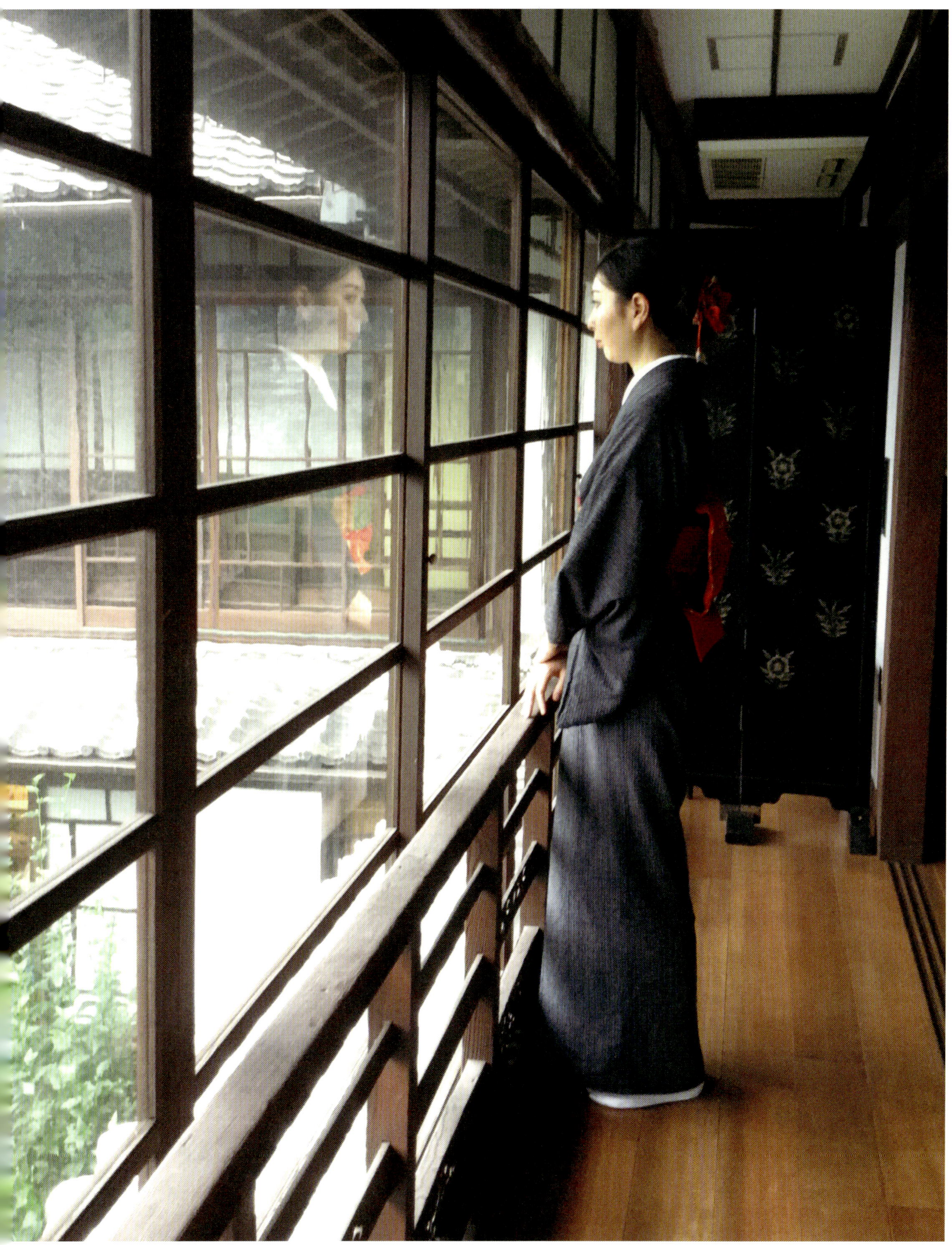

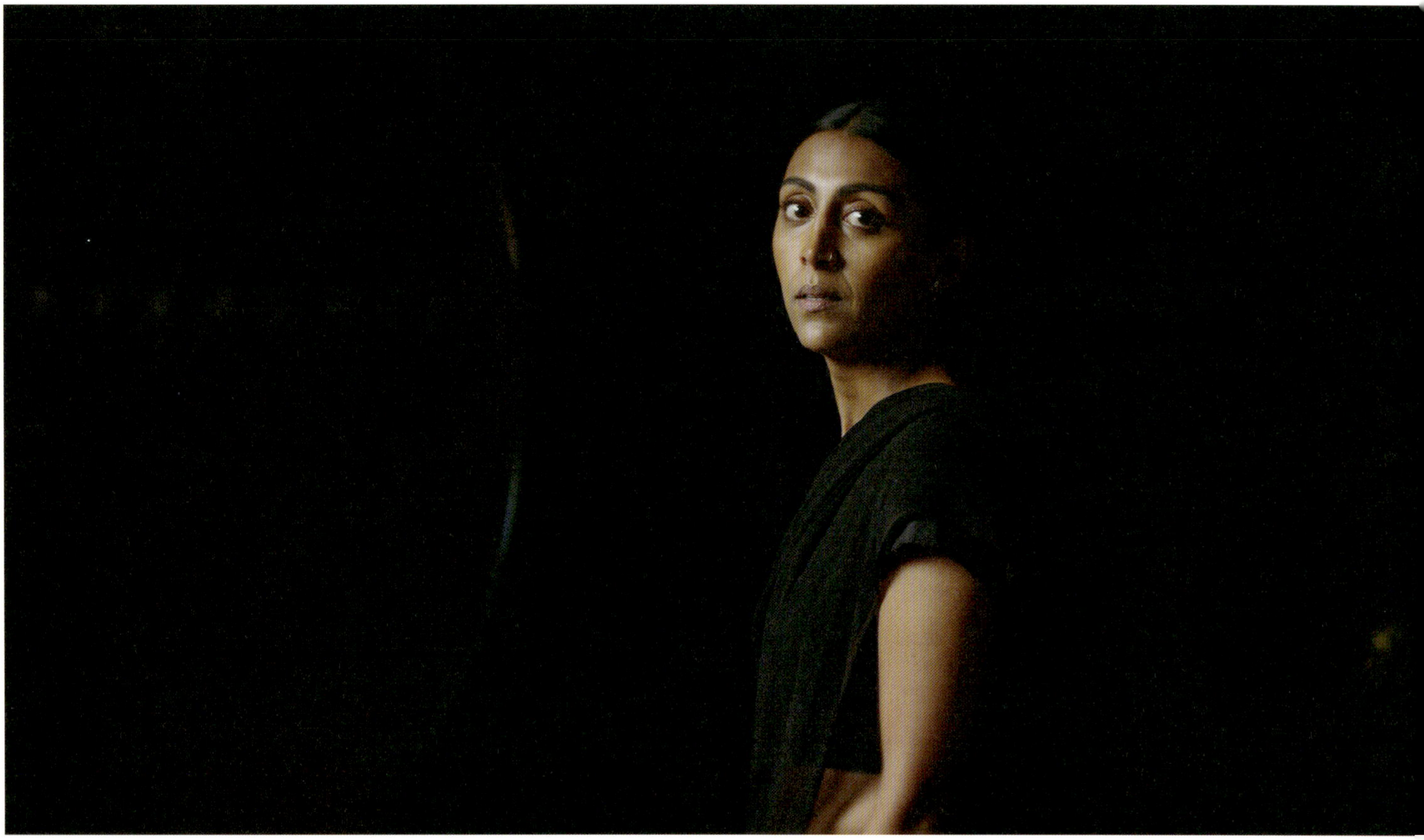

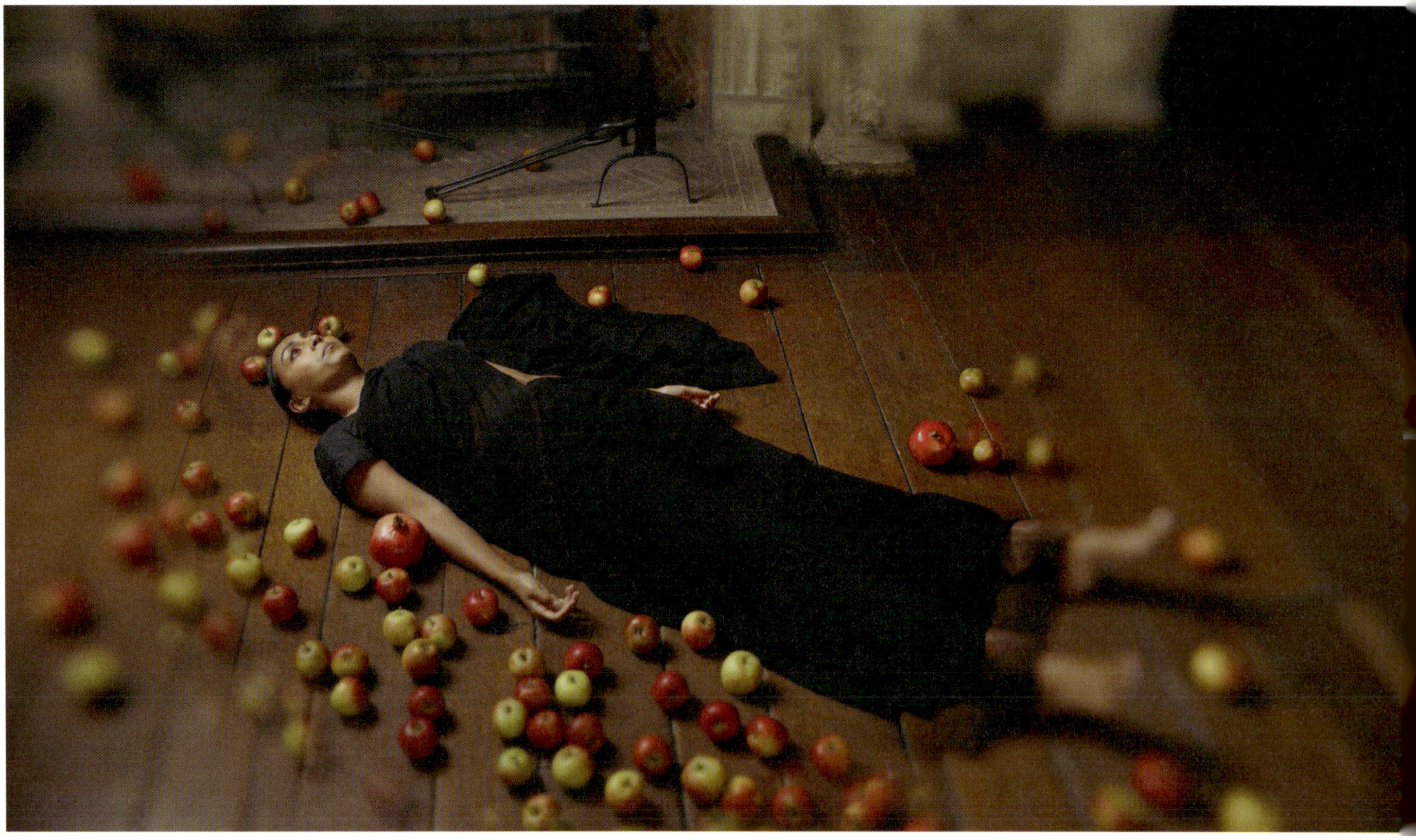

Plates XXX–XXXI
from *Lumen*, 2021

Lumen

Sutapa Biswas in conversation with Alessandro Vincentelli

Lumen is a thirty-minute film by Sutapa Biswas that draws upon the personal experience of her family's departure from India in the mid-1960s. It is a work that explores the phenomenon of migration and the feelings of rupture, dislocation, longing and belonging that such a journey brings. The sea journey is a formative memory for Biswas; the vivid images she has retained of that crossing, as well as her mother's anxieties for her children and her fears for their future are revisited through the narrative threads of a scripted monologue delivered by the actor Natasha Patel.

The script gives expression to a resonant matrilineal voice that has all too often been neglected in the telling of histories. The monologue combines Biswas's own frames of experience with those of her mother and her grandmother. As well as the family's displacement from one continent to another, the film traces the passage of various historic artefacts (paintings, fabrics and other objects) emblematic of the remnants of India's colonial past. The film oscillates almost in tidal motion between aural space and pictorial sequences comprising archival footage from the British Empire and Commonwealth Collection in Bristol, and passages shot on location at multiple locations in India in January 2020 and in Red Lodge, a historic house in Bristol, once home to abolitionist Mary Carpenter. The film weaves together intimate and global histories of passage, trade and migration and the dynamics of belonging, dispossession and trauma left in their wake.

Alessandro Vincentelli: How significant are your memories of childhood? What role do they play in *Lumen*?

Sutapa Biswas: I remember watching my mum when she received letters from India, and they were always on that distinctive blue aerogram paper, the type that very few people use these days. As my father travelled some months ahead of us, I tried to imagine how she may have felt in anticipation of receiving letters from him in that time. This is referenced in the monologue, where the protagonist, who is a fictionalised version of my mum, says: 'Chitti, Chitti, Chitti, I did not want to look, for in it was not even half my heart'.

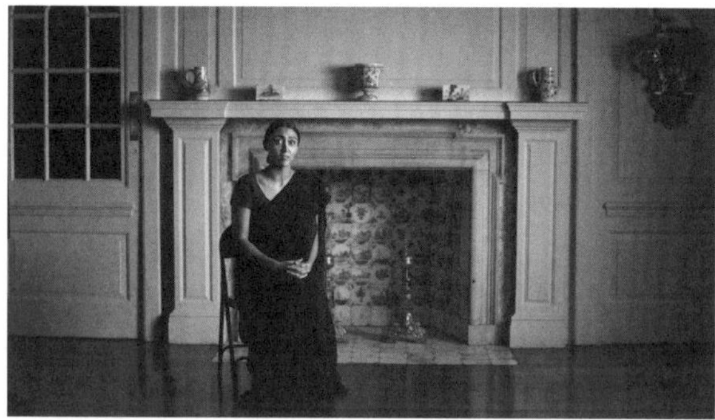

Figure 18
from *Lumen*, 2021

Figure 19
from *Lumen*, 2021

My mother must have been filled with fear of having to leave India. She was leaving everything — the love of her people, the love of her family, the love of her home, the love of the landscape — to go to the land of the same people who were responsible for bankrupting and violating her own place of birth. So, she must have been really ambivalent about making that journey. Had it not been for the fact that she had five children, I've often wondered whether she would have ever left India. I don't know that she would have.

So that scene, and the film itself, imagines what my mum must have felt and the longer histories, both told and untold, that surround her experience. While I'm working with personal memories, I also make references to other texts, images and films. For instance, the letter sequence reflects a scene from Satyajit Ray's film *Pather Panchali* (1955), in which the young son Apu is running through the forest to the gates of the house waving a letter. Through a play of camera shots, the anxiety and longing felt by Apu's mother, who has anxiously been awaiting word from her husband/lover, is made palpable. Ray's film brilliantly articulates the complexity of the impact of British colonial rule, even in its aftermath, on familial relations within Indian society, something that is also articulated in *Lumen*.

I'm also interested in the role of the child, and this is implicit in *Lumen*. Although the film is told from my mother's perspective, it is based on my memories and as such recognises the violence I experienced and the trauma that emerged from it. I was quite susceptible to sensing my mother's trauma when we arrived from India; somewhere in the witnessing of her own grief, I recognised something even though I was only four years old. There is a disposition in me to be storyteller, an artist, and perhaps this comes from sensing violence too early in life. At least it has shaped the stories I tell.

AV: What role does sound have in the film?

SB: Sound plays an important role in *Lumen*. In writing the monologue I imagined the narrator speaking as if reciting prose or poetry. Consequently, the monologue is structured to create a rhythm which when spoken feels tidal, in places Shakespearean and resonant of various poetry, all of which have been literary influences. These were guiding presences during rehearsals with Natasha Patel. Shakespeare in particular was an important reference because my parents and grandparents, born under colonial rule in British India, were educated in English and taught Shakespeare, Milton and the work of many British poets, while also being forbidden from speaking in public in their own mother tongue. When we arrived in England, I discovered that they were more fluent in these works than many of our neighbours schooled in England. There was one poem in particular that my mother often recited and that stopped me in my tracks: a poem by William Henry Davies called *Leisure* (1911) that seemed so embedded in a conversation about capitalism. It begins:

> What is this life if, full of care
> We have no time to stand and stare?[1]

On the lips of my mother and father, whether in India or in England, it speaks of racial capitalism.

Sound further functions in *Lumen* as having a haunting presence, overlapping and interacting with images that are both archival and contemporary as a triggering presence; I was keen to use sound in such a way that effected an ebb and flow taking the viewer back and forth across time. In some places it underscores archival footage of the British Raj, for example, to accentuate the violence of its colonial rule and its arrogant ambivalence to the enslaved Indian subjects over whom they ruled. Sound in this context is used to unpick the myth that British colonial rule in India was there to profit the Indian subjects. Research and archival sources tell us that, under colonial rule, vast sums of wealth were made by the British through the trade system and the enslaved labour of the Indians. The economist Utsa Patnaik argues that Britain drained an estimated $45 trillion from India during the period from 1765 and the founding of the British East India Company, and subsequently the British Raj in 1858, through to 1938.[2]

Another guiding influence for *Lumen*'s sound is my own sense of being in the world, and the profound connection sounds and smells provide. My interest in the experiential is perhaps an influence of my birthplace Santiniketan, where my father taught at the Tagore Institute. A place in which the performing arts, visual arts, literature, philosophy, economics, agriculture and the sciences were considered interconnected disciplines. I also inherited this sensibility from my father, a Marxist but also a romantic who felt a deep connection with nature and the wider cosmos.

AV: Do you have sonic memories, as well as visual ones?

SB: Yes, particularly the last conversation I had with my father before he passed away from cancer in hospital. I had been thinking about his imminent death on the day before he passed away, and in trying to think what I might read after his death to console myself I recalled Marcel Proust's powerful evocation of

1. W.H. Davies, 'Leisure', *Songs Of Joy and Others*, London: A.C. Fifield, 1911.

2. See Utsa Patnaik, *Agrarian and Other Histories: Essays for Binay Bhushan Chaudhuri*, ed. Shubhra Chakrabarti and Utsa Patnaik, New York: Columbia University Press, 2018.

time through his use of metaphor and the sound of the wood pigeon cutting through a forest. Proust's evocation was the subject of my last conversation with my dad, saying 'I won't forget you, because you are like the wood pigeon in Proust's forest'; I will remember you and all the words you've spoken with me in your lifetime, when I hear the sound of a bird. While for Proust the wood pigeon punctuates distance, time and space, in *Lumen* it is the crow. The idea that wind carries sound is really important to me, as well as how birdsong can cut through or over the wind too. This is important to earlier works, like *Magnesium Bird* (2004) (pl. XXII) where the haunting image of birds sculpted out of magnesium ribbon and ignited at dusk in the Victorian walled gardens of Harewood House in Leeds, is underscored by the sound of gale force winds and the voices of children.

AV: Could you say more about the character of the crow?

SB: There are different characters in the monologue. The crow is one of these characters, an apparition that haunts the story — like Banquo's ghost in *Macbeth* — or a talisman. I have memories of meeting a crow when I first returned to India in November 1986. I recall the chill of the foggy mornings, the sound of the whistle of the early morning night watchmen, and then hearing the piercing sound of the crow at dawn. The 'Kak, Kak, Kak' is a sound that is awakening but at the same time it is quite disturbing and shrill; it has a resonance that cuts through space. The crow is a fearless, sentient being that will just land right in front of you at the most unexpected moments. They are very brave and unafraid of humans. As mentioned in the monologue, they will steal the leftover scraps of food from the table if you let them; they sweep in and sweep out again. The crow is part of life; it will come when it needs to and leaves when it is good and ready.

AV: What role do circular forms, such as the moon, the chandelier, the mirror, have in the film?

SB: 'Lumen' is the name for the measure of a unit of light visible to the human eye. It also describes a cavity or structure in the body such as an artery. *Lumen*, as the film's producer Steven Bode has commented, is the site where these two meanings metaphorically converge in a dialogue around what is visible in the light, and what comes to light through bodily trauma.

From my early childhood, the moon has provided a navigational pull in my imagination, and whether this began with my own sea journey from India to England, looking for it out of a circular portal, I don't know. It is also interesting to me that early navigation was dependent on the position of the moon and constellations in the night sky. But the moon and circular forms also disrupt orientation and measurement through horizontal and vertical coordinates. In an earlier work called *Frieze* (1992) I disrupted the horizon line, randomly exposing and developing photographic fragments from the series *Synapse I* (1987–92) (pls. XI–XIV), creating a fluctuating line; it's like a wave.

In *Lumen* the horizon line is still implicit as a measuring device, but disordering circular forms are also persistent. The

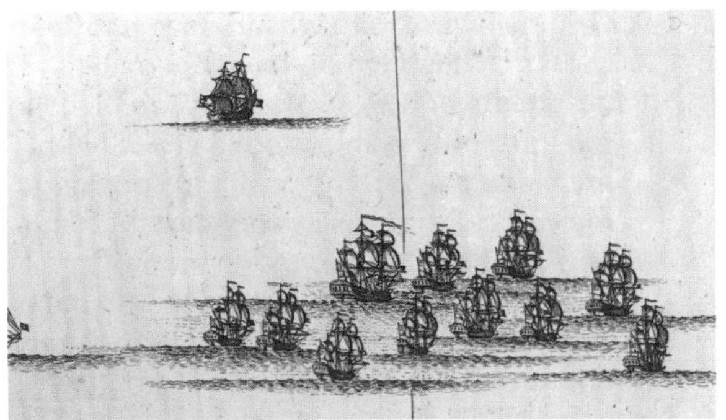

Figure 20
from *Lumen*, 2021

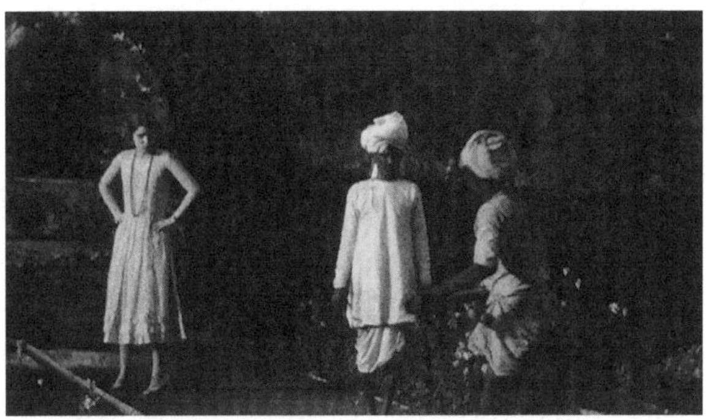

Figure 21
from *Lumen*, 2021

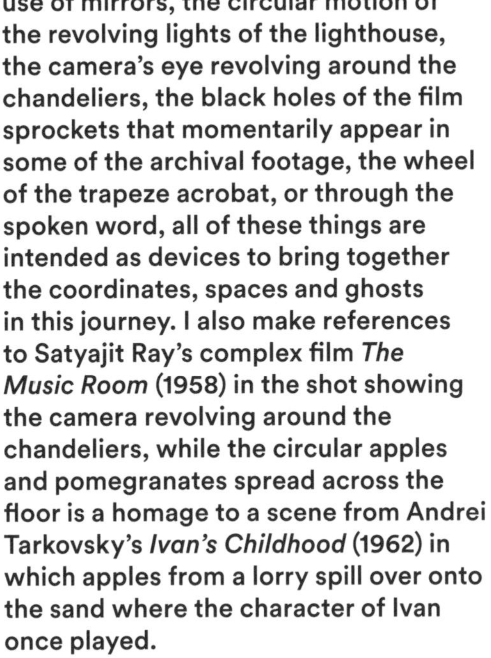

use of mirrors, the circular motion of the revolving lights of the lighthouse, the camera's eye revolving around the chandeliers, the black holes of the film sprockets that momentarily appear in some of the archival footage, the wheel of the trapeze acrobat, or through the spoken word, all of these things are intended as devices to bring together the coordinates, spaces and ghosts in this journey. I also make references to Satyajit Ray's complex film *The Music Room* (1958) in the shot showing the camera revolving around the chandeliers, while the circular apples and pomegranates spread across the floor is a homage to a scene from Andrei Tarkovsky's *Ivan's Childhood* (1962) in which apples from a lorry spill over onto the sand where the character of Ivan once played.

AV: There are certain colours, such as blue in particular, that recur in this work: the blue sari, the blue aerogram letter. How do you use colour in your film?

SB: Colour has been significant to my moving image works since *Untitled (Woman in Blue Weeping)* (1996) (pl. XX). This piece references the first painting I recall seeing as a child. It was a reproduction of *Woman in Blue Reading A Letter* (c. 1663) (fig. 17), by Johannes Vermeer. I think it struck a chord because it reminded me compositionally of a memory I had of my mother reading letters from India, stood at a window looking outwards. With her back towards me, unaware that I was watching, I had seen her weeping as she read. The letters were on blue aerograms, and she wore a blue fine silk sari brought with her from India. In 1996 I recreated this memory in film-form, but the sari also appears in *Lumen* (pl. XXXXV).

The scene with my mother's sari was filmed at Red Lodge in Bristol, and its atmospheric quality was an intentional reference to Vermeer's and Rembrandt's portraits. There are several reasons for this but primarily it is because, many years after first encountering Vermeer's painting, I began, as an undergraduate student at Leeds, to deconstruct the symbolism in the painting. Not only in terms of gender, but also paying close attention to the representation of the

large map filling the wall behind the woman portrayed. This map symbolises the expansion of the Dutch colonial empire in the seventeenth century when the Dutch East India Company (1602–1799) was not only founded, but also amassed enormous wealth on the backs of the Indian subjects. So in *Lumen*, blue refers to the trade in indigo, sourced from India, which was highly prized by the Europeans, as well as the trade in lapis, from Afghanistan, which was most likely used by Vermeer. Colour is very significant in *Lumen*, linking histories of colonialism, art history, family history and the history of my own work.

AV: You have mentioned in the past that your works are kind of 'spatial stories' that cross time and place. Is *Lumen* another spatial story for you?

SB: In short, yes. As with many of my works, I do see *Lumen* as a 'spatial story' that has roots in earlier works. The journey began in the works I made while a postgraduate student at the Slade, specifically the *Synapse* (1987–92) (fig. 1, pls. XI–XVI) series in which I overlaid images I had taken of Indian cultural sites onto a woman's body, my own. In this series I wanted to invoke both imagined and material histories that I was situated within, but that also went beyond that. In *Birdsong* (2004) (pls. XXIII–XXV), which is an homage to my father and my son mediated through my perspective, I connected the intimacy of mother–son and father–daughter relationships with English landscape painting and the brutality of property relations.

Originally *Birdsong* was to have another section, which would have been my perspective. It would have taken place in the interior of a ship, with a chest, with my niece playing the part and speaking my voice. But the film was shot on 16mm and we didn't raise enough money to shoot the third section; *Lumen* is in part a realisation of this. It has sat with me for about two decades, at least. I am glad to be making it now because I've lived life longer, maybe understand life better, and I'm wiser.

AV: *Lumen* concerns colonial histories of exploitation and extraction, and in particular the aftermath of post-independence India. You have included references and citations, both text and footage, to tell some of these histories, often subverting the material along the way. I was struck by this quotation in dialogue: 'Patterns we set — they do not heed'. Where did this come from?

SB: This comes from an 1813 satirical poem that I found in a book by Richard Drayton called *Nature's Government: Science, Imperial Britain and the Improvement of the World.*[3] The poem is a lament for the Duke of Bedford's paternalistic attempts to establish standard agricultural farming methods, and the failures of Whig politics. Although in *Lumen* the context is different, the sentiment feels true to the archival footage in the film, which evidences the prevailing and indignant attitude of the British Raj towards Indian subjects. I included it to highlight that there was nothing generous about Empire, but that rather it was punitive, violent and violating on every level.

3. Richard Drayton, *Nature's Government: Science, Imperial Britain and the Improvement of the World*, New Haven and London: Yale University Press, 2000, p.149.

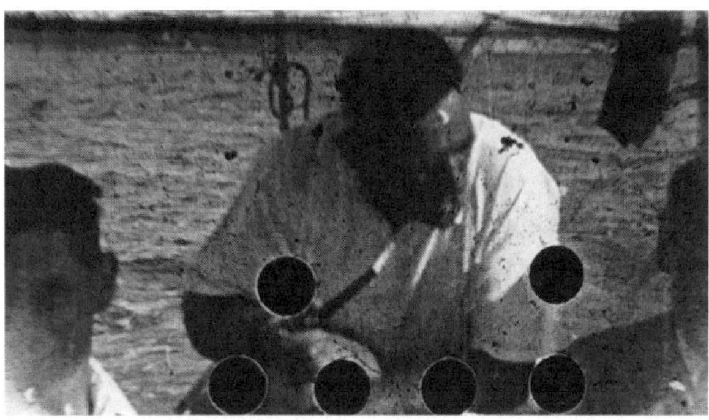

Figure 22
from *Lumen*, 2021

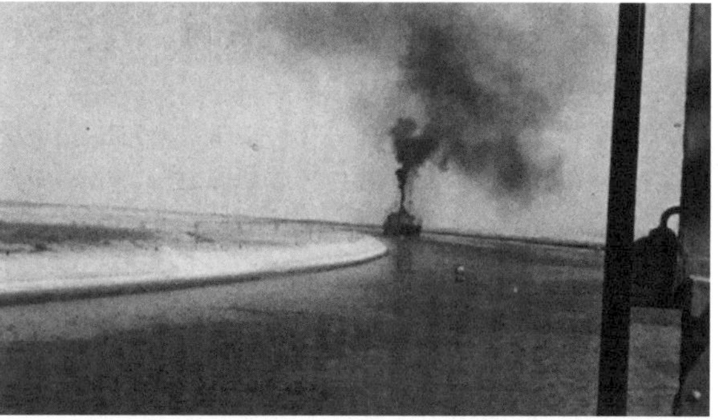

Figure 23
from *Lumen*, 2021

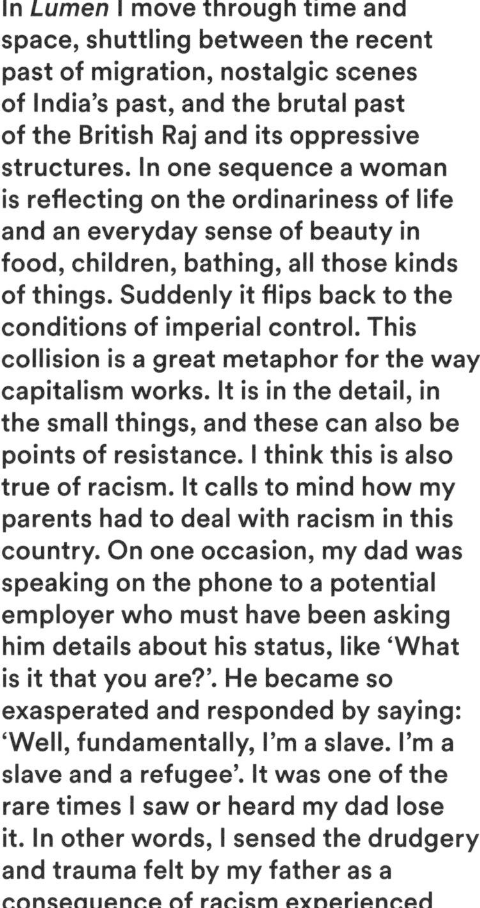

In *Lumen* I move through time and space, shuttling between the recent past of migration, nostalgic scenes of India's past, and the brutal past of the British Raj and its oppressive structures. In one sequence a woman is reflecting on the ordinariness of life and an everyday sense of beauty in food, children, bathing, all those kinds of things. Suddenly it flips back to the conditions of imperial control. This collision is a great metaphor for the way capitalism works. It is in the detail, in the small things, and these can also be points of resistance. I think this is also true of racism. It calls to mind how my parents had to deal with racism in this country. On one occasion, my dad was speaking on the phone to a potential employer who must have been asking him details about his status, like 'What is it that you are?'. He became so exasperated and responded by saying: 'Well, fundamentally, I'm a slave. I'm a slave and a refugee'. It was one of the rare times I saw or heard my dad lose it. In other words, I sensed the drudgery and trauma felt by my father as a consequence of racism experienced daily at a systemic level. Regardless of this, he instilled in us a sense of ownership and belonging. During a visit to the Victoria and Albert Museum, as we excitedly took in all that was before us, he told us 'Remember, this collection belongs to the public tax payers and because your mother and I pay our taxes, it means that everything here belongs to you'. These words hold a double meaning. In *Lumen* I've tried to bring that sense of the everyday into a relation with the space of history.

AV: What comes through the script is a sense of being unmoored in both time and space, and the fear of the sea journey. Of course the sea is both terrifying and has the potential to make you seasick, being unfixed from the horizon. Does that fear of the unknown relate for you?

SB: I really love your phrase 'being unmoored'. It is exactly right, because it encompasses the literal unmooring of the boat, the departure from one place, the nausea of the voyage and the psychic loss of belonging. It is a different sense of perspective. The desire to find

one's self, while fighting against the waves. There is nothing firm, it is not 'terra firma'. It may be terrifying until you see land again. It is like experiencing vertigo, where you feel like you're being swallowed whole. The fearsomeness of 'being swallowed whole', which I brought into that monologue for *Lumen* at the end, is another reference to an earlier work. It is a line from a new sculpture. It is a line from a new sculpture I made during my residency in Japan, the title of which is *silver green against dark navy* (2015) (pl. XXVII).

It was inspired by the haiku form, although it is not precisely a haiku. I wanted to take the idea of saying something poetic but lean. It has something Old English about it, but it refers to a moment when I felt exposed physically and emotionally, but also in great despair about the contemporary migrant crisis reported in newspapers and social media. So the poem is about the desire and the urgency to be accepted for who we are, to be taken whole and not spat out.

I think my mum must have felt that. When you look into the black of the sea, and all you can see are falling stars, or waves or the moon, the lights seen from afar, when you might be approaching Suez, or wherever, that somehow, in the pit of your stomach, there is the sense of the unknown and this is just the deepest fear really, of not living, and you know the darkest of spaces, like being swallowed whole. Your desire is that you are accepted for all your idiosyncrasies and the human being you are, that you don't have to change. Colonial histories have taught us that power seeks control, subservience and change. But at the same time 'a wog was always going to be a wog'; racism was always there.

AV: Lastly, a final question: why *Lumen*?

SB: I think we say in the opening sequences of the film that lumen is a unit of light. Light represents a kind of hopefulness, because light, as we all are, is a part of the cosmos, which may be quite small in relation to time and space, but is part of it nonetheless.

Plates XXXII–XXXXIV
from *Lumen*, 2021

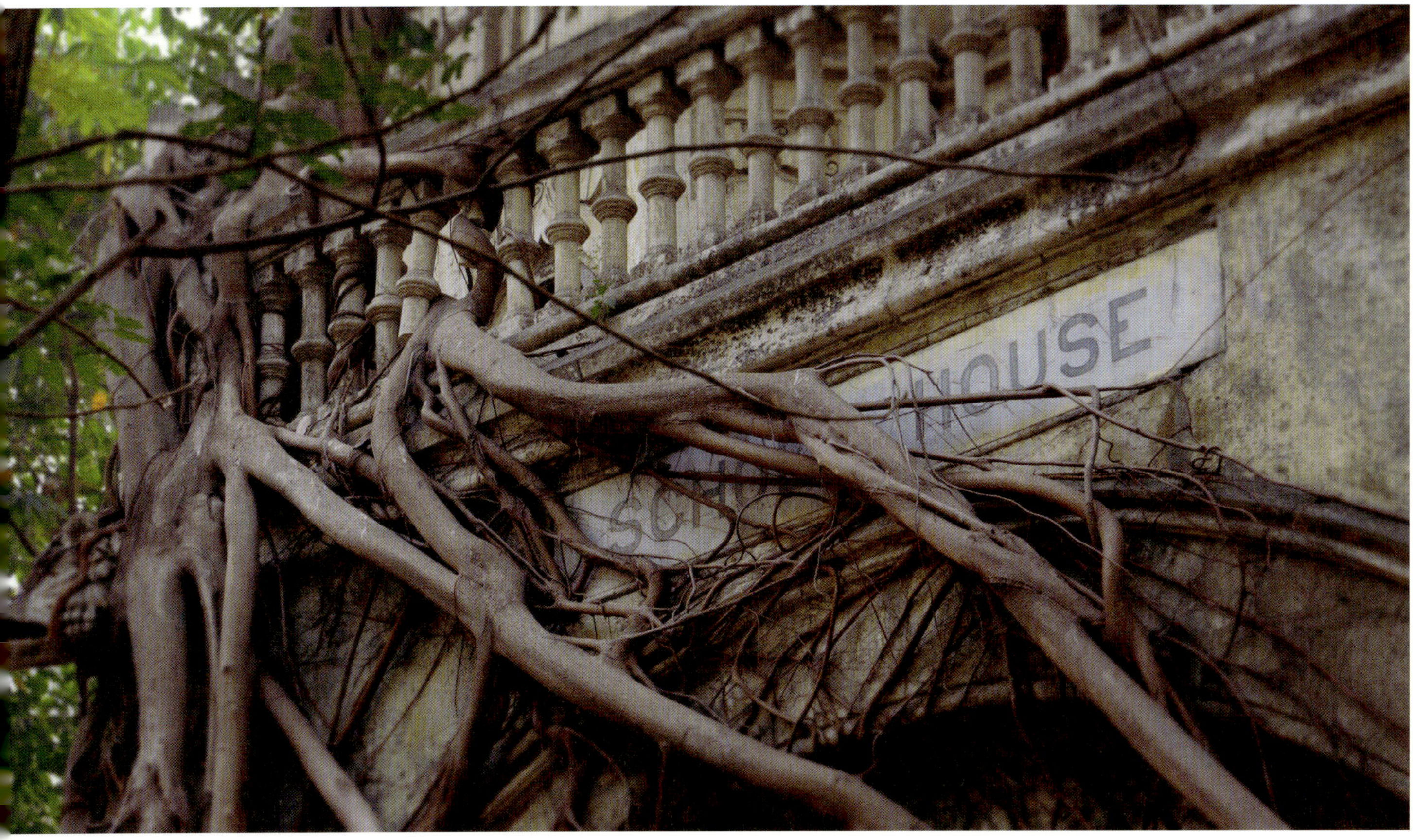
HOUSE

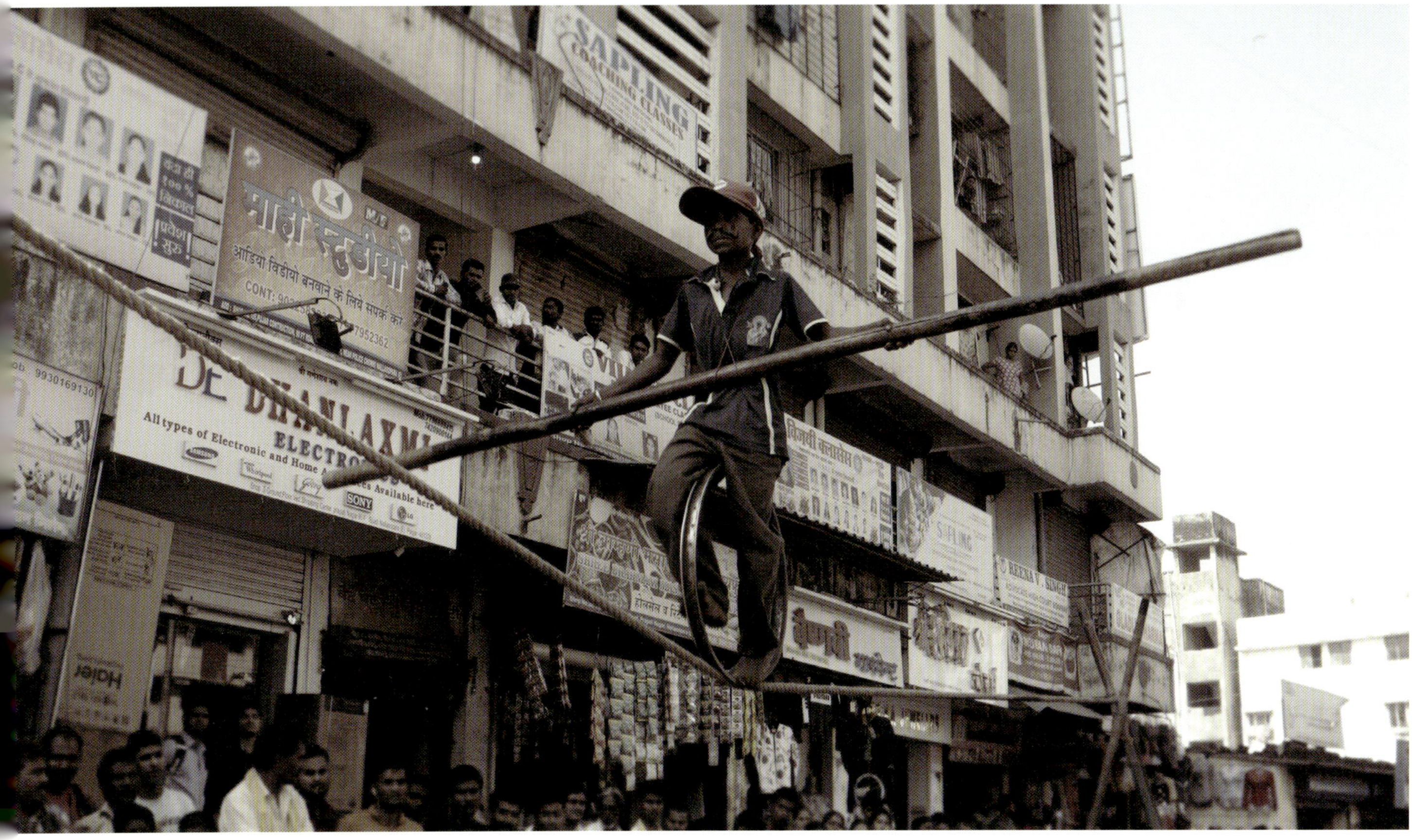
SAPLING
COACHING CLASSES
All types of Electronic and Home A
SONY
SAPLING

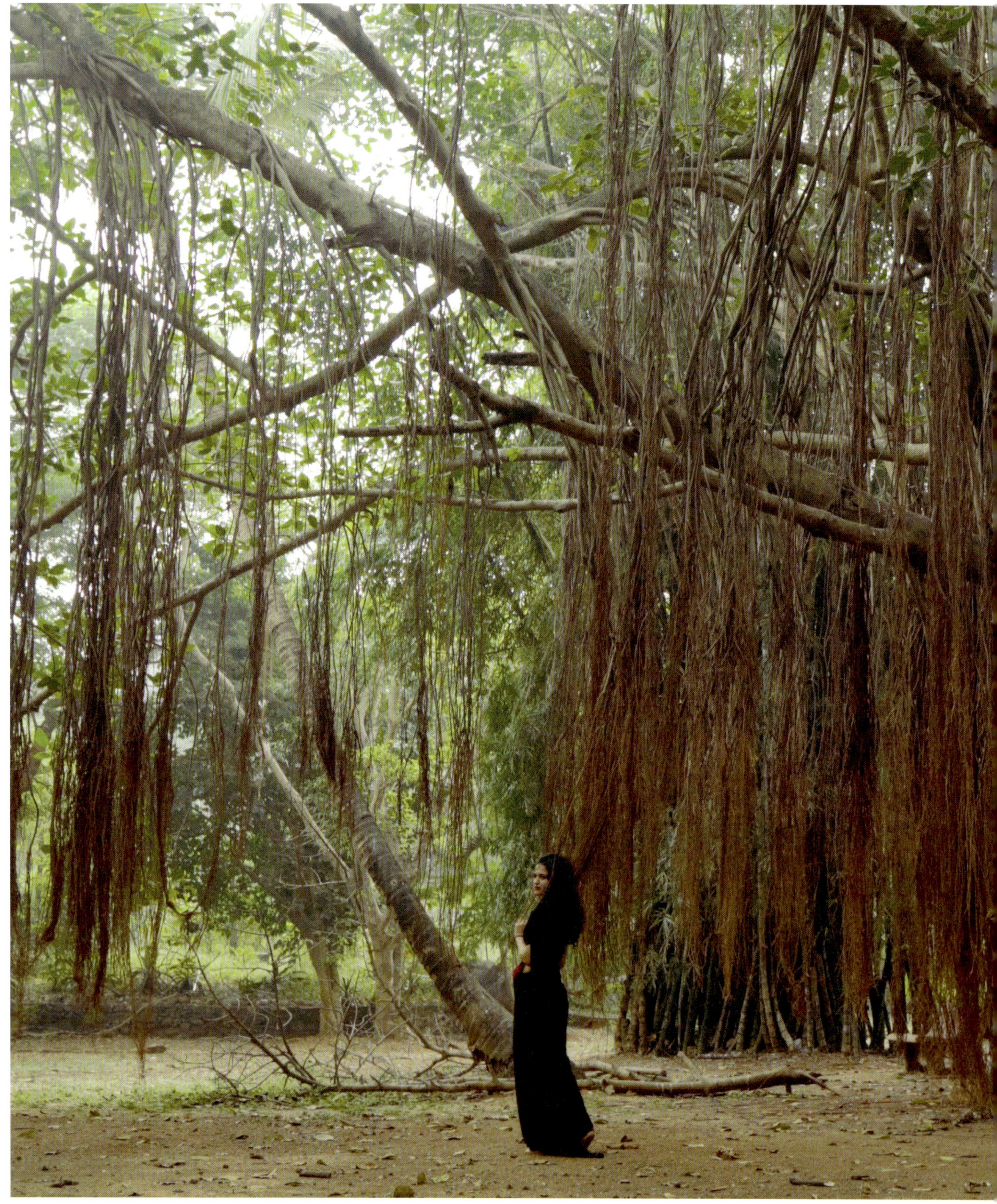

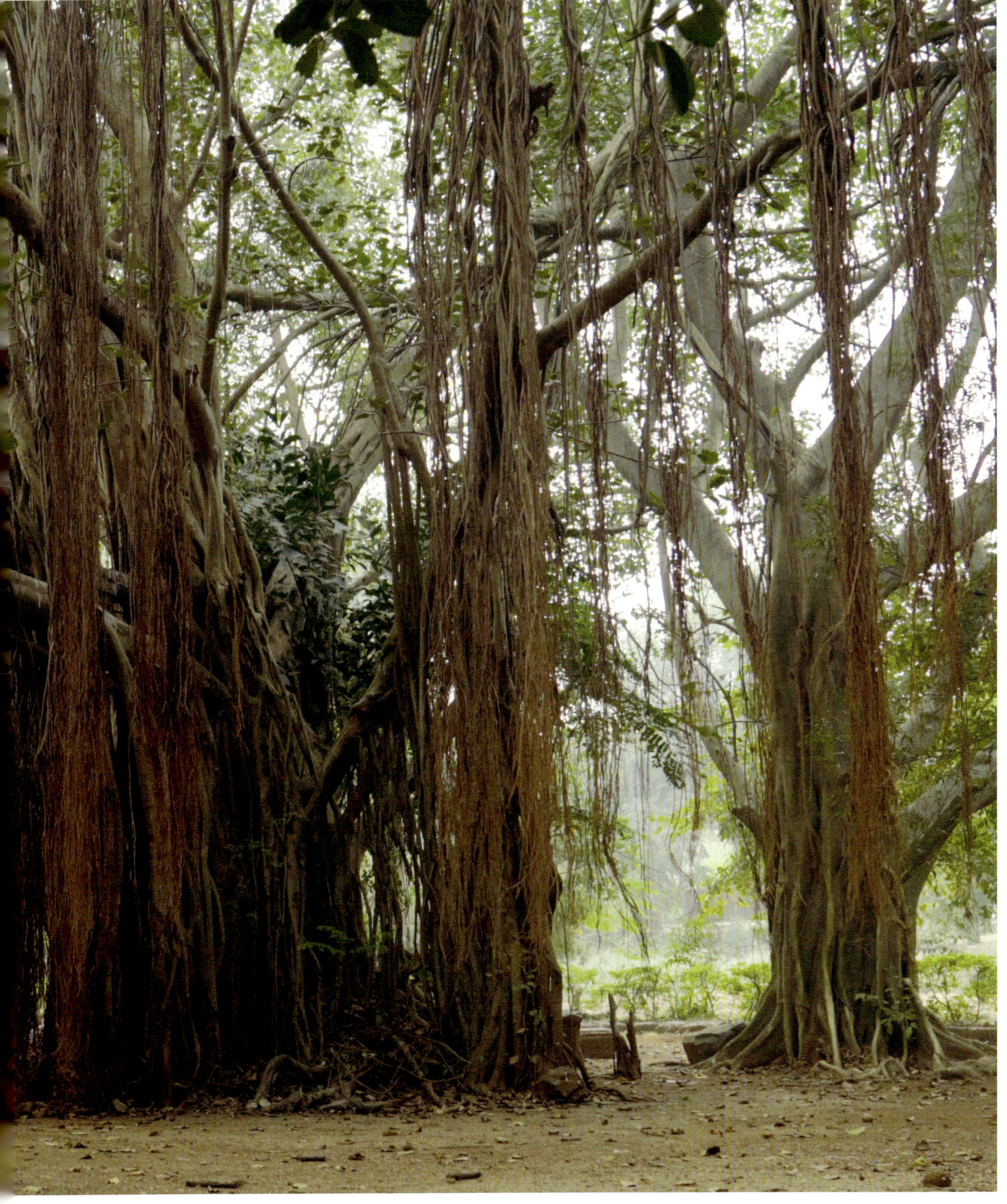

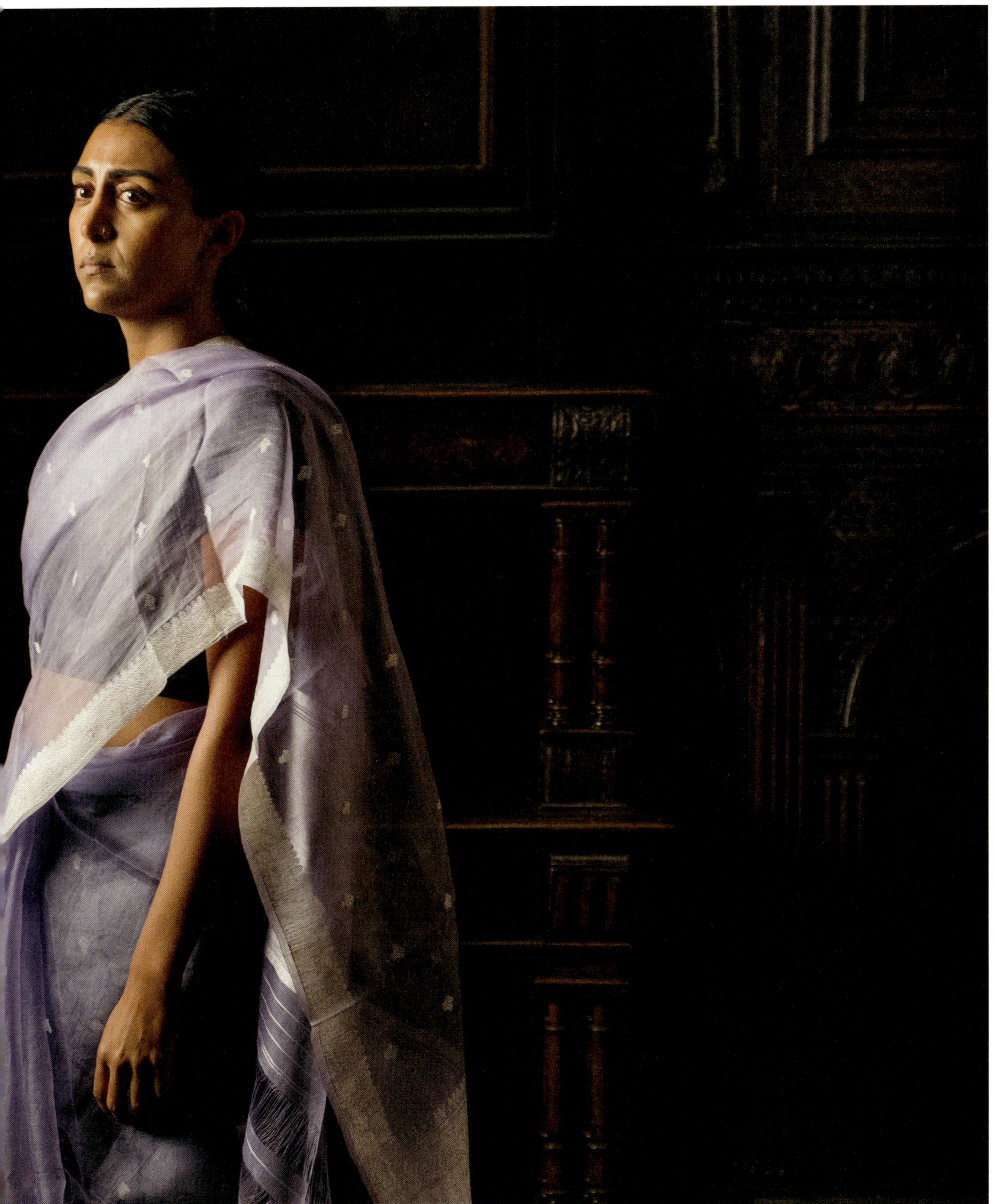

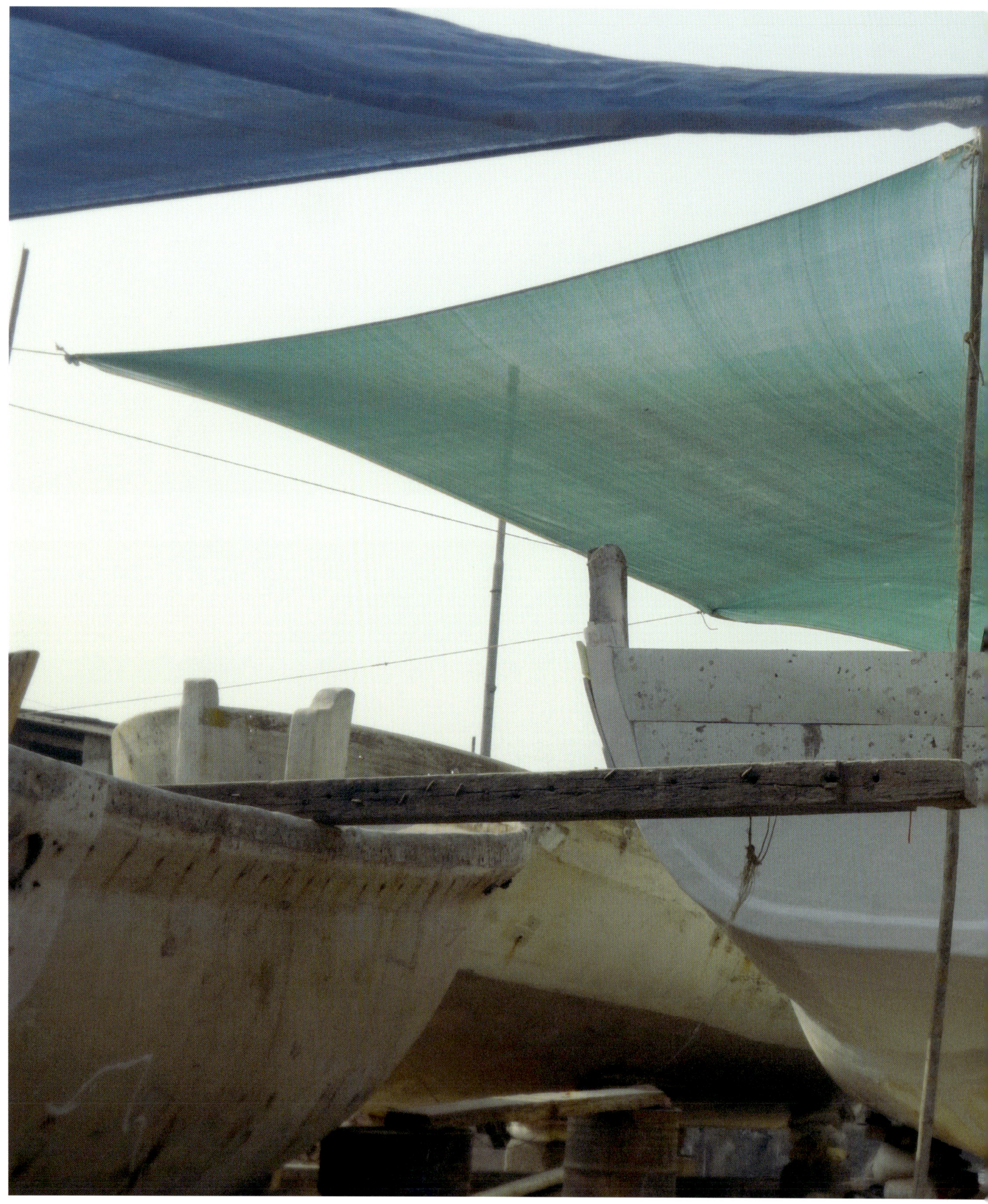

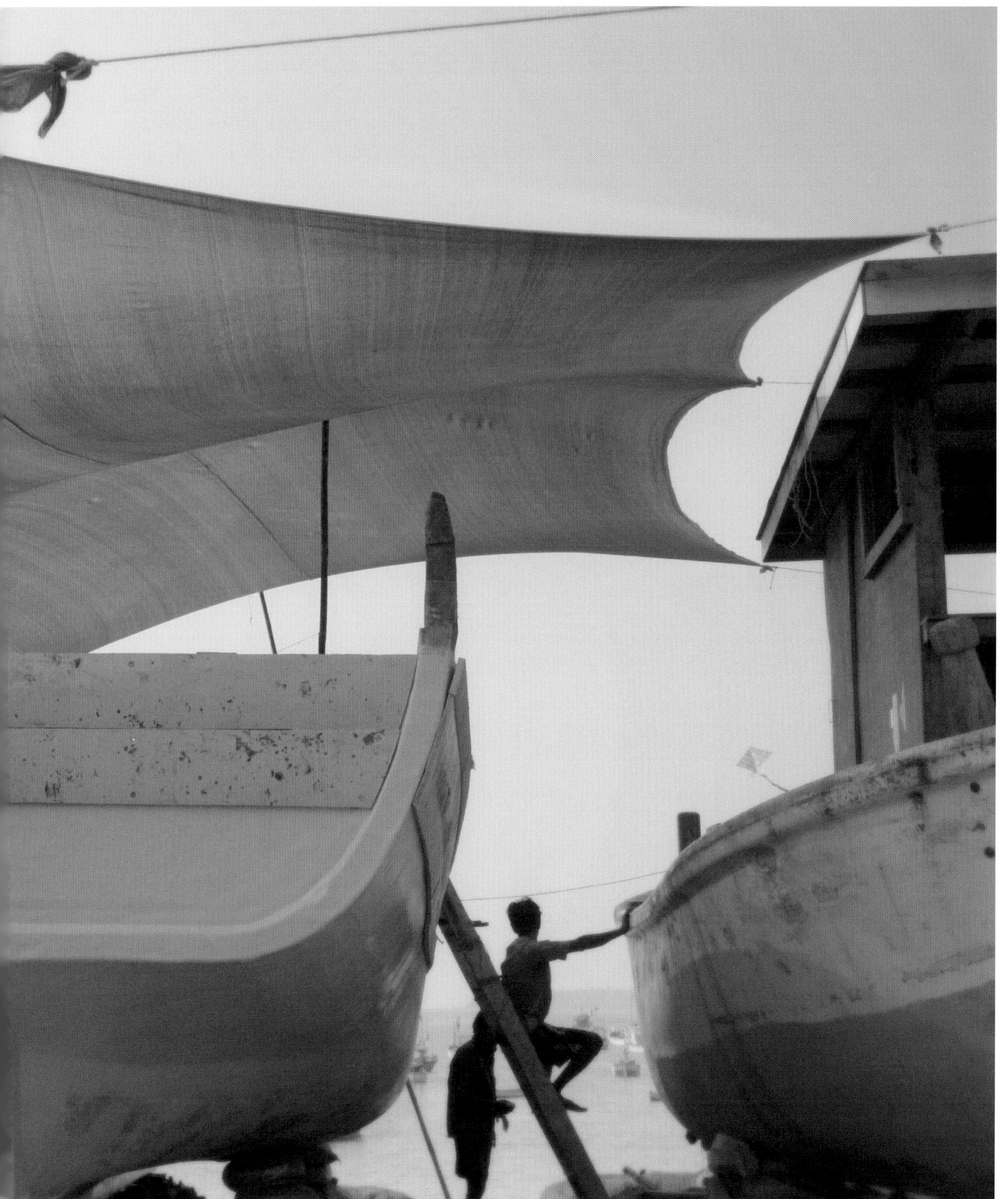

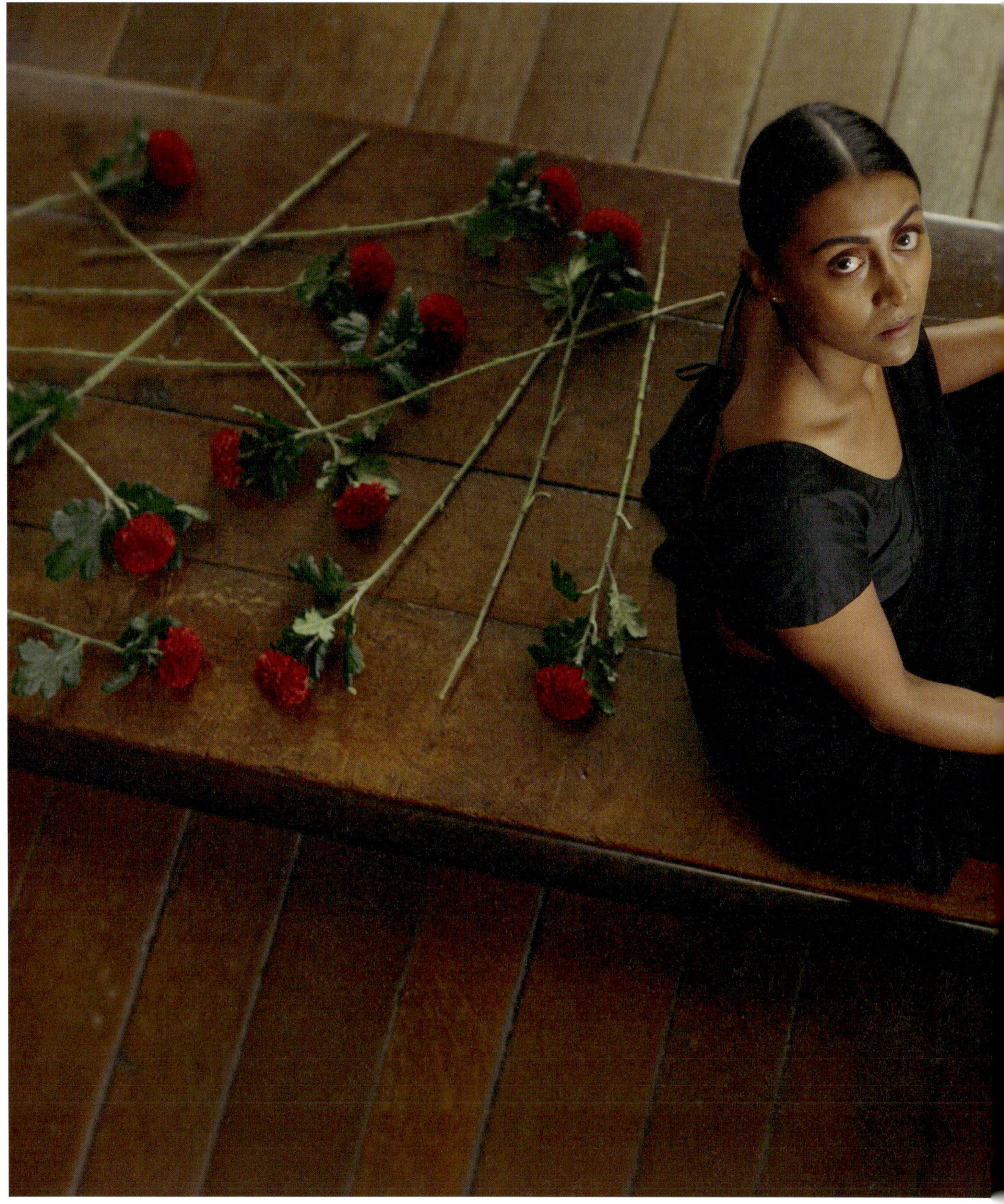

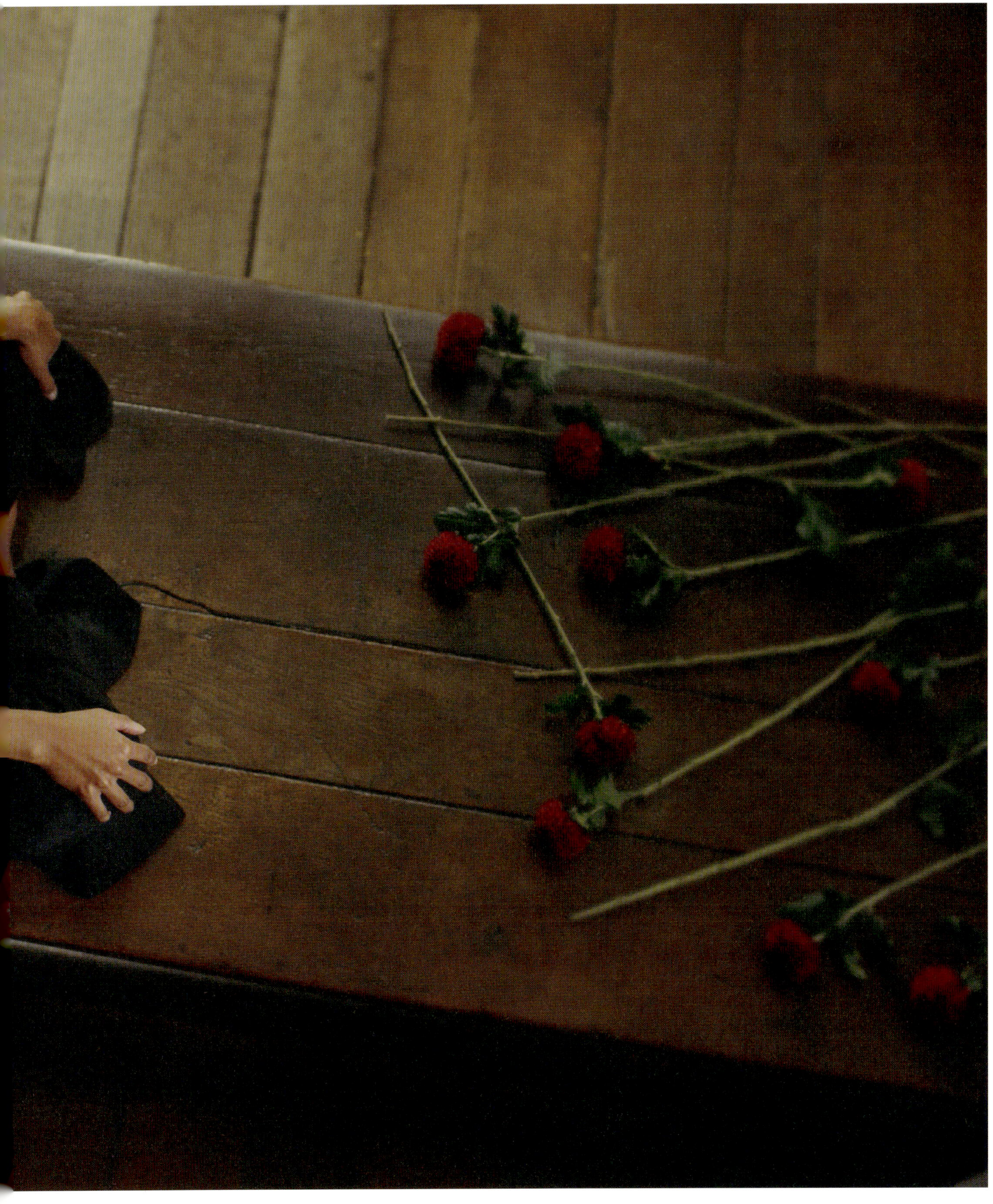

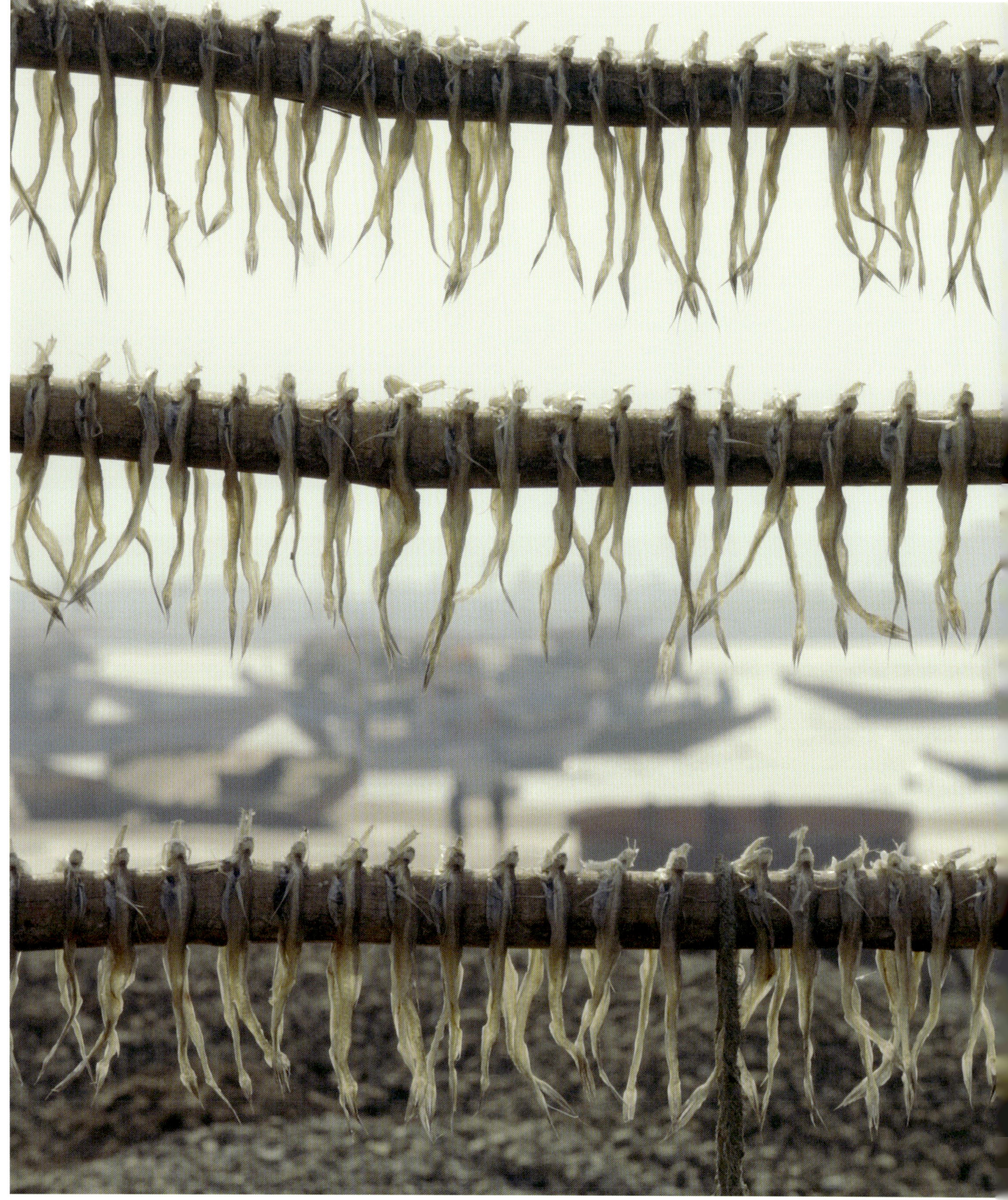

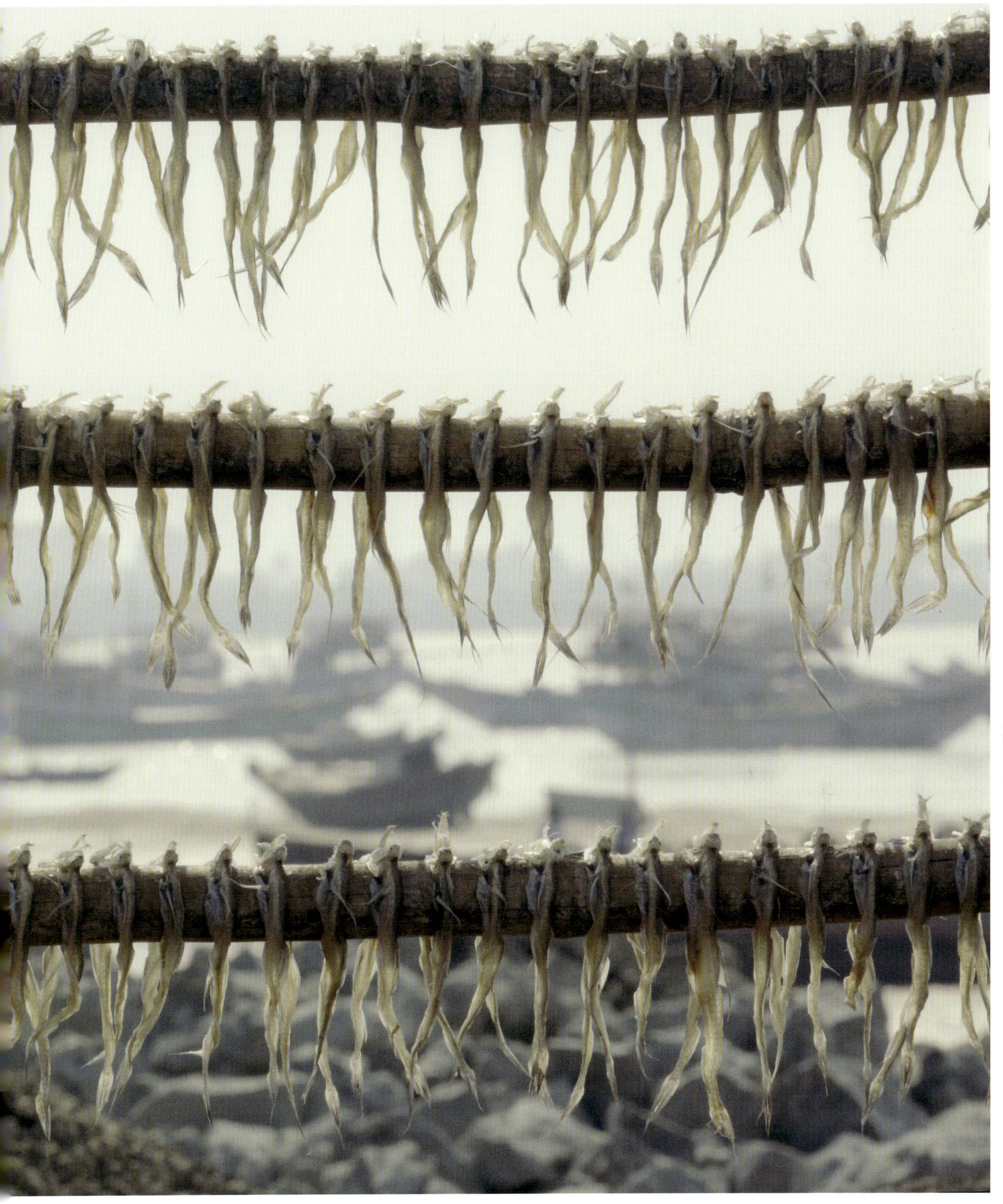

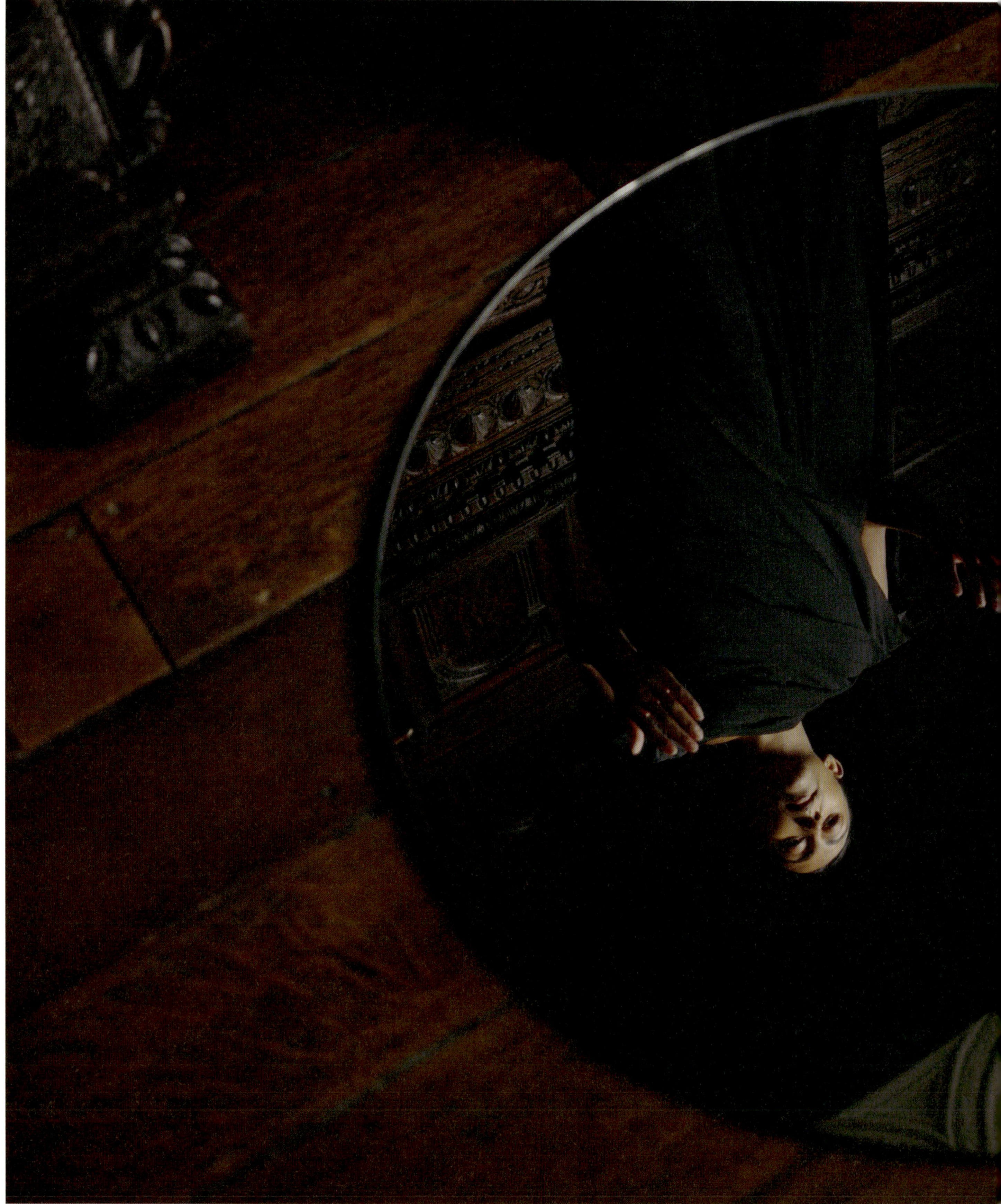

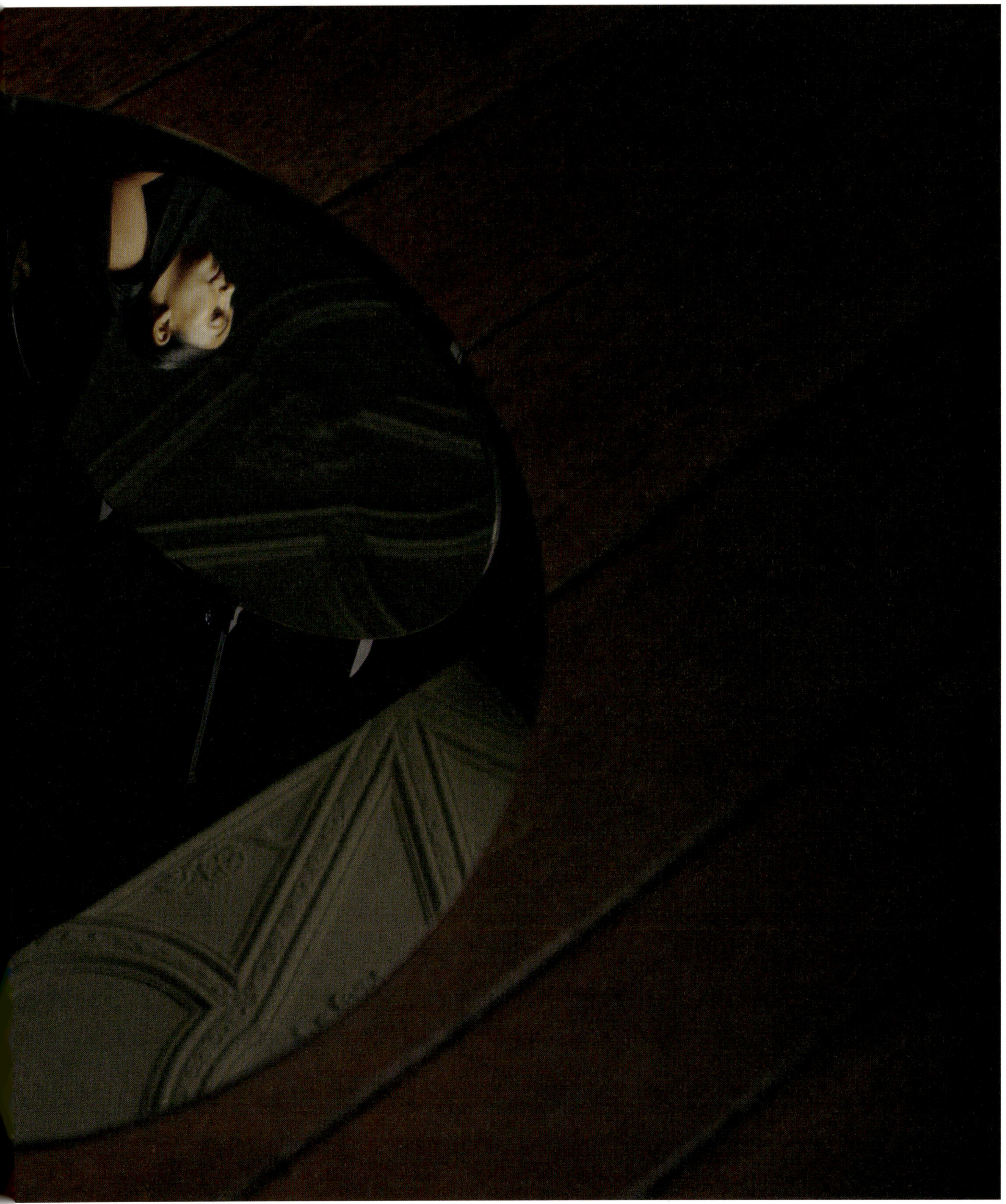

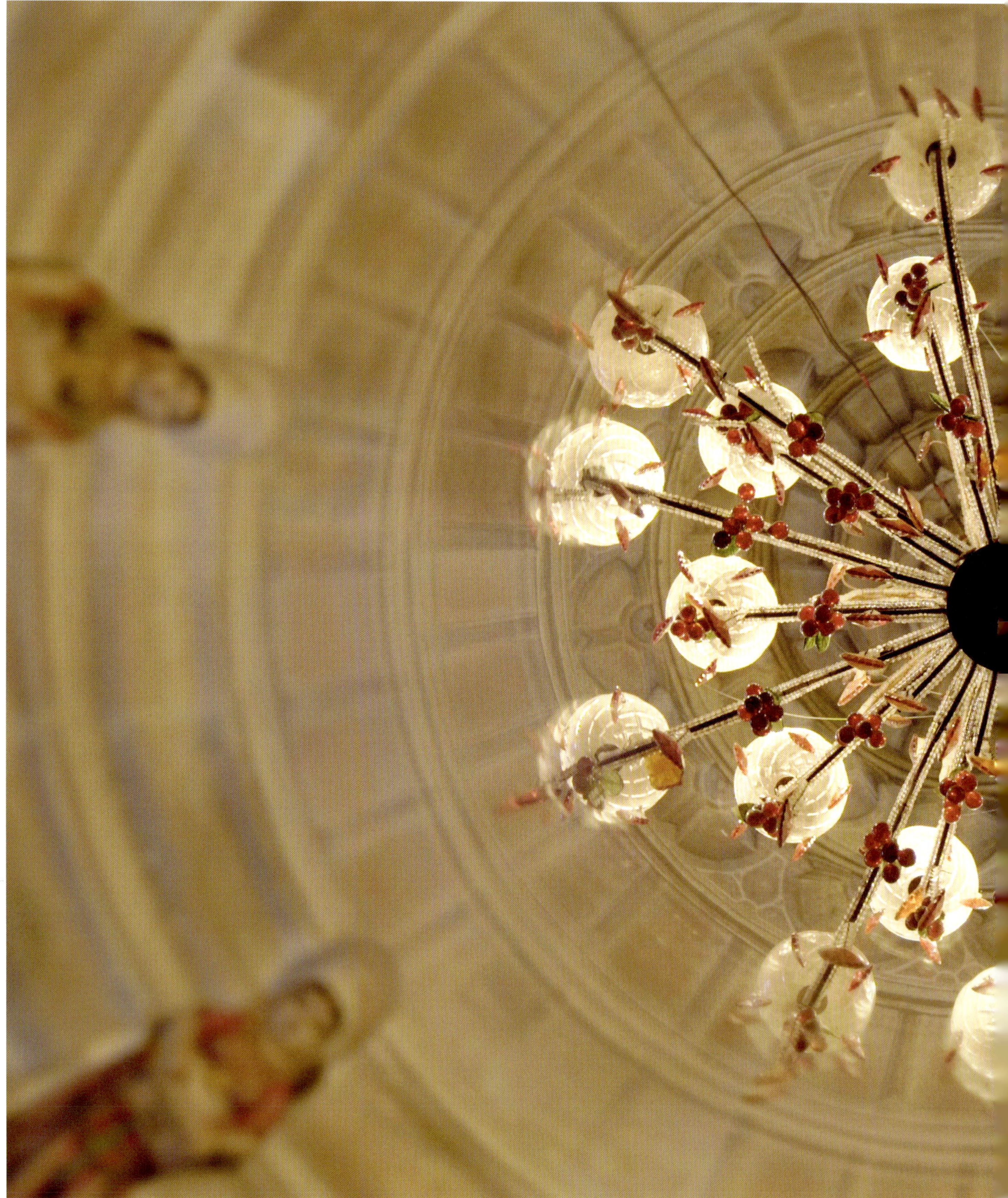

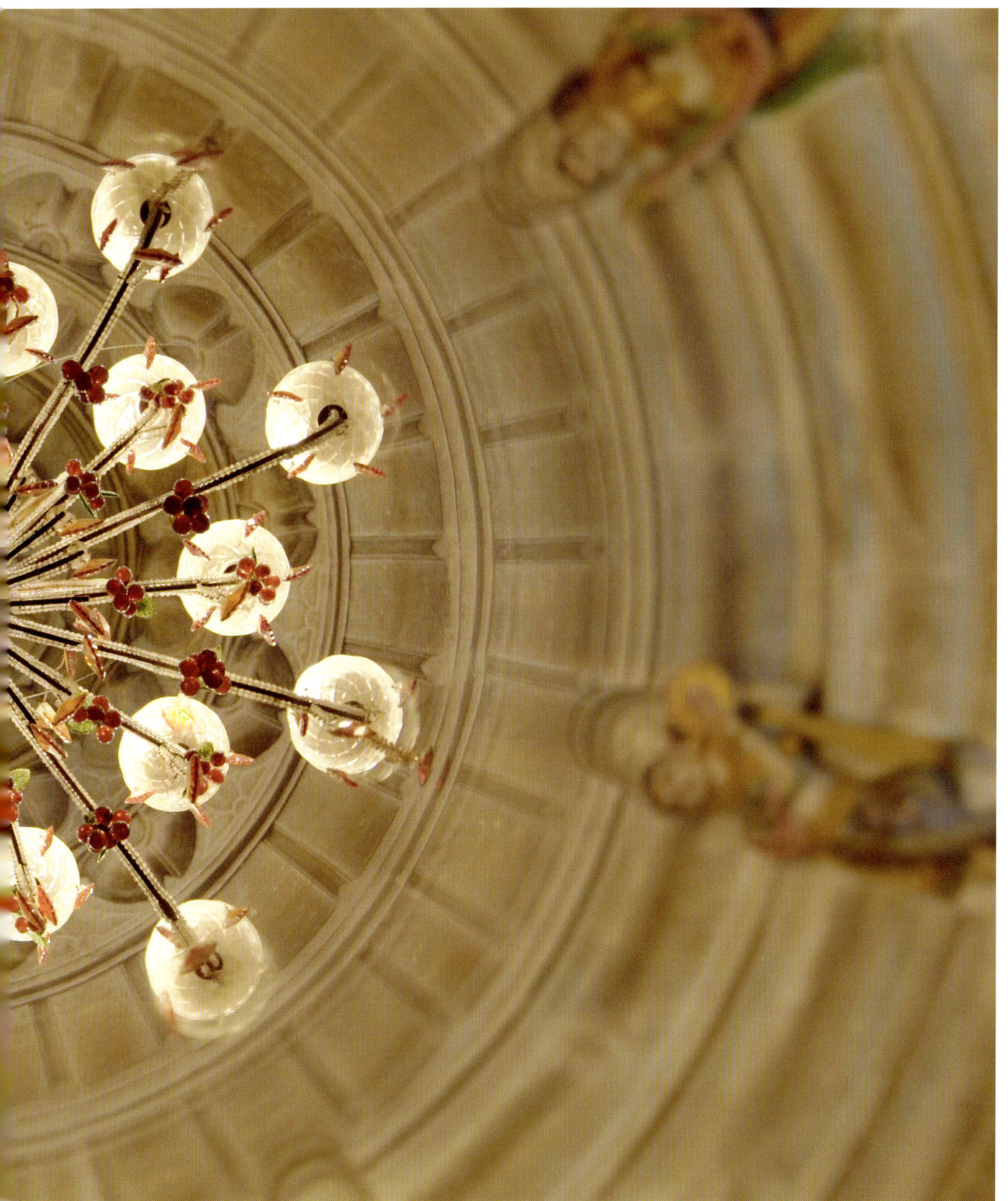

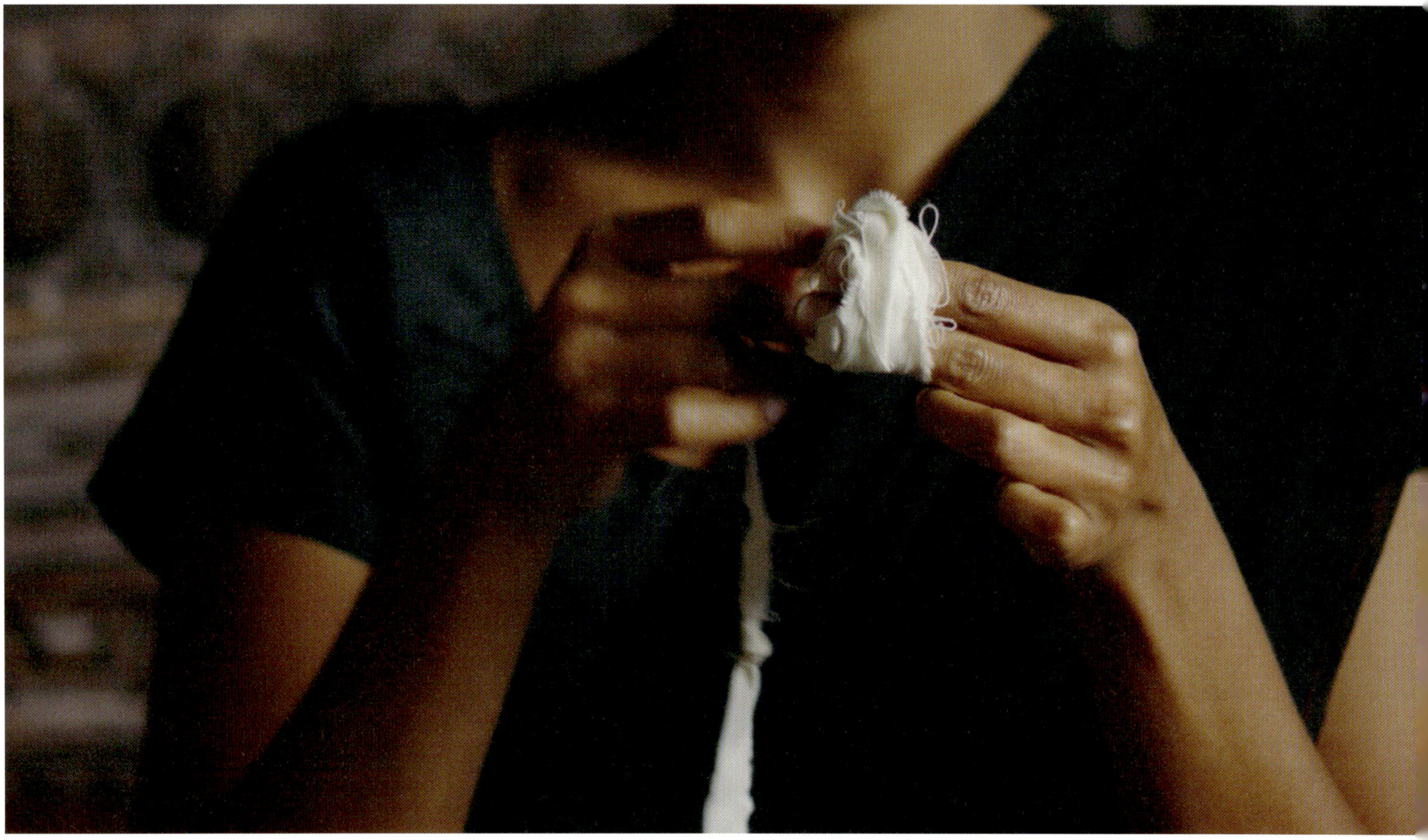

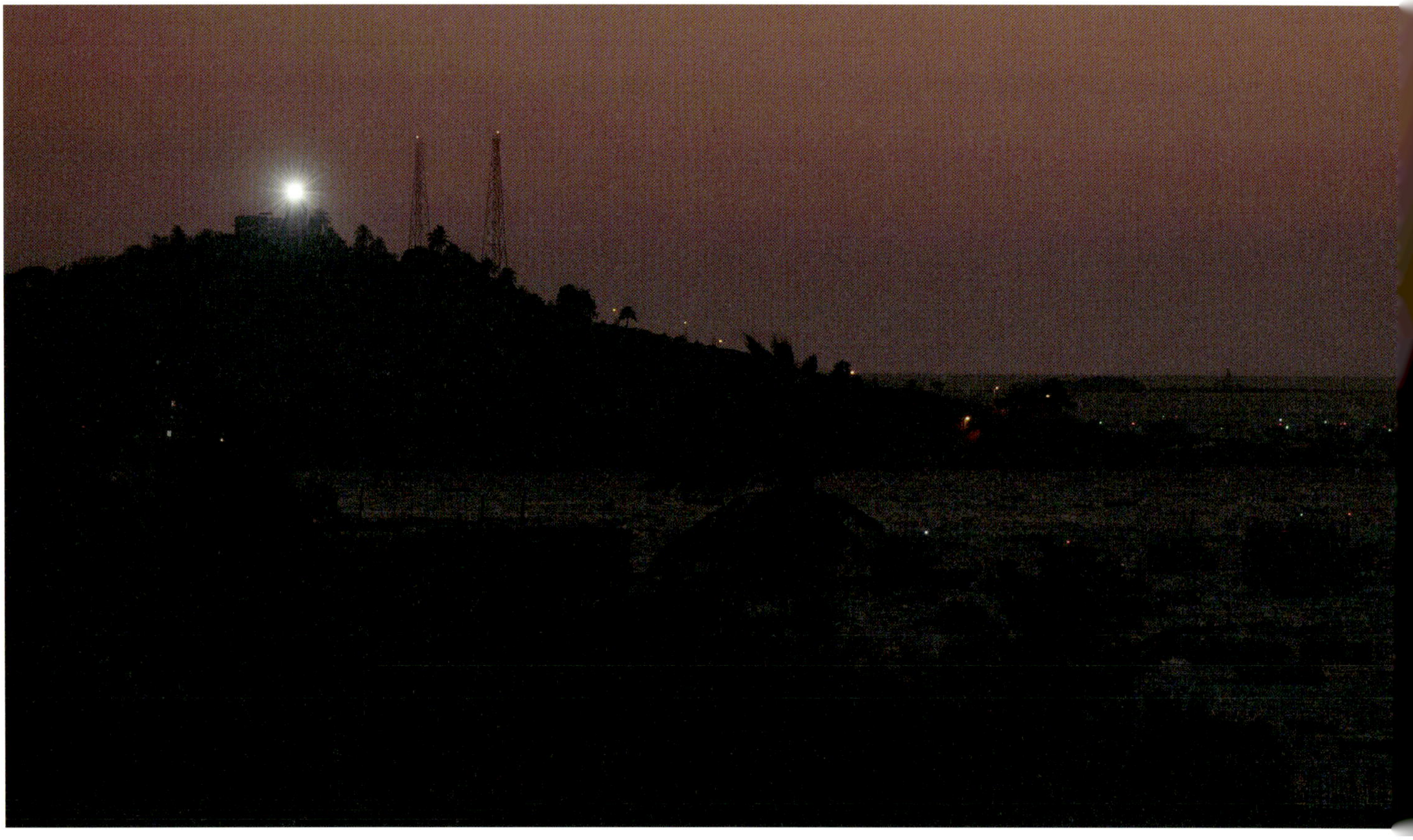

LIST OF ILLUSTRATIONS

FIGURES

Co-commissioned by Film and Video Umbrella, Bristol Museum & Art Gallery, Kettle's Yard, University of Cambridge and BALTIC Centre for Contemporary Art with Art Fund support through the Moving Image Fund for Museums. This programme is made possible thanks to Thomas Dane Gallery and a group of private galleries and individuals. The commission has been additionally supported by Autograph. Supported by Arts Council England.

Figure 24, p.128
Lumen, 2021
Still
Single-channel HD digital video, colour, sound, 30 minutes
Co-commissioned by Film and Video Umbrella, Bristol Museum & Art Gallery, Kettle's Yard, University of Cambridge and BALTIC Centre for Contemporary Art with Art Fund support through the Moving Image Fund for Museums. This programme is made possible thanks to Thomas Dane Gallery and a group of private galleries and individuals. The commission has been additionally supported by Autograph. Supported by Arts Council England.

PLATES

Plate I, p.33
Housewives with Steak-knives, 1984–5
Oil, acrylic, pastel, pencil, collage and house paint on paper mounted onto canvas, 245 x 222 cm
Collection of Cartwright Hall Art Gallery, Bradford Museums and Galleries
Photo credit: Andy Keate

Plate II, pp.34–5
As I Stood, Listened and Watched, My Feelings Were This Woman Is Not For Burning, 1985–6
Pastel, pencil and acrylic on paper, 183 x 91 cm
Collection of Cartwright Hall Art Gallery, Bradford Museums and Galleries
Photo credit: Paul Thompson

Plate III, pp.36–7
The Pied Piper of Hamlyn – Put Your Money Where Your Mouth Is, 1987
Gouache, acrylic, pastel and photocopy collage on paper and board, 216.5 x 300 cm
Arts Council Collection
Photo credit: Andy Keate

Plate IV, pp.38–9
To Touch Stone, 1989–90
Graphite on paper, 183 x 243 x 3.5 cm
Tate
Photo credit: © Tate

Plates V–X, p.40
Kali, 1983–5
Stills
Video transferred to digital, colour and sound (stereo), 25 minutes, 28 seconds
Tate
Photo credit: © Tate

Plates XI–XIV, p.81
Synapse I (1–4), 1987–92
Hand-printed black-and-white photographs (four-part work), 112.2 x 132.5 cm (each)
The Stanley & Audrey Burton Gallery, University of Leeds

Plates XV–XVI, pp.82–3
Synapse II, 1987–92
Hand-printed black-and-white photographs (two-part work), 112 x 130 cm each
Collection of Gallery Oldham

Plate XVII, p.84
Flights of Passage, 2014–15
Installation, saris loaned from family, friends and by the artist, wire, sound, dimensions variable
Radio City, Tate Britain
Photo credit: Sutapa Biswas

Plate XVIII, p.84
Stitch by Stitch, 2015
Donated kimono materials, antique indigo-dyed silk and silk thread, 126 cm x 164 cm
Installation view
Beppu Contemporary Art Triennial, 'Mixed Bathing World', Japan, curated by Keith Whittle, 2015
Artist's Collection

Plate XIX, p.85
Untitled (The Trials and Tribulations of Mickey Baker), 1997
Still
Video, colour, re-edited and re-mastered 2002, 10 minutes
Tate
Photo credit: © Tate

Plate XX, p.85
Untitled (Woman in Blue Weeping), 1996
Installation view
Video, colour, no sound, 14 minutes, 14 seconds
Artist's Collection

Plate XXI, p.87
Under my table, 2006
Still
Video, colour, no sound, 3 minutes, 16 seconds
Artist's Collection

Plate XXII, pp.88–9
Magnesium Bird, 2004
Still
Single-channel digital video work, colour with sound, 9 minutes, 27 seconds
Made possible with the generous support of inIVA, FVU, Grants for National Touring (ACE), AHRC, Harewood House (Yorkshire, UK), Reed College (Douglas Cooley Gallery, Portland, Oregon, USA), Chelsea College of Art and Design (UK). Collection of Sheffield Museums and Art Galleries supported by the Contemporary Art Society (UK)
Artist's Collection

Plates XXIII–XXIV, p.89
Birdsong, 2004
Stills
Two-channel video, 16mm film transferred to digital format, colour, no sound, 7 minutes, 7 seconds
Made possible with the generous support of inIVA, Film and Video Umbrella (London), Grants for National Touring (ACE), AHRC (UK)
Artist's Collection

Plate XXV, pp.90–1
Birdsong, 2004
Still
Two-channel video, 16mm film transferred to digital format, colour, no sound, 7 minutes, 7 seconds
Made possible with the generous support of inIVA, Film and Video Umbrella (London), Grants for National Touring (ACE), AHRC (UK)
Artist's Collection
Photo credit: Toby Granville

Plate XXVI, pp.92–3
Light rain, 2015–21
Production still, C-type photograph
Double-channel projection, digital video, colour with sound, 10 minutes, 10 seconds
Made possible with the generous support of The Kashima Artist in Residence, Japan, and the Agency for Cultural Affairs, Government of Japan
Artist's Collection

Plate XXVII, p.93
silver green against dark navy, 2015
Neon
Installation view
Beppu Contemporary Art Triennial, 'Mixed Bathing World', Fujiya Gallery and Historic Museum, Kanawa, Oita, Japan. Curated by Keith Whittle, commissioned in collaboration with Beppu Project NPO. Funded by the Agency for Cultural Affairs, Japan
Collection of Beppu Projects, Beppu, Oita, Japan
Photo credit: Beppu Projects

Plate XXVIII, p.94
mata ne, 2015–21
Production still, detail
Single-channel work, digital video, 35 minutes, 25 seconds
Made possible with the generous support of The Kashima Artist in Residence (Japan), and the Agency for Cultural Affairs, Government of Japan
Artist's Collection

Plate XXIX, p.95
mata ne, 2015–21
Still
Single-channel work, digital video, 35 minutes, 25 seconds
Made possible with the generous support of The Kashima Artist in Residence (Japan), and the Agency for Cultural Affairs, Government of Japan
Artist's Collection

Plates XXX–XXXI, p.96
Lumen, 2021
Still
Single-channel HD digital video, colour, sound, 30 minutes
Co-commissioned by Film and Video Umbrella, Bristol Museum & Art Gallery, Kettle's Yard, University of Cambridge and BALTIC Centre for Contemporary Art with Art Fund support through the Moving Image Fund for Museums. This programme is made possible thanks to Thomas Dane Gallery and a group of private galleries and individuals. The commission has been additionally supported by Autograph. Supported by Arts Council England.

Plates XXXII–XXXIV, pp.105–107 & XXXVI–XXXXII, pp.110–120
Lumen, 2021
Stills
Single-channel HD digital video, colour, sound, 30 minutes
Co-commissioned by Film and Video Umbrella, Bristol Museum & Art Gallery, Kettle's Yard, University of Cambridge and BALTIC Centre for Contemporary Art with Art Fund support through the Moving Image Fund for Museums. This programme is made possible thanks to Thomas Dane Gallery and a group of private galleries and individuals. The commission has been additionally supported by Autograph. Supported by Arts Council England.

Plate XXXXV, pp.108–9
Lumen, 2021
Production still
Single-channel HD digital video, colour, sound, 30 minutes
Photo credit: Carlotta Cardana
Co-commissioned by Film and Video Umbrella, Bristol Museum & Art Gallery, Kettle's Yard, University of Cambridge and BALTIC Centre for Contemporary Art with Art Fund support through the Moving Image Fund for Museums. This programme is made possible thanks to Thomas Dane Gallery and a group of private galleries and individuals. The commission has been additionally supported by Autograph. Supported by Arts Council England.

Sutapa Biswas Biography

Born in India and educated in the UK since the age of four, Sutapa Biswas graduated with a BA in Fine Art with Art History from the University of Leeds in 1985. She completed a postgraduate degree at the Slade School of Art in 1990 and was a research student at the Royal College of Art. She is now Reader in Fine Art at Manchester Metropolitan University, UK.

Venues that have hosted Biswas's works include: Tate Modern (London), Tate Britain (London), Tate Liverpool, Yale University Art Gallery (New Haven), The British Museum (London), *Mixed Bathing World*, Beppu Contemporary Art Triennial (Japan), 6th Havana Biennial, Neuberger Museum (New York), Art Gallery of Ontario (Toronto), Melbourne International Arts Festival, Whitechapel Gallery (London), Arnofini (Bristol), inIVA (London) and ICA (London). Biswas has also held solo exhibitions at Nara Roesler (Brazil), inIVA (UK touring), Douglas Cooley Gallery (Reed College, USA), Plug In Gallery, Institute of Contemporary Art (Winnipeg, Canada) in collaboration with Locus+ (Newcastle upon Tyne, UK), Leeds City Art Gallery and The Photographers' Gallery (London). In 2021 Biswas has two major UK solo exhibitions, at BALTIC, Gateshead and Kettle's Yard, University of Cambridge.

Biswas is a recipient of the Yale Center for British Art Visiting Scholars Award 2019–20 (Yale University), and most recently is also a recipient of the Art Fund Award made possible through the Moving Image Fund for Museums, in support of an ambitious new film co-commissioned with FVU (London), Bristol Museum & Art Gallery, Kettle's Yard, BALTIC and additionally supported by Autograph and Arts Council England. Biswas was the Andrew W. Mellon Fellow at the Yale Center for British Art (2008), and received the Correnah W. Wright Endowment Fund and The National Endowment for the Arts Award, Visiting Artist, Mills College, USA (1994), and is a European Photography Award 1992 nominee. Her artworks are represented in collections including: Tate; Arts Council England; Reed Gallery, USA; Graves Gallery, Sheffield Museums and Galleries, UK; Cartwright Hall, Bradford Museum and Art Gallery; Gallery Oldham; Rochdale Art Gallery; Stanley & Audrey Burton Gallery, University of Leeds, UK.

Author Biographies

Anna Arabindan-Kesson is an assistant professor of Black Diasporic art with a joint appointment in the Departments of African American Studies and Art and Archaeology at Princeton University. Born in Sri Lanka, she completed undergraduate degrees in New Zealand and Australia and worked as a Registered Nurse before gaining her PhD in African American Studies and Art History from Yale University. Arabindan-Kesson focuses on African American, Caribbean and British Art, with an emphasis on histories of race, Empire and transatlantic visual culture in the long nineteenth century. Her first book, published with Duke University Press, is called *Black Bodies White Gold: Art, Cotton and Commerce in the Atlantic World* (2021).

Courtney J. Martin is the director of the Yale Center for British Art. Previously, she was the deputy director and chief curator at the Dia Art Foundation, taught at Brown University and worked at the Ford Foundation. In 2012 Martin curated *Drop, Roll, Slide, Drip . . . Frank Bowling's Poured Paintings 1973–1978* at Tate Britain. At Dia she curated an exhibition of works by the painter Robert Ryman and oversaw exhibitions of works by Dan Flavin, Sam Gilliam, Blinky Palermo, Dorothea Rockburne, Keith Sonnier and Andy Warhol. She co-edited *Lawrence Alloway: Critic and Curator* (Getty Publications, 2015, winner of the 2016 Historians of British Art Book Award) and edited *Four Generations: The Joyner Giuffrida Collection of Abstract Art* (Gregory R. Miller & Co., 2016). In 2015 she received an Andy Warhol Foundation Arts Writers Grant. She received a doctorate from Yale University.

Alina Khakoo is a PhD candidate in Criticism and Culture at the University of Cambridge. She is interested in the South Asian diaspora in the British Black Arts Movement, in British Black intellectual production, and in British Black feminist and lesbian organising from the 1950s. Her PhD — supervised by Priya Gopal and advised by Amy Tobin — focuses on the 1980s. Alongside her doctoral studies, she has worked as a curatorial assistant at Kettle's Yard.

Amy Tobin is lecturer in the Department of History of Art and Curator, Contemporary Programmes at Kettle's Yard, University of Cambridge. She is the curator of *Sutapa Biswas: Lumen* as well as *Linderism* (2020). Her research and publications focus on art and feminism in the twentieth century.

Alessandro Vincentelli is a curator and writer, and former Curator of Exhibitions & Research at BALTIC Centre for Contemporary Art, Gateshead, where he worked for fifteen years. There he curated exhibitions with many international artists including RAQS Media Collective, Bani Abdi and Hajra Waheed. Recent significant projects have included solo exhibitions with Susan Philipsz, John Akomfrah, and the group shows *Disappearance at Sea — Mare Nostrum*, *Idea of North*, and *Digital Citizen — The Precarious Subject*. He has been curatorial advisor for numerous projects and has developed exhibitions and publications with artists Yinka Shonibare, Jasmina Cibic, Heather Phillipson and Rodney Graham. He previously worked as curator at Ikon Gallery, Birmingham and also in roles at the Arts Council England. He is currently developing and curating an Eco-themed triennial, EKO8, in Maribor, Slovenia, with some twenty international artists, titled *A Letter to the Future*, for summer 2021.

Griselda Pollock is Professor Emerita of Social and Critical Histories of Art, Director of the Centre for Cultural Analysis, Theory & History (CentreCATH) at the University of Leeds. She is the 2020 Laureate of the Holberg Prize for her contribution to feminist-postcolonial-queer-international-socio-historical studies in art history and cultural analysis. She has written on a wide range of twentieth-century and contemporary artists as well as on cinema. In addition to her now classic texts *Old Mistresses: Women, Art & Ideology* (1979/1981 new edition 2020) and *Framing Feminism* (1985) co-authored with Rozsika Parker and *Vision and Difference: Feminism, Femininity and the Histories of Art* (1988), publications include *Encounters in the Virtual Feminist Museum: Time, Space and the Archive* (2007) and *After-affects/After-images: Trauma and Aesthetic Transformation in the Virtual Feminist Museum* (2013), *Art as Compassion: Bracha L. Ettinger*, edited with Catherine de Zegher (2011) and a monograph *Charlotte Salomon in the Theatre of Memory* (2018). Forthcoming is *Killing Men and Dying Women: 1950s New York Painting and Imag(in)ing Difference* (2022) and a book on Marilyn Monroe.

Lumen

Lumen was written and directed by Sutapa Biswas. It is a Film and Video Umbrella Production, produced by Elizabeth Benjamin and Beccy McCray and co-produced by Leah McGurk, FVU. Steven Bode was Executive Producer.

Martin Testar was Director of Photography, Editor was Daniel Goddard and Online Editor Natalia Jaeger, who was also colourist along with Pat Wintersgill. Daniel Goddard was responsible for the music and sound design, and Ben Young for the sound mix.

Lumen included Natasha Patel as the lead actor, Namrata Sanghani as the Young Woman Beneath the Banyan Tree, with Nandini Nath, Nashik Nath and Shyam Nath as the acrobats.

Filmed at Mumbai and various locations in India, as well as The Red Lodge, Bristol, UK, with archival footage provided by British Empire and Commonwealth Collection: Bristol Archives, and Yale Center for British Art, Paul Mellon Collection.

Co-commissioned by Film and Video Umbrella, Bristol Museum & Art Gallery, Kettle's Yard, University of Cambridge and BALTIC Centre for Contemporary Art with Art Fund support through the Moving Image Fund for Museums. This programme is made possible thanks to Thomas Dane Gallery and a group of private galleries and individuals. The commission has been additionally supported by Autograph ABP. Supported by Arts Council England.

Sutapa Biswas: Lumen

at BALTIC

Curated by Alessandro Vincentelli and Emma Dean
Registrar and Production Manager: Adrianne Murray-Neil
Technical Manager: Thomas Newell
Programme Assistant: Emily Holmes
Communications: Craig Astley and Louise Todd

BALTIC Centre for Contemporary Art
Gateshead Quays
South Shore Road
Gateshead NE8 3BA
United Kingdom

Director: Sarah Munro
Chair of Trustees: Kirsty Lang
Vice Chair of Trustees: Louise Hunter

Lender to the exhibition:
Gallery Oldham

BALTIC Centre for Contemporary Art is supported by Arts Council England and Gateshead Council.

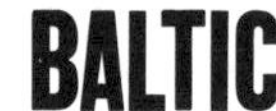

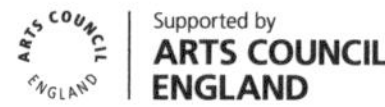

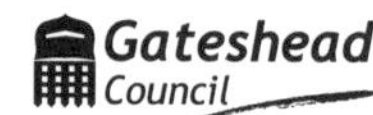

Art Fund_

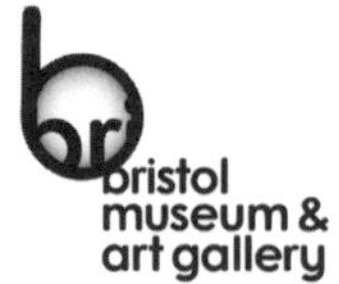

KETTLE'S YARD

BALTIC

AUTOGRAPH

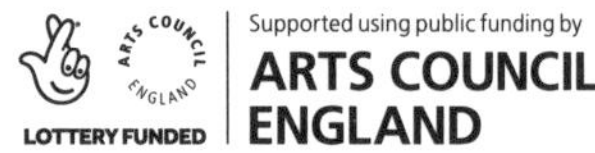

at Kettle's Yard

Curated by Amy Tobin, with Jennifer Powell
Assistant Curator: Guy Haywood, with contributions by Daniela Riva Rossi and Eliza Spindel
Programme Technician: Tom Noblett
Curatorial Assistant: Alina Khakoo
Communications: Helen Dickman

Kettle's Yard
University of Cambridge
Castle Street
Cambridge CB3 0AQ
United Kingdom

Director: Andrew Nairne OBE
Assistant Director: Susie Biller
Chair: Bridget Kendall MBE

Lenders to the exhibition:
Cartwright Hall, Bradford
University of Leeds
Tate
Touchstones, Rochdale

Support

Kettle's Yard relies on the generosity of supporters to care for the collection and historic buildings, and enable us to offer a full programme of activities, from exhibitions, learning activities and music, to publications and research. All gifts, large and small, help to safeguard the collection for future generations, and enable others to enjoy Kettle's Yard now and in the future.

There are a variety of ways in which you can help support Kettle's Yard and also benefit as a UK or US taxpayer. For more information please visit kettlesyard.co.uk/supporters.

Director's Circle

Carol Atack and Alex van Someren, Sir Charles and Lady Chadwyck-Healey, John and Jennifer Crompton, Claudio Köser, and those who wish to remain anonymous

Ede Circle

Michael Allen OBE and Marjolein Wytzes, Stuart Ansell, Helaine Blumenfeld OBE, Sophie Bowness, David and Rosalind Cleevely, Jennifer Crouch, Claire and Martin Daunton, Peter Gerrard, Sean Gorvy and Gael Gorvy Robertson, Jenny Little, Tim Llewellyn OBE, Anne Lonsdale CBE, Nicki and Christie Marrian, Suling Mead, Keith Moffat, Jonathan and Nicole Scott, Elizabeth Simpson, Toby Smeeton and Anya Waddington, Alan Swerdlow and Jeremy Greenwood, Stuart Wilkinson, and those who wish to remain anonymous

Corporate Supporters

Cheffins
EY
Tayabali & White
Eve Waldron Design
Anna's Flower Farm
Langham Press

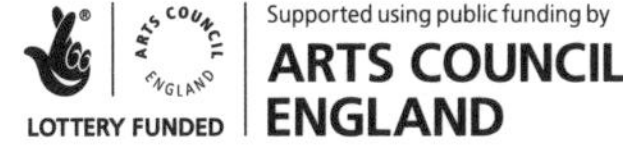

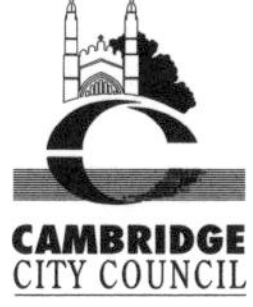

KETTLE'S YARD

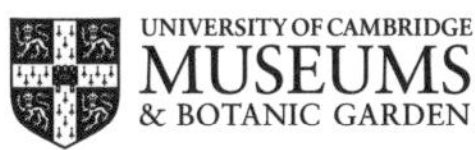

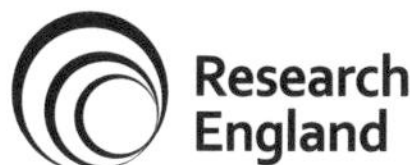

Acknowledgements
Sutapa Biswas

In life there is a point where one asks who, ever, will listen to my poetry. Not so much as a question. But a statement. And if some ear or eye takes a moment to hear, or see, and speak, will a page of thanks come at the beginning or at the end. As the Irish poet Paul Muldoon has recalled, it will be two places at once, or the same place, twice.*

I would like to thank the following:
Ma, Baba, my son Enzo, my companion Andrew, my sisters (especially Sujata), Rahoul, and Moira Roth. No paragraph in brief can mark this time.

To all those who unwaveringly and generously supported this project, including through a pandemic: Amy Tobin, Jenny Powell, Emma Dean, Alessandro Vincentelli, Andrew Nairne, Sarah Munro, Steven Bode, Julia Carver, Mike Jones, Susanna Chisholm, Guy Haywood, Eliza Spindel, Mark Sealy, Susie Biller, Louise Todd, Irene Aristizábal, Adrianne Murray-Neil, Thomas Newell, Rose McMurray, Daniela Riva Rossi, Tom Noblett, Kajsa Ståhl, Sophie Kullmann, Courtney J. Martin, Tim Barringer, Sarah Victoria Turner, Anna Arabindan-Kesson, Alina Khakoo, Martin Testar (my cinematographer on *Birdsong*, 2004, *Remembrance of Things Past*, 2006, and *Lumen*, 2021), The Art Fund through the Moving Image Fund for Museums.

To my wonderful film production team on *Lumen*: Steven Bode, Mike Jones, Martin (Teddy) Testar (again), Leah McGurk, Beccy McCray, Elizabeth Benjamin, my brilliant actress Natasha Patel, Daniel Goddard, Natalia Jaeger, Pat Wintersgill, Ben Young, all the beautiful people at Harkat Studios and my India crew — Karan Talwar, Michaela Talwar, Namrata Sanghani, Prachi Krishnakant Chandarana, Konal Lolitkar, Sheba Alexander, Tanya Dixit, Ram Bahadur Sahu, Ramesh Mondal, Mata Shankar Mishra — Amrit Gangar, Nandini Nath, Nashik Nath, Shyam Nath; my fabulous UK crew — Trevor Murphy, Andy Wain, Damien Gray, Sergejs Božoks, Graeme Willets, Maddelena McNicholas, Natalie Sloth Richter, Kate's Kitchen (Bristol), Pierre Tucker, Carlotta Cardana, Georgie Goddard. To Bristol Museum & Art Gallery for their amazing hospitality and support of *Lumen*: Frances Coles, Linda Gordon, Catherine Littlejohns, Jayne Pucknell. To Bristol Archives. To the Yale Center for British Art for the respectful generosity extended to me whilst undertaking research for *Lumen*, especially: Courtney J. Martin, Elisabeth R. Fairman, Martina Droth, Sarah Kraus, Laura Callery, Francis Lapka, Anne Markowski, Kraig Binkowski, Adrianna Bates, Bayla Arietta, Amelia Giordano. To the kindness of Martin J. McGlone, Kodak Laboratory London, Ruhan Lottering, and Dan Redrup, Digital Orchard. To Guy Brett, Ian Baucom, Stephanie Sakellaris-Snyder, Laura Mulvey, Gilane Tawadros, Lubaina Himid, Eddie Chambers, Donald Rodney, Rasheed Araeen, Mary Kelly, David Medalla, Stuart Hall who made *Birdsong* (2004) possible with his gift of a reference, Richard Drayton, Judith Mastai, Fred Orton, and to David Lascelles and Diane Howse for their loan of an apple orchard and the magnesium fires I lit therein.

In my journey there are many who joined along the way, and who still keep space in my heart. Some who have made this part of my journey a place to cherish are listed above. But one who is not yet written is the woman I met when she was aged thirty-one. A woman who, in her smiles, came to meet me outside a beautiful library as a prospective student. A woman I mistook in her kindness to be a student. And so, we both were. My thanks at the beginning and at the end of this passage, to my sister, friend and fellow student Griselda Pollock, whose kindest gift was to teach me that to unlearn was to learn.

The last word and thanks here are in honour of my dearest friends Moira Roth and Guy Brett. The art historian and cultural activist Moira Roth supported me with constancy in all of my endeavours since we first came to know each other in 1989. She sadly passed away on 25 June 2021, before I was able to send her a copy of this my second monograph; Guy too left this mortal world this year. Both had a profound impact on modes of thinking about art and the framing of practice, which transformed the landscape of art history globally. It has been an honour to have known and worked alongside both.

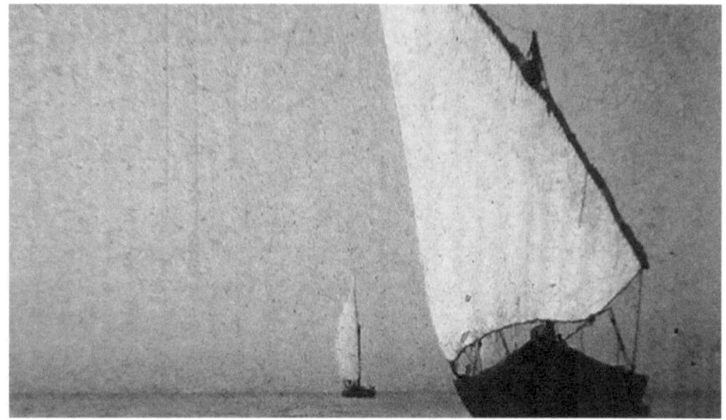

Figure 24
from *Lumen*, 2021

* Ian Baucom, 'Two Places at Once, or the Same Place Twice: The Art of Sutapa Biswas', in *Sutapa Biswas*, exh. cat., London and Portland: inIVA and Reed College, 2004, pp.58–65. An essay in which Baucom explores the nuances of my work drawing parallels with Muldoon's recollection of the school photograph in which his former classmate Lefty Clery appears twice.